Post-Analytic Philosophy

POST-ANALYTIC PHILOSOPHY

Edited by
JOHN RAJCHMAN
and CORNEL WEST

New York Columbia University Press *1985*

Library of Congress Cataloging in Publication Data
Main entry under title:

Post-analytic philosophy.

Includes bibliographies.
1. Philosophy, American—20th century—Addresses,
essays, lectures.   2. Philosophy—Addresses, essays,
lectures.   I. Rajchman, John.   II. West, Cornel.
B935.P67   1985   191   85-377
ISBN 0-231-06066-1
ISBN 0-231-06067-X (pbk.)

B
935
P67
1985

Columbia University Press
New York   Guildford, Surrey
Copyright © 1985 Columbia University Press
All rights reserved

Printed in the United States of America

*Clothbound editions of Columbia University Press books are
Smyth-sewn and printed on permanent and durable acid-free paper.*

CONTENTS

PREFACE

IN THIS VOLUME we have brought together philosophers widely regarded as among the most important or influential in America today. Surely other philosophers might have been included. However, the group we have selected is unified by familiarity: most of these authors have been engaged in "conversation" with each other. We have included in this conversation noted thinkers from outside the profession narrowly defined. The fact that these authors are all white males is a fact not about our selection but about the profession or about the society in which it figures.

It would seem that there is a diversity in philosophy today that contrasts with the uniformity of logical positivism and analytic philosophy, the programs which formed these philosophers, but from which, in various ways and to various degrees, they have all departed. What is new about what they are thinking; is there in fact still *one* philosophy in which they are all engaged? These are questions some have asked themselves and each other. They are the questions we are asking in this volume. Is their work the start of something new, or rather a continuation, or maybe a moment of fragmentation and transition? Is there then a new philosophy in America? What does it mean for other disciplines and for the coming generation of philosophers; what are its consequences: cultural, historical, political?

John Rajchman
Cornel West

Philosophy in America

JOHN RAJCHMAN

I think that in no country in the civilized world is less attention paid to philosophy than in the United States. The Americans have no philosophical school of their own, and they care but little for all the schools into which Europe is divided, the very names of which are scarcely known to them.*

M ORE THAN A CENTURY has elapsed since Tocqueville opened the second volume of his *Democracy in America* with this categorical contention. Within these hundred years, there has been more than one philosophy in America. Within a generation Peirce and James were to baptize a philosophy recognized even in Europe as specifically American, the first American philosophy to name itself: pragmatism. At the heart of this philosophy was a conception of truth which vigorously sought to depart from the schools that divided Europe. James was widely read and attracted large audiences. It was an era of public philosophy in America.

Pragmatism, however, was not to survive the triumph of the more specialized philosophical programs introduced by the Austrian and German émigrés: Carnap, Riechenbach, Fiegl, Hempel. Under their influence, by the late 1950s, mainstream American philosophy had become a specialized occupation with precise formal problems, one that eschewed public debate, disclaimed the requirements of literary or historical erudition, dismissed phenomenological and existential thought, and found little scientific and nothing philosophical in either psychoanalysis or Marxism. Philosophy became a recondite recluse.

Now this may be changing. Influential philosophers are emerging from their specialized preoccupations, challenging the "professionalized" character of the discipline, and wondering openly whether, in the words of Putnam, their basic programs have not come to a dead end.

*Alexis de Tocqueville, *Democracy in America* (New York: Vintage; 1945), 2: 3.

In the nineteenth century, as the "queen of the sciences," philosophy may have prided itself on supplying the foundations and the systematic unity of all other disciplines or endeavors. But when, in America, philosophy emerged from professional seclusion, it no longer related to other disciplines in this grand old Germanic manner. It has proceeded by proliferation and merger rather than by unification and the drawing of boundaries. Together with other disciplines, its analyses have given rise to new lines of thought. This volume is about this movement.

Analytic philosophy has produced brilliant technical work and enjoyed a stunning institutional success. It may be, as Danto and Putnam contend, the dominant philosophy in capitalist countries today. Yet in America it is being increasingly argued that the basic programs of this philosophy have been undermined precisely by its own technical work, leaving some doubt about how it may now continue. The very idea of logical analysis has been challenged. There may be no such thing as the method or logic of science, nothing "philosophical" to study. There may be no such thing as analytic sentences, and nothing for analytic philosophers to analyze. Rorty puts it bluntly: "The notion of 'logical analysis' turned upon itself and committed slow suicide."[1]

Putnam may thus not be alone, he may be expressing the view of an influential part of a generation, when he declares in "After Empiricism": "The accomplishments of analytic philosophy are only negative; it destroyed the very problems with which it started by successive failure even to determine what would count as a solution." The negative accomplishment was to show in great technical detail that the problem of "how words hook onto the world" does not admit of a solution, and that rationality in science or in ethics does not consist in the possession of a formal method for appraisal and adjudication.

In 1980, Danto put the matter in other terms: "The history of analytic philosophy may be read as a history of failed reforms . . . it may soon dawn upon us that we do not really know what philosophy is . . . Right now at least I doubt we can say what we are without our own self-misconceptions."[2] Danto says a basic assumption in analytic philosophy was that one could provide what he calls an Analytic of Concepts. That entailed a sharp distinction between first- and second-order discourse; philosophers would do what others did meta- . It assumed a representational relation of first-order discourse to the world, and finally that one could find primitive concepts, a core of privileged representations, in each first-order domain. None of these assumptions would survive successive scrutiny and reform, and the very concept of philosophy would be undermined.

Rorty's *Philosophy and the Mirror of Nature* reviews the objections to the search for foundations or privileged representations and the arguments through which the distinctions between the conceptual and the empirical, scheme and content, were gradually eroded: and he declares that: "Analytic philosophy *cannot* . . . be written without one or the other of these distinctions."[3] For Rorty, exposure of the "dogmas of empiricism" by Quine and Davidson are the self-refutation of the program of analytic philosophy. It is the refutation of a particular *kind* of philosophy: "academic neo-Kantian epistemologically-centered philosophy."[4] The significance of the demise of the analytic program ties in with a larger historical ending of this kind of philosophy.

In 1981, Rorty offers a portrait of the state of professional philosophy in America. "There is no more consensus about the problems and methods of philosophy in America today than there was in Germany in 1920,"[5] when logical positivism emerged. New problems come and go with increasing rapidity, and what remains constant is only a style: a sort of generalized legalistic expertise, a skill with cases, claims and arguments, "the ability to construct a good brief or conduct a devastating cross-examination or find relevant precedents."[6]

In particular, American professional philosophy no longer has a historical account which relates its problems with those of previous philosophy. Analytic philosophy at least had that. It introduced a revision of the history of philosophy, one that apparently appealed to Americans, for there were after all other forms of European philosophy which came to the United States at about the same time. It made the problems of classical empiricism into the central problems of philosophy and represented the idealist turn in post-Kantian thought as an excursus into something that ought never to have called itself philosophy: something metaphysical, a fuzzy thinking, a false historicism, an irrationalism, something that might be repudiated with the help of the analytic of concepts.

Rorty introduces a new history which allies American pragmatism with recent French and German philosophy—against "Kantian epistemology." He sees pragmatism at the center of an uncompleted revolution in the very nature of philosophy, which the triumph of the émigré program interrupted, but which its internal collapse now allows us to state in a sharper form. He has a selective reading of pragmatism, one which stresses Dewey's notion of many communities of inquirers at the expense of Peirce's notion of a single logic of inquiry.[7] The Deweyan idea is to be linked to the questioning of truth and rationality influenced by Heidegger, to the antisystematic, antifoundational strain in European thought found primarily in France—the European country most resistant to the international success of analytic philosophy.[8] The pragmatist form of this new philosophy would spare us what Rorty sees as the pessimistic, antisocial and antidemocratic consequences of French philosophy; he names it "neopragmatism." It is the philosophy of "solidarity" not "objectivity."

The Analytic of Concepts was meant to solve the set of specialized problems that characterized philosophy as a profession. Not only have there been internal difficulties with the very idea of logical analysis; there have been questions about this "professionalized" conception of the discipline.

At the beginning of the century, one wrote books with titles like *The Problems of Philosophy* (Russell), *Some Main Problems of Philosophy* (Moore), and *Some Problems of Philosophy* (James). In Britain and America, philosophy became a cluster of problems for which there existed increasingly sophisticated methods of solution as well as a tradition of previous attempts: the problems of induction, the free will, other minds, the external world, and so forth.

Nagel preserves the idea that the "problems of philosophy" are perennial ones which have always confronted reflective thought. But he is sanguine about whether formal techniques can be devised to resolve them. His *Mortal Questions* is a map of some of the motivating issues in philosophy and the inconclusive efforts to settle them. One such "mortal question" is the question of subjective and objective which he discusses in his contribution to this volume.

Cavell, Hacking, and Rorty take rather more decisive steps away from the idea of the "problems of philosophy." Cavell focuses on skepticism about the traditions and the world in which we find ourselves. Far from being a specialized problem, such skepticism would be the very source of reflective thought. Hacking starts from the assumption that many of the problems of philosophy derive from the emergence of various kinds of science and reasoning. Thus, in his *The Emergence of Probability*,[9] he provides a historical or "archeological" account for how the "problem of induction" could arise in Hume.

Rorty thinks there was a "hidden agenda" behind the central problems in analytic philosophy: the defense of the values of science, democracy and art on the part of secular intellectuals. He takes this to be the source of the philosophical debates of the seventeenth and eighteenth centuries, from which analytic philosophy was to extract its technical problems and for which it devised its formal solutions. This rethinking of the discipline—both conceptual and institutional or historical—has led to questions about what should come after analytic philosophy. What is "after empiricism"? Rorty asks: what are the "successor subjects"? He conjures a race of edifying philosophers who, armed with the assurance that there exists no privileged discourse or manner of reasoning, would create new and useful discourses, incommensurable with those of their predecessors. Those dissatisfied with analytic philosophy have not, however, found Rorty's alternative very attractive. It nevertheless constitutes a first attempt to make the internal difficulties of analytic philosophy the starting point for a new philosophy.

This volume is not about the agonies of the analytic profession. It does not simply rehearse the arguments that have led analytic philosophers to rethink the assumptions of their discipline. It is rather about new directions in American philosophy after analysis. It is not about an end to philosophy, but about new kinds of philosophy that may revitalize American intellectual debate.

It focuses on three main areas of thought and research around which a post-analytic philosophy has crystallized: literary theory, history of science, and political philosophy. Other disciplines are involved in each case, and this volume includes representatives from them: a literary critic, a historian of science, and a political theorist. The move to other fields, however, has been more "de-disciplinizing" than "interdisciplinary": less a collaboration between specialized fields than a questioning of basic assumptions in those fields and an attempt to create new ones. There are the post-analytic mergers or amalgamations: philosophy-literary theory, philosophy-history of science, philosophy-public moral debate; they have supplied the principal subjects of inquiry or reflection, the *topoi* of post-analytic philosophy. The creation of such new fields constitutes a challenge to the great Kantian distinctions between them: the distinction between science, morals and aesthetics. It is a challenge to the attempt to find grounds for this distinction in a philosophical anthropology or a theory of language. In each case, therefore, part of the debate has surrounded the claim that there exists a single or unified sort of rationality appropriate to each domain. In portraying post-analytic philosophy as anti-Kantian, Rorty's new pragmatism has been important: it has offered an overall analysis and argument for these changes and thus has sought a place for post-analytic philosophy in American intellectual history.

Literary Theory

One topic in post-analytic philosophy might be called by the title of Danto's contribution to this volume: "philosophy as/and/of literature." Parts of the philosophical tradition which the period of analysis had disowned survived in certain literature departments. Marx, and particularly Freud, sometimes received places of honor, and Idealist or Romantic aesthetics and the later Heidegger were not ignored. But it was primarily French structuralism and post-structuralism which caused American critics to question basic assumptions in their discipline: conceptions of writing, reading, tradition, indeed of literature itself. Under the French impetus, an influential group of critics produced not simply a new program of literary criticism but a conception of philosophy itself as a kind of writing or literature. They reexamined Plato's condemnation of rhetoric and invented a new "literary theory" which was largely ignored or dismissed by analytic philosophers.

Post-analytic philosophy responded to literary theory in at least two ways.

1. It recast debates within that theory in a terminology it had devised in its own preoccupations, for example, in terms of its preoccupation with reference. Putnam had applied Kripke's seminal work on reference to questions about the senses in which theoretical entities such as electrons or acids can be said to be real. Against Frege, Kripke had shown that reference can remain fixed through changes in meaning. Putnam used Kripke's theory to show how reference to real entities remains fixed through Kuhnian changes in scientific vocabulary; he thus sought to dispute what he saw as Kuhn's "relativism." Eventually, however, Putnam acknowledged that a theory of references must itself be indeterminant, and that it is only from within a theory that we can suppose we know what we are referring to. It was assumed that literary theorists had been engaged in the same kinds of debate about realism and relativism. Thus, Derrida's remark "there is no outside-the-text" was turned into a sort of general slogan for all literary theory.[10] The remark was taken to express controversial claims (such as the view that there is no single thing to which all scientific or literary traditions must refer) as well as absurd or ridiculous ones (such as the view that texts are the only kind of thing which exists).

2. In the second place, an attempt was made to create a homegrown American version of philosophy-literary theory. Its roots would lie in Emerson and American pragmatism rather than in French structuralism.

A post-analytic philosophy would rediscover and continue pre-analytic American literary traditions which had been cast aside in the development of professional philosophy. Both kinds of post-analytic discussion are represented in this volume.

One line of argument Danto brings to the hybrid "philosophy of/and/as literature" lies in his objections to a French literary theorist he simply calls R. R. is a proponent of "the intertext," the web of allusions and literary presuppositions which binds texts one to another. R. advances a philosophical thesis, to which Danto takes exception, which says that texts refer only to other texts, and that it is a "referential fallacy" to think that they refer to the world. Danto not only debunks this thesis, he advances one of his own: that texts refer to readers (and so to the world). Intertextual theorists had referred to a sort of Ideal reader. But Danto's picture of the way texts refer to real readers has the effect of returning to a familiar humanism, the general outlook of the pre-theoretical consensus among American literary critics.

Rorty applies the "pragmatist" lessons he drew from recent discussion in the philosophy of science to literature and criticism. He exhorts us to replace the Kantian image of a single fixed cultural framework or vocabulary with an image of many different corrigible and changeable vocabularies; he exhorts us to replace the values of foundation and system with those of proliferation and plurality. Thus he interprets the debates about the concept of literature and criticism: he calls "modernism" that writing and criticism which accepts the "mortality" of vocabularies and embraces the aim of proliferating new ones: "There is no constant vocabulary in which to describe the values to be defended or the objects to be imitated or the emotions to be expressed . . . We don't *want* works of literature to be criticizable within a terminology we already know; we want those works, and the criticism of them, to give us *new* terminologies."[11]

Rorty fits this definition of modernism into his story about philosophy since Kant; it contributes to the undoing of Kantian distinctions between science and literature. Analytic philosophy rejects the dogma of the distinction between fact and language, and Kuhn argues that there is no single neutral vocabulary to be extracted from our various scientific traditions and used to adjudicate conflicts between them. Modernist literary theory rejects the related dogma in its domain: the distinction between literary and critical languages, or the view that there exists a single neutral vocabulary—a "metalanguage"—to be extracted from our changing literary traditions. In both cases, the idea of a single commensurating framework is rejected in favor of many incommensurable "mortal vocabularies," subject to no deeper constraints than those embodied in our pragmatic purposes. Both thus lead to a pragmatism of changing traditions, for which the Kantian division between science and literature no longer makes sense.

Bloom adopts this pragmatism of mortal vocabularies. His definition of poetry as "a loving conflict with previous poetry rather than a conflict with the world" may seem a version of the intertextualist view which Danto rejects.[12] Bloom, however, calls it a pragmatist view. He preserves an internalist conception of tradition as changing from within by revising its own self-conceptions. But he rejects the structuralist emphasis on language as the source of such internal revision. He declares that the "Franco-Heideggerian and monolithic" idea of "language-as-Demiurge" is "at best gorgeous nonsense, and at worst only another residuum of the now wearisome perpetual crusade of intellectual Paris against its own upper middle class, and this just has no relevance to, or in, our perpetually Emersonian America."[13]

Bloom rejects the "Kantian" view of culture as a museum of great works that refer to something timeless or objective in the human imagination. Rather he sees the cultural tradition as a perpetual struggle over the very terms of tradition, over how things are written and read, with no other foundation than the acts of reading and writing themselves. Writing and reading are precisely the *agon* over the mortal vocabularies we inherit. There are "strong" readings and writings (but there is no writing which does not suppose some reading). A strong reading is one that interprets previous or alternative readings and starts a new tradition. By the lights of the old ones it is always a "misreading." Poetry *is* the loving struggle to introduce such new revisionary vocabularies. Thus:

> Rorty is splendidly useful when he sees that pragmatism and currently advanced literary criticism come to much the same cultural enterprise and I add only that Emerson . . . is the largest precursor of this merger . . . on a pragmatic view there is no language of *criticism* but only of an individual critic, because again I agree with Rorty that a theory of strong misreading denies that there is or should be any common vocabulary in terms of which critics argue with one another.[14]

For Cavell, Emerson is the forgotten source from which springs what is best in American thought; he is the "largest precursor" of philosophy in America. In the work of Emerson and Thoreau, Cavell finds a skepticism which would be the American counterpart to Heidegger's return to the everyday life world and Wittgenstein's return to ordinary language.

Cavell's Emersonian skepticism is directed against the "immortality" or false naturalness of the vocabularies a thinker inherits. Community lies in "con-dition," a common mortal language or form of life. Emersonian self-reliance is the thinking, writing or action which withdraws from such con-ditions and tries to find "what works and is" for oneself. It embodies a kind of philosophical ethic: "the endless responsibility for one's own dis-course, for not resting with words you do not happily mean."[15] It aban-dons the metaphysical solace of familiarity with traditions; it defamiliar-izes the con-ditions of one's day. It is the "civil disobedience" within received conditions of thought or action. The language of the self-reliant thinker can thus never be the language into which he is born. Cavell would be such an Emersonian maverick.

For Bloom, Emerson is also our great "American original." He starts an American literary "religion": a religion without a fixed language or church, a religion of constantly sparking new tongues, a religion of crit-ical and philosophical self-reliance.

The "self" in self-reliance would break from previous conceptions of authorship or writing. It would be found not in authentic self-relation but in endless self-experimentation. What the writer would rely on would be the singularity of an experience strong enough to spark new tradi-tions. Emerson would thus introduce a sort of "radical empiricism" into the heart of the American literary experience. One Emersonian aphorism Bloom cites with approval is: "The only sin is limitation."

Bloom employs a special brand of allegorical interpretation. He reads themes, images and symbols as allegories of the *agon* of tradition which he takes to be constitutive of literature. Emersonian self-reliance would be allegorical in this sense: it would introduce a mythology of America itself. It is the mythology of constant renewal with no fixed tradition, of an endless youth with no father, of always starting afresh. Emersonian self-reliance would be that "strong" reading and writing in which a my-thology of change and diversity replace a mythology of a common lan-guage that expresses the spirit, blood, or destiny of a people. The poem of America itself would be an Emersonian poem. Bloom cites Whitman: "These states are the greatest poem."

In his contribution for this volume, Bloom formulates a problem for Jewish culture in an Emersonian America. The Emersonian "religion" was launched before the great Jewish emigration. It had no place for the messianic elements in the conception of culture which the German Jewry brought with them. The myth of exile had been reformulated in the context of "a Germany that had leaped straight out of a barbaric, mythological and romance conception of itself to a rather shaky Post-Enlightenment idealizing self-vision." In America the reformulated myth of exile would come to a "pragmatic ending." It could not take root in an America which "is a theological and philosophical conception of itself, a conception with much Puritanism but little ethnic mythology at the root." Thus the problem of Jewish "memory"—of cultural preservation through textual exegesis—which Bloom claims Freud and Kafka formulated in the German context, is raised again in an American context. The "pragmatics of contemporary Jewish culture" would lie in the problem of rethinking Jewish memory within the pragmatist and Emersonian conception of literary tradition. Perhaps Bloom's own "strong misreading" is his attempt to do this.

Scientific Theory

A second topic in post-analytic philosophy is the topic of scientific rationality. Kuhn's historicist challenge to the positivist philosophy of science reopened the general debate about the critical values enlightened opinion had associated with modern science. For the first time in American philosophy, rationality seemed to be questioned. There has ensued a long debate about the nature of rationality with wide-ranging intellectual consequences.

In 1962, in his highly influential *The Structure of Scientific Revolutions,* Kuhn announced that the study of history would change the "image of science of which we are now possessed."[16] A predominant assumption in the philosophy of science was that history did not matter at all; Reichenbach's distinction between the contexts of justification and of discovery in science was widely adopted. Philosophy would only be about justification. Kuhn did help change that style in the philosophy of science. Debates ensued over whether the process which replaced one fundamental scientific theory with another could be made on the basis of rational standards, could retain reference to a common world, or could make progress towards an ideal truth. Kant had made the correspondence theory of truth seem untenable; Peirce turned correspondence into consensus within a hypothetical enduring community of inquirers. Now philosophers found a surrogate for rationality within the history of science: in terms of the way that history deals with its anomalies or solves its problems. Quine's challenge to the dogmas of empiricism was brought in along with a long series of qualifications of the distinction between observation and theory required by the deductive model of scientific explanation, which had been at the heart of the ahistorical philosophy of science. In his essay in this book Putnam comes to the view that we have labored under a misguided picture of science and rationality—a form of "scientism," the awareness of which "is bound to effect the way in which the culture generally views all questions of general intellectual procedure." In particular it qualifies the division between science and morals, or fact and value, promoted by the logical positivists.

These discussions were often cast in the form of discussions about language; for Kuhn that is still an important way of thinking about science. Quine had talked about "semantic ascent"—moving up to language—and he proposed a theory of "stimulus-meaning." He pictured science as a network of sentences with a central theoretical core and a periphery, the two being adjusted to one another in a complex process of revision. A "conceptual scheme" was a network of such sentences a community held to be true. One debate was about "meaning invariance"—whether the meaning of terms in a science could survive a basic change in theory—which led to discussion about the mutual "translatability" among theories. There was also the problem about whether there existed something independent of the network of sentences, the reference to which could survive changes in schemes—the problem of "realism."

Davidson's challenge to the very idea of a conceptual scheme could therefore assume the force of a challenge to a new dogma of empiricism. Davidson argues that the idea of an alternative conceptual scheme is not thinkable, and neither therefore is the idea of a conceptual scheme itself. For to understand an alien scheme is to "translate" it into what one knows. One can never completely disagree with another since one must attribute some true beliefs to him in order to attribute some false ones.

Hacking proposes to redefine incommensurability in another way. He disputes Davidson's assumption that to understand is to translate into what one knows. Rather, to understand is to learn how to reason. To learn how to reason is to see how a domain of objective discourse is possible. One can learn a style of reasoning without believing any of the propositions it yields, as in the case of Paracelsus. A style of reasoning defines a field of objective discourse, but there may be no common ground between such fields; thus they may be incommensurable. Such incommensurability is not between totalizing Quinean networks of sentences held for true (conceptual schemes), but between different worlds of objective discourse. It involves a relativism not about what is true but about what *may* be true. A style of reasoning is therefore not a scheme that confronts reality, and indeed it is not the sort of thing about which it is useful to have a philosophy of *language*.

Statistical reasoning comes from counting practices that determine an idea of what a law and a fact is;[17] experiments determine objects of science through highly artificial "interventions." In neither case is an analysis of sentences of much importance. Hacking thinks the philosophy of meanings and language has had a misleading influence on the new philosophy of science. It has led to a false enthusiasm for theory, an indifference to experiment and practice, and to a peculiar linguistic idealism that wonders whether there is a world outside the sentences of science.

Hacking revives Comte's term "positivity" to refer to the domains of objective discourse he associates with styles of reasoning. In this way he interprets the discussion of the "constitution of objects of sciences" in the French tradition of Bachelard, Althusser, and Foucault. He sees the plurality of styles of reasoning or of "positivities" as a challenge to the unity of science, and the centrality of the model of physics, but not as a challenge to objectivity. In that sense he remains a "positivist."

Putnam and Rorty expose the "scientism" which consists in assuming that all sciences are possessed of a single procedural method of appraisal, the possession of which makes them rational. Hacking is against unity. Along with Kuhn he wants to dispute the "scientism" which consists in assuming Reason and Science are unified things. There is no one thing "Nature" for all our sciences to be about; there is no one thing "Reason" found in all kinds of objective discourse. Hacking holds we can admit this and embrace a proliferation of incommensurable domains of objective research, while remaining rationalist or positivist within them. He thinks society is best off when many different incommensurable traditions of reason and science proliferate.

Kuhn explains that his thesis of the disunity of sciences came from an attempt to synthesize the two leading models of science which had been devised to account for the origins and consequences of the "scientific revolution."[18] There was a historiographical conflict between the two that could be resolved only when the models were seen to apply to different sorts of scientific tradition. From the experimental and the mathematic traditions we derive two different images of scientific development, one which stresses external factors, the other which analyzes an internal intellectual dynamic.

There was a German tradition growing out of Marxist and Weberian sociology, centered on the problems of the relations of modern science with technology, Protestantism, and the industrial revolution, resulting in what Kuhn calls "the Merton Thesis." There was a French tradition that employed exegetical or hermeneutical techniques in intellectual history (particularly the history of philosophy) and which was exemplified in Duhem's demonstration that the roots of the scientific revolution are found in medieval science, long before the Reformation. The German tradition understood the origin of modern science in external sociological terms; the French tradition in internal intellectual terms, but in fact the "scientific revolution" was not a unified event, and each model was primarily useful only in explaining a part of it.

Rather like the social sciences, the Baconian or experimental sciences remained much longer tied to external conditions and their pattern of development was not modeled on a progressive modification of a theoretical core in relation to a recalcitrant periphery. The tie-in between the experimental and mathematic traditions which is shown in Silicon Valley, really only begins in the nineteenth century, symbolized by the I. G. Farben chemical plant.[19]

Thus the debate over the origins of modern science arose within a framework of a general history of a single monolithic development. That framework underlies many of the terms in which the discussion of the "rationality" of science in contemporary society has been carried on: is the scientific revolution progress towards a better world, a great mastery of nature and society for our purposes, the end to the thrall of superstitions; or is it the uprooting of tradition and community, the reinforcement of capitalism, the loss of our relation to the life world and to nature? The philosophical attempt to demarcate *the* single logic or structure of all science belongs to such universalist historical questions.

Kuhn's thesis of the disunity of sciences and Hacking's thesis of the proliferation of styles of reasoning propose another conception of the relation between the philosophy and history of science. The philosophy of science gives up the attempt to determine a general theory of scientific rationality; the history of sciences gives up the attempt to find the origins of science in a single great narrative. Both start from the assumption that the different kinds of science and the different styles of reasoning have different sorts of external histories. The proliferation of traditions replaces their systematic unity. A new philosophy is then directed to reconstituting the forgotten sources for current conceptual controversy from within the history of sciences and styles of reasoning.

Moral Theory

A third focus for debate in post-analytic philosophy has been the issue of rationality in moral theory. It derives in part from the far-reaching consequences Putnam associates with the demise of the conception of scientific rationality propounded by the logical positivists: in particular, the attempt to deny any rational context to moral discourse at all. Should the image of the diversity of sciences and of styles of reasoning, and the values of proliferation, be applied to moral as well as to literary theory? In the case of moral theory, this question moves into the territory of classical political thought.

Central in this debate is the Kantian theory of equality which Rawls advances in his contribution to this volume. Rawls argued for the independence of moral theory from the linguistic and epistemological preoccupations in analytic philosophy.[20] He then formulated and defended an equalitarian principle, rooted in the tradition of liberal thought in America, with a Kantian theory which identifies "morally right" with "justified to any rational agent." He devised a kind of procedural or formal scheme for the application of the principle.

Basically Rawls proposes to justify a qualified egalitarian principle on the basis of a contractualist thought experiment in which people are imagined to make choices from behind a "veil of ignorance" or on the assumption that they might be anyone in society. This device was meant to separate interest in what is right from interest in what is good, morality from prudence. A number of questions were raised about it.

There was some doubt as to whether one *would* choose the egalitarian principle in the thought experiment. Nagel raised another kind of question: why such a choice would *justify* the principle or make it right.[21] Those who reject the idea of egalitarian distribution on principled grounds, he suggests, are in effect appealing to other conceptions of equality. He thinks egalitarianism no longer has aristocratic enemies; no longer does anyone find aristocratic principles legitimate. There are only *kinds* of principles of equality. As distinct from distributive equality, there is the equality of the aggregate good and the equality of individual rights. Rawls' thought-experiment supposes a particular kind of justification: one that appeals to results that would be acceptable to each person involved. But other kinds of equality involve other kinds of justification, and there may be no way of deciding between them.

Scanlon's analysis of contractualism and utilitarianism in this volume moves in a similar direction. He sees these two moralities not simply as competing moral principles, but as different accounts or pictures of what morals are and of what motivates people to adopt them. For contractualism, morals are thought to lie in action which proceeds from principles which are acceptable (or at least not reasonably rejectable) by others.

Rorty contends that Scanlon thus moves contractualism away from a Kantian appeal to "humanity in general" to an appeal to a particular historical tradition. Solidarity with our Jeffersonian tradition is enough; we need not appeal to the Nature of Man to account for our political rights. We should adopt a "pragmatic view about how social institutions match with our enjoyment of political liberties."[22] To back up this match we do not need a Hegelian history or a "German ideology."

To read contractualism in terms of a historical tradition rather than in terms of the general nature of human rationality, however, is to open questions about the nature and limits of that tradition. Conservatives had long held that it was fundamentally misguided to picture individuals as constituted prior to a State that exacted obligations solely in terms of the needs of the individuals and the contracts into which they entered. For, it was argued, individuals cannot be separated from the social wholes in which they find themselves and which make them who they are. Liberalism is therefore a reflection of alienation from such "constitutive communities."

We find this line of argument in Sandel's objections to Rawls.[23] Sandel argues that *no* choice could be made from behind a veil of ignorance. It is incoherent to ask us to imagine choosing a life plan when ignorant of who we are. Without the traditions and communities which supply us with our identities, we cannot choose anything at all. Perhaps there is no *single* distributive principle that applies to all persons and goods in every situation. Perhaps we are *never* benevolent utility-calculators, rational choosers, or participants in a tradition-free discussion, and the proceduralism of a moral theory which rests on such conceptions of ourselves must remain empty. Rawls cannot naturalize Kant and maintain his distinction between morality and prudence, rationality and tradition.

For Bernstein and Wolin, such arguments lead to political considerations about the nature of "community." Bernstein is influenced by a critical thought which holds that our identities have been "socially produced" in ways we don't realize and with results we would not approve. He advances a pragmatism which combines an analysis of the social production of our self-conceptions with an attempt to create new "communities" in which they would no longer have any constitutive role. Bernstein proposes to associate such a community-oriented politics with a Deweyan conception, which finds the roots of democracy not in our nature as Kantian agents, but in our capacity to create such communities.

Wolin worries that the liberal protection of abstract rights by law and opinion has in fact introduced a decline in civic culture and political action. He attempts to redefine the concept of revolutionary action, separating it from the Jacobin model of a capture of state as a prelude to a global social transformation.

In his contribution to the volume, Wolin argues that the reduction of government to the adjudication and participation in interest-group politics has led to an erosion in civic action and public space. The welfarist compromise which would supplement the liberal rights, that can be enforced by the correlative duties, with economic or "positive" rights (entitlements), has resulted in a further depoliticization. The centralized redistributive agencies in fact have led to a radically discouraged and undemocratic underclass of race, poverty, crime, and unemployment, an underclass whose life is so fragmented into the categories of bureaucratic dependence as to become incapable of any genuine political action. Hence the passivity toward the cuts in benefits which came when the economy was no longer expanding, and the "pessimism" of what to do about them.

Wolin thinks we have to "reinvent the forms and practices that will express a democratic conception of collective life." That would be a revolution, if revolution were to mean the right to invent new forms when those who rule have perverted the old ones. For this *inventio* from within our traditions, we need a new kind of political and philosophical theory.

In post-analytic philosophy we thus find a challenge to the Kantianism that holds that morality consists in what can be justified to all rational agents, a challenge to the scientism which postulates a single kind of rationality, and a challenge to the humanism that assumes all works appeal the universality of the human imagination. Philosophy turns to proposals of a civic or community-based democratic politics, to a historical analysis of the philosophical problems which arise in the proliferation of sciences, and to a revival of the Emersonian tradition in letters. For Rorty, these post-analytic developments return us to the great issues of liberalism, scientism and modernism at the heart of Dewey's public philosophy.

Philosophy of America

Pragmatism was widely assumed to be a native American philosophy that grew out of and expressed specifically American traditions: Fordism, Taylorism, American ingenuity, American experimental and entrepreneurial spirit, American "exceptionalism." The debate over pragmatism was in part a debate over those traditions and the way pragmatism expressed them: was pragmatism a reduction of all problems to standards of efficiency, performance and management, did it serve the interests of a managerial class, did it deny the role of class conflict or the irreducibly religious nature of the human community? In 1922, Dewey replied to Russell's quip that

> The two qualities which I consider superlatively important are love of truth and love of our neighbor. I find the love of truth in America obscured by commercialism of which pragmatism is the philosophical expression; and love of our neighbor kept in fetters by Puritan morality.[24]

Introducing another conception of "commercialism," Dewey retorts:

> Commerce itself, let us dare to say it, is a noble thing. It is intercourse, exchange, communication, distribution, sharing of what is otherwise secluded and private.[25]

No such historical debate surrounded American analytic philosophy. Nobody cared what might make it an "American" philosophy; nobody thought that great social questions were at stake in it. Not so with post-analytic philosophy. Cavell wants to revive the Emersonian tradition in letters; Bloom is wondering how "text-centeredness" can survive in America; Wolin wants to derive a concept of revolutionary action from American political traditions.

Rorty urges "solidarity" with Dewey; his post-analytic pragmatism would restore pride in the moral worth of our intellectual heritage. He sees the eclipse of Dewey as part of a misguided moralistic reaction to the "loss of America's hope to lead the nations" which set in with Vietnam: "the sense that we have been found *morally* unworthy of the role we once thought we might play. Such self-indulgent *Schadenfreude* is, I think, the origin of the idea that Deweyan experimentalism, the dominant intellectual movement of a more hopeful time, was not "real" philosophy, but merely a rationalizing apology for certain institutions."[26] Rorty asks a good question: in what sense is philosophy in America a philosophy of America, in what sense does it form part of our intellectual traditions?

Rorty's answer is rather traditional. His idea that "anti-ideological liberalism is the most valuable tradition in American intellectual life"[27] seems a version of a historical thesis defended in 1955 by Louis Hartz, in his once seminal *The Liberal Tradition in America*. Hartz, who strongly influenced Wolin, goes back to Tocqueville's famous claim that: "The great advantage of the Americans is that they have arrived at a state of democracy without having to endure a democratic revolution; and that they are born equal instead of becoming so." Toqueville thought that emigration had done for the Englishmen who became Americans what the monarchy had done for the French: the removal of society from feudal conditions. The Atlantic had done the job of the French State, and its distance, the work of centuries. Thus, democracy was a revolutionary state in the Old World, but a normal one in the New. Americans experienced no social revolution in '76. In America, Lockean traditions together with the absence of an *ancien régime* precluded an aristocracy on the right and a radical working class on the left. The Lockean principle that power be subject to consent combined with the Puritan virtues of ambition, enterprise, and opportunity, to form the great liberal tradition in America.

Rorty's moral patriotism, inasmuch as it rests on a historical view, is thus Tocquevillian. America is the civilized country least concerned with philosophy, declared Tocqueville in 1840. The country least concerned with Kantian epistemologically centered philosophy and with "ideology," adds Rorty in 1984. We must side with our great anti-ideological liberalism and join with contemporary European "post-Marxists" in reversing the question "why is there no socialism in America?" and asking "why *is* there socialism in Europe?"

To read Rorty's pronouncements in this way, however, is to confront his philosophical pride with the long historical and historiographical debate in American history since Hartz and the liberal consensus of the 1950s. The examination of the institutions of slavery in the South, the discovery of the civic republican sources for our Jeffersonian inheritance and our political institutions, and the analysis of the welfare state, have served rather to disrupt that consensus. Rorty's question thus points to a renewed discussion about the basic patterns and traditions in American history. One senses a larger debate which might allow us to separate what is valuable in our intellectual traditions from an official nationalism which presents American democracy as the universal future for the rest of the world.

NOTES

1. Richard Rorty, *Consequences of Pragmatism* (Minneapolis: University of Minnesota Press, 1982), p. 227.

2. Arthur Danto, "Analytic Philosophy" *Social Research* (Winter 1980), 47(4):615–616.

3. Richard Rorty, *Philosophy and the Mirror of Nature* (Princeton: Princeton University Press, 1979), p. 172.

4. Richard Rorty, *Consequences of Pragmatism*, p. 160.

5. *Ibid.*, p. 216.

6. *Ibid.*

7. For Rorty's remarks on Peirce see "Pragmatism, Relativism, and Irrationalism" in *Consequences of Pragmatism*, pp. 160–162. Rorty wants to deny that pragmatism only "suggested various holistic corrections of the atomistic doctrines of the early logical empiricism"; what we now see as most important was a new conception of philosophy itself. This leads him to a selective reading even of Dewey. In "Dewey's Metaphysics" (pp. 72–90) he thus describes a "tension in Dewey's thought." This tension matches what, in an admirable clear introduction to Dewey, Sidorsky describes as the "major discontinuity in philosophical discussion since Dewey wrote. . . . His philosophical theses have not been refuted; yet they have been abandoned by a shift in philosophical interest and a transposition of philosophical method" (Introduction to John Dewey: *The Essential Writings*, p. lv). Rorty thinks this transposition has led to an impasse and wants to revise our philosophical interests accordingly. Thus he has a controversial interpretation even of Dewey.

8. Jacques Bouveresse gives a good sense for the dissidence of doing analytic philosophy in France in "Why I am so very unFrench" in A. Montefiore, ed. *Philosophy in France Today* (Cambridge: Cambridge University Press, 1983).

9. Ian Hacking, *The Emergence of Probability* (Cambridge: Cambridge University Press, 1976.

10. Rorty, "Philosophy as a Kind of Writing," in *Consequences of Pragmatism*, pp. 90–110. In fact, Derrida was *not* advancing a theory about reference with this remark. It was rather directed against the picture of a complete or self-contained unity of a work, which would allow us to speak of what is "inside" and what is "outside" of it. There can be no *hors-texte*, because works do not possess this kind of integrity. Derrida makes the remark in the course of an analysis of Hegel's attempt in his preface to the *Phenomenology of Spirit* to occupy such an external position and comment on what is inside his own book. The analysis "prefaces" Derrida's book, *Dissemination* (Chicago: University of Chicago Press,

1981). Derrida might find our debates about reference and realism rather puzzling.

11. Rorty, *Consequences of Pragmatism*, p. 142. I don't find that the consequence of this pragmatism is the one which Walter Ben-Michel and Steven Knapp infer in "Again Theory," *Critical Inquiry* (Summer 1982): that literary critics should give up reflection about their discipline and content themselves with turning out more readings. Rorty's point is that literary theory should give up the attempt to fix a general frame that specifies the nature of works and their interpretations; it should not start from a conception of what works are, but should look at which particular mortal conceptions of works our traditions in fact suppose. The assumption that works *are* only objects for endless academic readings is precisely the sort of general assumption which Rorty would have literary theory abandon.

12. Bloom, *Agon*, p. viii.

13. Bloom, *Agon*, p. 19. In his social history of the "symbol of America," Bercovitch argues that our "perpetually Emersonian America" in fact refers to middle-class culture: "to declare oneself the symbol of America is by definition to retain one's alliance to middle class culture." *The American Jeremiad* (Madison: Wisconsin University Press, 1978). Emerson thought self-reliance incompatible with socialism; and his "disgust with the 'pushing' Jacksonian 'masses' is well-known; his solution was to train a new leadership, essentially drawn from the 'cultured' middle class 'to cope with the needs of [...] a new age.' " What Bloom's Emersonian modernism departs from is thus the anti-bourgeois sentiments of the European avant-garde.

14. Bloom, *Agon*, p. 20.

15. Stanley Cavell, "Politics as Opposed to What?" *Critical Inquiry* (September 1982), 9(7):

16. Thomas S. Kuhn, *The Structure of Scientific Revolutions* (Chicago: University of Chicago Press, 1964), p. 3.

17. See Ian Hacking, "How Should We Do the History of Statistics," *I & C* (1981), 8:15–26, and Ian Hacking, "Biopower and the Avalanche of Printed Numbers," in *Culture and History* (1983), pp. 279–295.

18. Retrospectively it may seem appropriate that *The Structure of Scientific Revolutions* was the last volume in an eminently logical-positivist series called the *International Encyclopedia of Unified Science*. Kuhn's book was about scientific revolutions in the plural. His "paradigm" or "disciplinary matrix" is a small professional group located anywhere with its journal, its "commitments," its ways of seeing things, and of defining its problems and so forth. It would take a lot of such communities to add up to something called *the* scientific revolution. Yet Kuhn's book suggests there is one *structure* for all change in science, a single or "essential tension." It may be doubted, however, whether all episodes in science in fact conform to his model of accumulation of anomalies leading to crisis and finally change.

19. See Thomas S. Kuhn, "History and History of Science," *Essential Tension* (Chicago: University of Chicago Press, 1977), pp. 140–147.

20. See John Rawls, "The Independence of Moral Theory," in *Proceedings and Addresses of the American Philosophical Association* (1974–75), pp. 5–22. Rorty also

says "*A Theory of Justice* . . . descends straight from Kant, Mill and Sidgwick. The same book could have been written if logical positivism had never existed. It is not a triumph of 'analytic' philosophizing. It is simply the best update of liberal social thought which we have." Richard Rorty, *Consequences of Pragmatism*, p. 216.

21. Thomas Nagel, *Mortal Questions* (Harvard University Press, 1979), pp. 106–128.

22. Richard Rorty, "Pragmatism Without Method," in *Essays in Honor of Sidney Hook.*

23. Cf. Michael Walzer, *Spheres of Justice.*

24. Freeman, as quoted by John Dewey in "Pragmatic America," *New Republic,* April 12, 1922, p. 185.

25. John Dewey, "Pragmatic America," in *Pragmatism and American Culture,* Gail Kennedy, ed. (Heath, 1950), p. 59.

26. Rorty, "Pragmatism Without Method."

27. *Ibid.*

Post-Analytic Philosophy

ONE
INTRODUCTION

[1]
Solidarity or Objectivity?

RICHARD RORTY

THERE ARE two principal ways in which reflective human beings try, by placing their lives in a larger context, to give sense to those lives. The first is by telling the story of their contribution to a community. This community may be the actual historical one in which they live, or another actual one, distant in time or place, or a quite imaginary one, consisting perhaps of a dozen heroes and heroines selected from history or fiction or both. The second way is to describe themselves as standing in immediate relation to a nonhuman reality. This relation is immediate in the sense that it does not derive from a relation between such a reality and their tribe, or their nation, or their imagined band of comrades. I shall say that stories of the former kind exemplify the desire for solidarity, and that stories of the latter kind exemplify the desire for objectivity. Insofar as a person is seeking solidarity, he or she does not ask about the relation between the practices of the chosen community and something outside that community. Insofar as he seeks objectivity, he distances himself from the actual persons around him not by thinking of himself as a member of some other real or imaginary group, but rather by attaching himself to something which can be described without reference to any particular human beings.

The tradition in Western culture which centers around the notion of the search for Truth, a tradition which runs from the Greek philosophers through the Enlightenment, is the clearest example of the attempt to find a

This paper is a revised version of a Howison Lecture given at the University of California at Berkeley in January 1983. A somewhat different version appeared in *Nanzan Review of American Studies*, vol. 6, 1984, and (in French translation) in *Critique*.

sense in one's existence by turning away from solidarity to objectivity. The idea of Truth as something to be pursued for its own sake, not because it will be good for oneself, or for one's real or imaginary community, is the central theme of this tradition. It was perhaps the growing awareness by the Greeks of the sheer diversity of human communities which stimulated the emergence of this ideal. A fear of parochialism, of being confined within the horizons of the group into which one happens to be born, a need to see it with the eyes of a stranger, helps produce the skeptical and ironic tone characteristic of Euripides and Socrates. Herodotus' willingness to take the barbarians seriously enough to describe their customs in detail may have been a necessary prelude to Plato's claim that the way to transcend skepticism is to envisage a common goal of humanity—a goal set by human nature rather than by Greek culture. The combination of Socratic alienation and Platonic hope gives rise to the idea of the intellectual as someone who is in touch with the nature of things, not by way of the opinions of his community, but in a more immediate way.

Plato developed the idea of such an intellectual by means of distinctions between knowledge and opinion, and between appearance and reality. Such distinctions conspire to produce the idea that rational inquiry should make visible a realm to which nonintellectuals have little access, and of whose very existence they may be doubtful. In the Enlightenment, this notion became concrete in the adoption of the Newtonian physical scientist as a model of the intellectual. To most thinkers of the eighteenth century, it seemed clear that the access to Nature which physical science had provided should now be followed by the establishment of social, political, and economic institutions which were in accordance with Nature. Ever since, liberal social thought has centered around social reform as made possible by objective knowledge of what human beings are like—not knowledge of what Greeks or Frenchmen or Chinese are like, but of humanity as such. We are the heirs of this objectivist tradition, which centers round the assumption that we must step outside our community long enough to examine it in the light of something which transcends it, namely, that which it has in common with every other actual and possible human community. This tradition dreams of an ultimate community which will have transcended the distinction between the natural and the social, which will exhibit a solidarity which is not parochial because it is the expression of an ahistorical human nature. Much of the rhetoric of contemporary intellectual life takes for granted that the goal of scientific inquiry into man is to understand "underlying structures," or, "culturally invariant factors," or "biologically determined patterns."

Those who wish to ground solidarity in objectivity—call them "realists"—have to construe truth as correspondence to reality. So they must construct a metaphysics which has room for a special relation between beliefs and objects which will differentiate true from false beliefs. They also must argue that there are procedures of justification of belief which are natural and not merely local. So they must construct an epistemology which has room for a kind of justification which is not merely social but natural, springing from human nature itself, and made possible by a link between that part of nature and the rest of nature. On their view, the various procedures which are thought of as providing rational justification by one or another culture may or may not really *be* rational. For to be truly rational, procedures of justification *must* lead to the truth, to correspondence to reality, to the intrinsic nature of things.

By contrast, those who wish to reduce objectivity to solidarity—call them "pragmatists"—do not require either a metaphysics or an epistemology. They view truth as, in William James' phrase, what it is good for *us* to believe. So they do not need an account of a relation between beliefs and objects called 'correspondence,' nor an account of human cognitive abilities which ensures that our species is capable of entering into that relation. They see the gap between truth and justification not as something to be bridged by isolating a natural and transcultural sort of rationality which can be used to criticize certain cultures and praise others, but simply as the gap between the actual good and the possible better. From a pragmatist point of view, to say that what is rational for us now to believe may not be *true,* is simply to say that somebody may come up with a better idea. It is to say that there is always room for improved belief, since new evidence, or new hypotheses, or a whole new vocabulary, may come along.[1] For pragmatists, the desire for objectivity is not the desire to escape the limitations of one's community, but simply the desire for as much intersubjective agreement as possible, the desire to extend the reference of "us" as far as we can. Insofar as pragmatists make a distinction between knowledge and opinion, it is simply the distinction between topics on which such agreement is relatively easy to get and topics on which agreement is relatively hard to get.

"Relativism" is the traditional epithet applied to pragmatism by realists. Three different views are commonly referred to by this name. The first is the view that every belief is as good as every other. The second is the view that "true" is an equivocal term, having as many meanings as there are procedures of justification. The third is the view that there is nothing to be said about either truth or rationality apart from descriptions of the familiar procedures of justification which a given society— *ours*—uses in one or another area of inquiry. The pragmatist holds the ethnocentric third view. But he does not hold the self-refuting first view, nor the eccentric second view. He thinks that his views are better than the realists, but he does not think that his views correspond to the nature of things. He thinks that the very flexibility of the word "true"—the fact that it is merely an expression of commendation—insures its univocity. The term "true," on his account, means the same in all cultures, just as equally flexible terms like "here," "there," "good," "bad," "you," and "me" mean the same in all cultures. But the identity of meaning is, of course, compatible with diversity of reference, and with diversity of procedures for assigning the terms. So he feels free to use the term "true" as a general term of commendation in the same way as his realist opponent does— and in particular to use it to commend his own view.

However, it is not clear why "relativist" should be thought an appropriate term for the ethnocentric third view, the one which the pragmatist *does* hold. For the pragmatist is not holding a positive theory which says that something is relative to something else. He is, instead, making the purely *negative* point that we should drop the traditional distinction between knowledge and opinion, construed as the distinction between truth as correspondence to reality and truth as a commendatory term for well-justified beliefs. The reason that the realist calls this negative claim "relativistic" is that he cannot believe that anybody would seriously deny that truth has an intrinsic nature. So when the pragmatist says that there is nothing to be said about truth save that each of us will commend as true those beliefs which he or she finds good to believe, the realist is inclined to interpret this as one more positive theory about the nature of truth: a theory according to which truth is simply the contemporary opinion of a chosen individual or group. Such a theory would, of course, be self-refuting. But the pragmatist does not have a theory of truth, much less a relativistic one. As a partisan of solidarity, his account of the value of cooperative human inquiry has only an ethical base, not an epistemological or metaphysical one. Not having *any* epistemology, *a fortiori* he does not have a relativistic one.

The question of whether truth or rationality has an intrinsic nature, of whether we ought to have a positive theory about either topic, is just the question of whether our self-description ought to be constructed around a relation to human nature or around a relation to a particular collection of human beings, whether we should desire objectivity or solidarity. It is hard to see how one could choose between these alternatives by looking more deeply into the nature of knowledge, or of man, or of nature. Indeed, the proposal that this issue might be so settled begs the question in favour of the realist, for it presupposes that knowledge, man, and nature *have* real essences which are relevant to the problem at hand. For the pragmatist, by contrast, "knowledge" is, like "truth," simply a compliment paid to the beliefs which we think so well justified that, for the moment, further justification is not needed. An inquiry into the nature of knowledge can, on his view, only be a sociohistorical account of how various people have tried to reach agreement on what to believe.

This view which I am calling "pragmatism" is almost, but not quite, the same as what Hilary Putnam, in his recent *Reason, Truth and History,* calls "the internalist conception of philosophy."[2] Putnam defines such a conception as one which gives up the attempt at a God's eye view of things, the attempt at contact with the nonhuman which I have been calling "the desire for objectivity." Unfortunately, he accompanies his defense of the antirealist views I am recommending with a polemic against a lot of the other people who hold these views—e.g., Kuhn, Feyerabend, Foucault, and myself. We are criticized as "relativists." Putnam presents "internalism" as a happy *via media* between realism and relativism. He speaks of "the plethora of relativisitic doctrines being marketed today"[3] and in particular of "the French philosophers" as holding "some fancy mixture of cultural relativism and 'structuralism' ".[4] But when it comes to criticizing these doctrines all that Putnam finds to attack is the so-called "incommensurability thesis": vis., "terms used in another culture cannot be equated in meaning or reference with any terms or expressions *we* possess."[5] He sensibly agrees with Donald Davidson in remarking that this thesis is self-refuting. Criticism of this thesis, however, is destructive of, at most, some incautious passages in some early writings by Feyerabend. Once this thesis is brushed aside, it is hard to see how Putnam himself differs from most of those he criticizes.

Putnam accepts the Davidsonian point that, as he puts it, "the whole justification of an interpretative scheme . . . is that it renders the behavior of others at least minimally reasonable by *our* lights."[6] It would seem natural to go on from this to say that we cannot get outside the range of those lights, that we cannot stand on neutral ground illuminated only by the natural light of reason. But Putnam draws back from this conclusion. He does so because he construes the claim that we cannot do so as the

claim that the range of our thought is restricted by what he calls "institutionalized norms," publicly available criteria for settling all arguments,
including philosophical arguments. He rightly says that there are no such
criteria, arguing that the suggestion that there are is as self-refuting as the
"incommensurability thesis." He is, I think, entirely right in saying that
the notion that philosophy is or should become such an application of
explicit criteria contradicts the very idea of philosophy.[7] One can gloss
Putnam's point by saying that "philosophy" is precisely what a culture
becomes capable of when it ceases to define itself in terms of explicit rules,
and becomes sufficiently leisured and civilized to rely on inarticulate know-
how, to substitute *phronesis* for codification, and conversation with for-
eigners for conquest of them.

But to say that we cannot refer every question to explicit criteria institutionalized by our society does not speak to the point which the people
whom Putnam calls "relativists" are making. One reason these people are
pragmatists is precisely that they share Putnam's distrust of the positiv-
istic idea that rationality is a matter of applying criteria.

Such a distrust is common, for example, to Kuhn, Mary Hesse, Wittgenstein, Michael Polanyi and Michael Oakeshott. Only someone who
did think of rationality in this way would dream of suggesting that "true"
means something different in different societies. For only such a person
could imagine that there was anything to pick out to which one might
make "true" relative. Only if one shares the logical positivists' idea that
we all carry around things called "rules of language" which regulate what
we say when, will one suggest that there is no way to break out of one's
culture.

In the most original and powerful section of his book, Putnam argues
that the notion that "rationality . . . is defined by the local cultural norms"
is merely the demonic counterpart of positivism. It is, as he says, "a
scientistic theory inspired by anthropology as positivism was a scientistic
theory inspired by the exact sciences." By "scientism" Putnam means the
notion that rationality consists in the application of criteria.[8] Suppose we
drop this notion, and accept Putnam's own Quinean picture of inquiry
as the continual reweaving of a web of beliefs rather than as the application of criteria to cases. Then the notion of "local cultural norms" will
lose its offensively parochial overtones. For now to say that we must work
by our own lights, that we must be ethnocentric, is merely to say that
beliefs suggested by another culture must be tested by trying to weave
them together with beliefs we already have. It is a consequence of this
holistic view of knowledge, a view *shared* by Putnam and those he criti-

cizes as "relativists," that alternative cultures are not to be thought of on the model of alternative geometries. Alternative geometries are irreconcilable because they have axiomatic structures, and contradictory axioms. They are *designed* to be irreconcilable. Cultures are not so designed, and do not have axiomatic structures. To say that they have "institutionalized norms" is only to say, with Foucault, that knowledge is never separable from power—that one is likely to suffer if one does not hold certain beliefs at certain times and places. But such institutional backups for beliefs take the form of bureaucrats and policemen, not of "rules of language" and "criteria of rationality." To think otherwise is the Cartesian fallacy of seeing axioms where there are only shared habits, of viewing statements which summarize such practices as if they reported constraints enforcing such practises. Part of the force of Quine's and Davidson's attack on the distinction between the conceptual and the empirical is that the distinction between different cultures does not differ in kind from the distinction between different theories held by members of a single culture. The Tasmanian aborigines and the British colonists had trouble communicating, but this trouble was different only in extent from the difficulties in communcation experienced by Gladstone and Disraeli. The trouble in all such cases is just the difficulty of explaining why other people disagree with us, of reweaving our beliefs so as to fit the fact of disagreement together with the other beliefs we hold. The same Quinean arguments which dispose of the positivists' distinction between analytic and synthetic truth dispose of the anthropologists' distinction between the intercultural and the intracultural.

On this holistic account of cultural norms, however, we do not need the notion of a universal transcultural rationality which Putnam invokes against those whom he calls "relativists." Just before the end of his book, Putnam says that once we drop the notion of a God's-eye point of view we realize that:

> we can only hope to produce a more rational *conception* of rationality or a better *conception* of morality if we operate from *within* our tradition (with its echoes of the Greek agora, of Newton, and so on, in the case of rationality, and with its echoes of scripture, of the philosophers, of the democratic revolutions, and so on . . . in the case of morality). We are invited to engage in a truly human dialogue.[9]

With this I entirely agree, and so, I take it, would Kuhn, Hesse, and most of the other so-called "relativists"—perhaps even Foucault. But Putnam then goes on to pose a further question:

Does this dialogue have an ideal terminus? Is there a *true* conception of
rationality, an ideal morality, even if all we ever have are our *conceptions*
of these?

I do not see the point of this question. Putnam suggests that a negative
answer—the view that "there is only the dialogue"—is just another form
of self-refuting relativism. But, once again, I do not see how a claim that
something does not exist can be construed as a claim that something is
relative to something else. In the final sentence of his book, Putnam says
that "The very fact that we speak of our different conceptions as different
conceptions of *rationality* posits a *Grenzbegriff,* a limit-concept of ideal
truth." But what is such a posit supposed to do, except to say that from
God's point of view the human race is heading in the right direction?
Surely Putnam's "internalism" should forbid him to say anything like that.
To say that *we* think we're heading in the right direction is just to say,
with Kuhn, that we can, by hindsight, tell the story of the past as a story
of progress. To say that we still have a long way to go, that our present
views should not be cast in bronze, is too platitudinous to require support by positing limit-concepts. So it is hard to see what difference is
made by the difference between saying "there is only the dialogue" and
saying "there is also that to which the dialogue converges."

I would suggest that Putnam here, at the end of the day, slides back
into the scientism he rightly condemns in others. For the root of scientism, defined as the view that rationality is a matter of applying criteria,
is the desire for objectivity, the hope that what Putnam calls "human
flourishing" has a transhistorical nature. I think that Feyerabend is right
in suggesting that until we discard the metaphor of inquiry, and human
activity generally, as converging rather than proliferating, as becoming
more unified rather than more diverse, we shall never be free of the motives which once led us to posit gods. Positing *Grenzbegriffe* seems merely
a way of telling ourselves that a nonexistent God would, if he did exist,
be pleased with us. If we could ever be moved solely by the desire for
solidarity, setting aside the desire for objectivity altogether, then we should
think of human progress as making it possible for human beings to do
more interesting things and be more interesting people, not as heading
towards a place which has somehow been prepared for humanity in advance. Our self-image would employ images of making rather than finding, the images used by the Romantics to praise poets rather than the
images used by the Greeks to praise mathematicians. Feyerabend seems

to me right in trying to develop such a self-image for us, but his project seems misdescribed, by himself as well as by his critics, as "relativism."[10]

Those who follow Feyerabend in this direction are often thought of as necessarily enemies of the Enlightenment, as joining in the chorus which claims that the traditional self-descriptions of the Western democracies are bankrupt, that they somehow have been shown to be "inadequate" or "self-deceptive." Part of the instinctive resistance to attempts by Marxists, Sartreans, Oakeshottians, Gadamerians and Foucauldians to reduce objectivity to solidarity is the fear that our traditional liberal habits and hopes will not survive the reduction. Such feelings are evident, for example, in Habermas' criticism of Gadamer's position as relativistic and potentially repressive, in the suspicion that Heidegger's attacks on realism are somehow linked to his Nazism, in the hunch that Marxist attempts to interpret values as class interests are usually just apologies for Leninist takeovers, and in the suggestion that Oakeshott's skepticism about rationalism in politics is merely an apology for the status quo.

I think that putting the issue in such moral and political terms, rather than in epistemological or metaphilosophical terms, makes clearer what is at stake. For now the question is not about how to define words like "truth" or "rationality" or "knowledge" or "philosophy," but about what self-image our society should have of itself. The ritual invocation of the "need to avoid relativism" is most comprehensible as an expression of the need to preserve certain habits of contemporary European life. These are the habits nurtured by the Enlightenment, and justified by it in terms of an appeal of Reason, conceived as a transcultural human ability to correspond to reality, a faculty whose possession and use is demonstrated by obedience to explicit criteria. So the real question about relativism is whether these same habits of intellectual, social, and political life can be justified by a conception of rationality as criterionless muddling through, and by a pragmatist conception of truth.

I think that the answer to this question is that the pragmatist cannot justify these habits without circularity, but then neither can the realist. The pragmatists' justification of toleration, free inquiry, and the quest for undistorted communication can only take the form of a comparison between societies which exemplify these habits and those which do not, leading up to the suggestion that nobody who has experienced both would prefer the latter. It is exemplified by Winston Churchill's defense of democracy as the worst form of government imaginable, except for all the others which have been tried so far. Such justification is not by reference to a criterion, but by reference to various detailed practical advantages. It is circular only in that the terms of praise used to describe liberal societies will be drawn from the vocabulary of the liberal societies themselves. Such praise has to be in *some* vocabulary, after all, and the terms of praise current in primitive or theocratic or totalitarian societies will not produce the desired result. So the pragmatist admits that he has no ahistorical standpoint from which to endorse the habits of modern democracies he wishes to praise. These consequences are just what partisans of solidarity expect. But among partisans of objectivity they give rise, once again, to fears of the dilemma formed by ethnocentrism on the one hand and relativism on the other. Either we attach a special privilege to our own community, or we pretend an impossible tolerance for every other group.

I have been arguing that we pragmatists should grasp the ethnocentric horn of this dilemma. We should say that we must, in practice, privilege our own group, even though there can be no noncircular justification for doing so. We must insist that the fact that nothing is immune from criticism does not mean that we have a duty to justify everything. We Western liberal intellectuals should accept the fact that we have to start from where we are, and that this means that there are lots of views which we simply cannot take seriously. To use Neurath's familiar analogy, we can *understand* the revolutionary's suggestion that a sailable boat can't be made out of the planks which make up ours, and that we must simply abandon ship. But we cannot take his suggestion seriously. We cannot take it as a rule for action, so it is not a live option. For some people, to be sure, the option *is* live. These are the people who have always hoped to become a New Being, who have hoped to be converted rather than persuaded. But we—the liberal Rawlsian searchers for consensus, the heirs of Socrates, the people who wish to link their days dialectically each to each—cannot do so. Our community—the community of the liberal intellectuals of the secular modern West—wants to be able to give a *post factum* account of any change of view. We want to be able, so to speak, to justify ourselves to our earlier selves. This preference is not built into us by human nature. It is just the way *we* live now.[11]

This lonely provincialism, this admission that we are just the historical moment that we are, not the representatives of something ahistorical, is what makes traditional Kantian liberals like Rawls draw back from pragmatism.[12] "Relativism," by contrast, is merely a red herring. The realist is, once again, projecting his own habits of thought upon the pragmatist when he charges him with relativism. For the realist thinks that the whole point of philosophical thought is to detach oneself from any particular community and look down at it from a more universal standpoint. When he hears the pragmatist repudiating the desire for such a standpoint he cannot quite believe it. He thinks that everyone, deep down inside, *must* want such detachment. So he attributes to the pragmatist a perverse form of his own attempted detachment, and sees him as an ironic, sneering aesthete who refuses to take the choice between communities seriously, a mere "relativist." But the pragmatist, dominated by the desire for solidarity, can only be criticized for taking his own community *too* seriously. He can only be criticized for ethnocentrism, not for relativism. To be ethnocentric is to divide the human race into the people to whom one must justify one's beliefs and the others. The first group—one's *ethnos*—comprises those who share enough of one's beliefs to make fruitful conversation possible. In this sense, everybody is ethnocentric when engaged in actual debate, no matter how much realist rhetoric about objectivity he produces in his study.[13]

What is disturbing about the pragmatist's picture is not that it is relativistic but that it takes away two sorts of metaphysical comfort to which our intellectual tradition has become accustomed. One is the thought that membership in our biological species carries with it certain "rights," a notion which does not seem to make sense unless the biological similarities entail the possession of something non-biological, something which links our species to a nonhuman reality and thus gives the species moral dignity. This picture of rights as biologically transmitted is so basic to the political discourse of the Western democracies that we are troubled by any suggestion that "human nature" is not a useful moral concept. The second comfort is provided by the thought that our community cannot wholly die. The picture of a common human nature oriented towards correspondence to reality as it is in itself comforts us with the thought that even if our civilization is destroyed, even if all memory of our political or intellectual or artistic community is erased, the race is fated to recapture the virtues and the insights and the achievements which were the glory of that community. The notion of human nature as an inner structure which leads all members of the species to converge to the same point, to recognize the same theories, virtues, and works of art as worthy of honor, assures us that even if the Persians had won, the arts and sciences of the Greeks would sooner or later have appeared elsewhere. It assures us that even if the Orwellian bureaucrats of terror rule for a thousand years the achievements of the Western democracies will someday be duplicated by our remote descendents. It assures us that "man will prevail," that something reasonably like *our* world-view, *our* virtues, *our* art, will bob up again whenever human beings are left alone to cultivate their inner natures. The comfort of the realist picture is the comfort of saying not simply that there is a place prepared for our race in our advance, but also that we now know quite a bit about what that place looks like. The inevitable ethnocentrism to which we are all condemned is thus as much a part of the realist's comfortable view as of the pragmatists' uncomfortable one.

The pragmatist gives up the first sort of comfort because he thinks that to say that certain people have certain rights is merely to say that we should treat them in certain ways. It is not to give a *reason* for treating them in those ways. As to the second sort of comfort, he suspects that the hope that something resembling *us* will inherit the earth is impossible to eradicate, as impossible as eradicating the hope of surviving our individual deaths through some satisfying transfiguration. But he does not want to turn this hope into a theory of the nature of man. He wants solidarity to be our *only* comfort, and to be seen not to require metaphysical support.

My suggestion that the desire for objectivity is in part a disguised form of the fear of the death of our community echoes Nietzsche's charge that the philosophical tradition which stems from Plato is an attempt to avoid facing up to contingency, to escape from time and chance. Nietzsche thought that realism was to be condemned not only by arguments from its theoretical incoherence, the sort of argument we find in Putnam and Davidson, but also on practical, pragmatic, grounds. Neitzsche thought that the test of human character was the ability to live with the thought that there was no convergence. He wanted us to be able to think of truth as:

> a mobile army of metaphors, metonyms, and anthromorphisms—in short a sum of human relations, which have been enhanced, transposed, and embellished poetically and rhetorically and which after long use seem firm, canonical, and obligatory to a people.[14]

Nietzsche hoped that eventually there might be human beings who could and did think of truth in this way, but who still liked themselves, who saw themselves as *good* people for whom solidarity was *enough*.[15]

I think that pragmatism's attack on the various structure-content distinctions which buttress the realist's notion of objectivity can best be seen as an attempt to let us think of truth in this Nietzschean way, as entirely a matter of solidarity. That is why I think we need to say, despite Putnam, that "there is only the dialogue," only *us*, and to throw out the last residues of the notion of "trans-cultural rationality." But this should not lead us to repudiate, as Nietzsche sometimes did, the elements in our movable host which embody the ideas of Socratic conversation, Christian fellowship, and Enlightenment science. Nietzsche ran together his diagnosis of philosophical realism as an expression of fear and resentment with his own resentful idiosyncratic idealizations of silence, solitude, and violence. Post-Nietzschean thinkers like Adorno and Heidegger and Foucault have run together Nietzsche's criticisms of the metaphysical tradition on the one hand with his criticisms of bourgeois civility, of Christian love, and of the nineteenth century's hope that science would make the world a better place to live, on the other. I do not think that there is any interesting connection between these two sets of criticisms. Pragmatism seems to me, as I have said, a philosophy of solidarity rather than of despair. From this point of view, Socrates' turn away from the gods, Christianity's turn from an Omnipotent Creator to the man who suffered on the Cross, and the Baconian turn from science as contemplation of eternal truth to science as instrument of social progress, can be seen as so many preparations for the act of social faith which is suggested by a Nietzschean view of truth.[16]

The best argument we partisans of solidarity have against the realistic partisans of objectivity is Nietzsche's argument that the traditional Western metaphysico-epistemological way of firming up our habits simply isn't working anymore. It isn't doing its job. It has become as transparent a device as the postulation of deities who turn out, by a happy coincidence, to have chosen *us* as their people. So the pragmatist suggestion that we substitute a "merely" ethical foundation for our sense of community—or, better, that we think of our sense of community as having no foundation except shared hope and the trust created by such sharing—is put forward on practical grounds. It is *not* put forward as a corollary of a metaphysical claim that the objects in the world contain no intrinsically action-guiding properties, nor of an epistemological claim that we lack a faculty of moral sense, nor of a semantical claim that truth is reducible to justification. It is a suggestion about how we might think of ourselves in order to avoid the kind of resentful belatedness—characteristic of the bad side of Nietzsche—which now characterizes much of high culture. This resentment arises from the realization, which I referred to at the beginning of this essay, that the Enlightenment's search for objectivity has often gone sour.

The rhetoric of scientific objectivity, pressed too hard and taken too seriously, has led us to people like B. F. Skinner on the one hand and people like Althusser on the other—two equally pointless fantasies, both produced by the attempt to be "scientific" about our moral and political lives. Reaction against scientism led to attacks on natural science as a sort of false god. But there is nothing wrong with science, there is only something wrong with the attempt to divinize it, the attempt characteristic of realistic philosophy. This reaction has also led to attacks on liberal social thought of the type common to Mill and Dewey and Rawls as a mere ideological superstructure, one which obscures the realities of our situation and represses attempts to change that situation. But there is nothing wrong with liberal democracy, nor with the philosophers who have tried to enlarge its scope. There is only something wrong with the attempt to see their efforts as failures to achieve something which they were not trying to achieve—a demonstration of the "objective" superiority of our way of life over all other alternatives. There is, in short, nothing wrong with the hopes of the Enlightenment, the hopes which created the Western democracies. The value of the ideals of the Enlightenment is, for us pragmatists, just the value of some of the institutions and practices which they have created. In this essay I have sought to distinguish these institutions and practices from the philosophical justifications for them provided by partisans of objectivity, and to suggest an alternative justification.

NOTES

1. This attitude toward truth, in which the consensus of a community rather than a relation to a nonhuman reality is taken as central, is associated not only with the American pragmatic tradition but with the work of Popper and Habermas. Habermas' criticisms of lingering positivist elements in Popper parallel those made by Deweyan holists of the early logical empiricists. It is important to see, however, that the pragmatist notion of truth common to James and Dewey is not dependent upon either Peirce's notion of an "ideal end of inquiry" nor on Habermas' notion of an "ideally free community." For criticism of these notions, which in my view are insufficiently ethnocentric, see my "Pragmatism, Davidson, and Truth," forthcoming in a festschrift for Davidson edited by Ernest LePore (to be published by the University of Minnesota Press in 1985), and "Habermas and Lyotard on Postmodernity" in *Praxis International,* 1984.

2. Hilary Putnam, *Reason, Truth, and History* (Cambridge: Cambridge University Press, 1981), pp. 49–50.

3. *Ibid.,* p. 119.

4. *Ibid.,* p. x

5. *Ibid.,* p. 114

6. *Ibid.,* p. 119. See Davidson's "On the very idea of a conceptual scheme," in his *Inquiries into Truth and Interpretation* (Oxford: Oxford University Press, 1984) for a more complete and systematic presentation of this point.

7. Putnam, p. 113

8. *Ibid.,* p. 126

9. *Ibid.,* p. 216

10. See, e.g., Paul Feyerabend, *Science in a Free Society* (London: New Left Books, 1978), p. 9, where Feyerabend identifies his own view with "relativism (in the old and simple sense of Protagoras)." This identification is accompanied by the claim that " 'Objectively' there is not much to choose between anti-semitism and humanitarianism." I think Feyerabend would have served himself better by saying that the scare-quoted word "objectively" should simply be dropped from use, together with the traditional philosophical distinctions between scheme and content (see the Davidson essay cited in note 6 above) which buttress the subjective-objective distinction, than by saying that we may keep the word and use it to say the sort of thing Protagoras said. What Feyerabend is really against is the correspondence theory of truth, not the idea that some views cohere better than others.

11. This quest for consensus is opposed to the sort of quest for authenticity which wishes to free itself from the opinion of our community. See, for example, Vincent Descombes' account of Deleuze in *Modern French Philosophy* (Cam-

bridge: Cambridge University Press, 1980), p. 153: "Even if philosophy is essentially demystificatory, philosophers often fail to produce authentic critiques; they defend order, authority, institutions, 'decency,' everything in which the ordinary person believes." On the pragmatist or ethnocentric view I am suggesting, all that critique can or should do is play off elements in "what the ordinary person believes" against other elements. To attempt to do more than this is to fantasize rather than to converse. Fantasy may, to be sure, be an incentive to more fruitful conversation, but when it no longer fulfills this function it does not deserve the name of "critique."

12. In *A Theory of Justice* Rawls seemed to be trying to retain the authority of Kantian "practical reason" by imagining a social contract devised by choosers "behind a veil of ignorance"—using the "rational self-interest" of such choosers as a touchstone for the ahistorical validity of certain social institutions. Much of the criticism to which that book was subjected, e.g., by Michael Sandel in his *Liberalism and the Limits of Justice* (Cambridge, Cambridge University Press, 1982), has centered on the claim that one cannot escape history in this way. In the meantime, however, Rawls has put forward a meta-ethical view which drops the claim to ahistorical validity. (See his "Kantian constructivism in moral theory," *Journal of Philosophy,* 1977, and his "Theory of Justice: Metaphysical or Political?" forthcoming in *Philosophy and Public Affairs.*) Concurrently, T. M. Scanlon has urged that the essence of a "contractualist" account of moral motivation is better understood as the desire to justify one's action to others than in terms of "rational self-interest." See Scanlon, "Contractualism and Utilitarianism" in A. Sen and B. Williams, eds., *Utilitarianism and Beyond,* ed. (Cambridge, Cambridge University Press, 1982). Scanlon's emendation of Rawls leads in the same direction as Rawls' later work, since Scanlon's use of the notion of "justification to others on grounds they could not reasonably reject" chimes with the "constructivist" view that what counts for social philosophy is what can be justified to a particular historical community, not to "humanity in general." On my view, the frequent remark that Rawls' rational choosers look remarkably like twentieth-century American liberals is perfectly just, but not a criticism of Rawls. It is merely a frank recognition of the ethnocentrism which is essential to serious, nonfantastical, thought. I defend this view in "Postmodernist Bourgeois Liberalism," *Journal of Philosophy,* 1983.

13. In an important paper called "The Truth in Relativism," included in his *Moral Luck* (Cambridge: Cambridge University Press, 1981), Bernard Williams makes a similar point in terms of a distinction between "genuine confrontation" and "notional confrontation." The latter is the sort of confrontation which occurs, asymmetrically, between us and primitive tribespeople. The belief-systems of such people do not present, as Williams puts it, "real options" for us, for we cannot imagine going over to their view without "self-deception or paranoia." These are the people whose beliefs on certain topics overlap so little with ours that their inability to agree with us raises no doubt in our minds about the correctness of our own beliefs. Williams' use of "real option" and "notional confrontation" seems to me very enlightening, but I think he turns these notions to purposes they will not serve. Williams wants to defend ethical relativism, defined as

the claim that when ethical confrontations are merely notional "questions of appraisal do not genuinely arise." He thinks they *do* arise in connection with notional confrontations between, e.g., Einsteinian and Amazonian cosmologies. (See Williams, p. 142.) This distinction between ethics and physics seems to me an awkward result to which Williams is driven by his unfortunate attempt to find *something* true in relativism, an attempt which is a corollary of his attempt to be "realistic" about physics. On my (Davidsonian) view, there is no point in distinguishing between true sentences which are "made true by reality" and true sentences which are "made true by us", because the whole idea of "truth-makers" needs to be dropped. So I would hold that there is *no* truth in relativism, but this much truth in ethnocentrism: we cannot justify our beliefs (in physics, ethics, or any other area) to everybody, but only to those whose beliefs overlap ours to some appropriate extent. (This is not a theoretical problem about "untranslatability," but simply a practical problem about the limitations of argument; it is not that we live in different worlds than the Nazis or the Amazonians, but that conversion from or to their point of view, though possible, will not be a matter of inference from previously shared premises.)

14. Nietzsche, "On Truth and Lie in an Extra-Moral Sense", in *The Viking Portable Nietzsche,* Walter Kaufmann, ed. and trans., pp. 46–47.

15. See Sabina Lovibond, *Realism and Imagination in Ethics* (Minneapolis: University of Minnesota Press, 1983), p. 158: "An adherent of Wittgenstein's view of language should equate that goal with the establishment of a language-game in which we could participate ingenuously, while retaining our awareness of it as a specific historical formation. A community in which such a language-game was played would be one . . . whose members understood their own form of life and yet were not embarrassed by it."

16. See Hans Blumenberg, *The Legitimation of Modernity* (Cambridge: MIT Press, 1982), for a story about the history of European thought which, unlike the stories told by Nietzsche and Heidegger, sees the Enlightenment as a definitive step forward. For Blumenberg, the attitude of "self-assertion," the kind of attitude which stems from a Baconian view of the nature and purpose of science, needs to be distinguished from "self-foundation," the Cartesian project of grounding such inquiry upon ahistorical criteria of rationality. Blumenberg remarks, pregnantly, that the "historicist" criticism of the optimism of the Enlightenment, criticism which began with the Romantics' turn back to the Middle Ages, undermines self-foundation but not self-assertion.

[2]
After Empiric

HILARY PUTN.

IF ANY PROBLEM has emerged as *the* problem for analytic philosophy in the twentieth century, it is the problem of how words "hook
onto" the world. The difficulty with A. J. Ayer, who has tried, in his recent book, to sum up Philosophy in the Twentieth Century is that there
is no acknowledgement of the difficulty of this problem.

A. J. Ayer's *Philosophy in the Twentieth Century* is pleasant and useful
reading in its first half. One encounters William James, C. I. Lewis, Bertrand Russell, G. E. Moore, and such lesser Oxford figures as W. D. Ross
and H. A. Pritchard, presented as they struck Ayer as a young man or as
they influenced his philosophical life, and not just as he now regards them
(although he tells us that as well). Ayer's description of the Wittgenstein
of the *Tractatus* is likewise pleasant and useful to read. But beginning
with the section on the later Wittgenstein the book becomes, for the most
part, disappointing.

It is obvious that something happened in philosophy after the *Tractatus* with which Ayer is profoundly out of sympathy. And while he tries
to present what happened conscientiously—and he is certainly fair
minded—he curiously fails to tell the reader *what* it is that he is unable
to sympathize with: perhaps he does not know himself. The result is that
a reader who had only this book to go by would have to see philosophy
after the early Wittgenstein as, for the most part, a series of empty and
confused ideas and arguments. Even the exposition becomes untrustwor-
thy. My own views (with which Ayer concludes) are misrepresented (I

This essay first appeared as "After Ayer, After Empiricism" in *Partisan Review* (1984), vol.
51, no. 2.

do not hold that it is inconceivable that one could discover that water is not H_2O as Ayer suggests), as are, for example, those of David Armstrong, the representative of contemporary materialism that Ayer chooses. (Ayer charges Armstrong with denying the existence of "appearances," i.e., sense-data. But Armstrong is quite clear on this point: he believes in the existence of appearances, but he does not take appearance-*concepts* as primitive and unanalyzable. Rather he regards appearances as functionally characterized brain-events.)

If the book only half succeeds in its aim to be a sequel to Russell's *A History of Western Philosophy*, it succeeds better in giving a picture of Ayer as a philosopher. From the time he first appeared on the scene as *the* British exponent of logical positivism to the present moment, Sir Alfred Jules Ayer has been somewhat of a paradox—always against the fashion, always rebellious, yet, also (and in a good sense) old-fashioned in his philosophical demeanor. While his views have changed considerably since he wrote *Language, Truth, and Logic,* he continues to philosophize in the style and spirit of Bertrand Russell. If that style and spirit no longer speak to the concerns of practicing philosophers, that is, I suspect, a fact of cultural importance and not just an event for professional philosophers to note.

On the one hand, Ayer still bases his philosophy—he remains an empiricist—on sense-data, which he now prefers to call "sense-qualia." He answers Wittgenstein's famous doubts about the possibility of accounting for public language and public knowledge in terms of supposedly private objects, by postulating a faculty he calls "primary recognition" which enables us to "straightforwardly identify" sense-qualia when they occur. Wittgenstein's treatment of scepticism about our ability to know other minds is seen as a "summary dismissal," rather than (as more appreciative readers of Wittgenstein would see it) as something which cannot be understood apart from the whole structure of Wittgenstein's philosophical work—which would make it just the opposite of "summary."

On the other hand, Ayer no longer holds to the positivist view that unverifiable statements are meaningless. (Statements about the distant past may be unverifiable, but according to Ayer, they are certainly meaningful.) Ayer has long since given up his former view that material objects are just a sort of logical fiction which we introduce to systematize our talk about sense-qualia. Like Russell in his later writings, Ayer now thinks that material objects are real things whose existence we are justified in inferring from the behavior of our sense-qualia.

There is even a hint—perhaps much more than a hint—of mind-body dualism in Ayer's current view. Ayer doubts that the statement that a sense-quale is "identical" with a brain-event is *intelligible;* and he further doubts that the evidence for a one-to-one correlation of sense-qualia and (some class of) brain-events, is more than fragmentary. He avoids having to say either that human bodily motions are exceptions to the laws of physics or that human wishes and desires are epiphenomenal by postulating that some physical events—bodily behaviors—can have more than one causal explanation. The motion of my arm can be causally explained by events in my nervous system, but since it can also be causally explained by my wish to hand someone an ashtray, there is no question of this wish being something which I feel before the arm moves, but which does not "really" cause the arm to move.

I have indicated that practicing philosophers today feel a strong sense of *déjà vu* when they read this sort of thing. Ayer will reply that he is quite aware that his views are "out of fashion." But is a change of fashion really all that is in question? A change of fashion is certainly part of what is involved. As Ayer remarks, materialism is again in vogue, at least in American and Australian philosophy, and "sense-qualia" are out of vogue. But more is also involved. What analytic philosophers of almost any per-suasion will regard as strange is that Ayer ignores an enormous amount of discussion of the issue of recognition of sense-qualia. Ayer has, so to speak, no interest in cognitive psychology. But a cognitive psychology of some sort—a theory of the mind—is what is needed to back his talk of "primary recognition." Thus, the possibility of misinterpreting one's sense-data is mentioned only in passing (they are qualitatively the same even if one misinterprets them, according to Ayer, who agrees with C. E. Lewis on this point). There are no entries under "corrigibility," "incorrigibil-ity," or "privileged access" in the index, although these are notions around which discussion has centered for the last forty years.

To see why this ought to be a problem for Ayer, let us recall that Ayer follows Hume in regarding causal statements as just a special class of reg-ularity-statements. Certain sorts of regularities may be especially impor-tant and useful, and we may call them "causal" for that reason, but this should not mislead us, Ayer argues, into believing that the event we call the "cause" somehow *necessitates* the event we call the "effect." This is why Ayer can think that two such different events (in his view) as an electro-chemical event in my brain, and a desire to hand someone an ashtray can both cause the motion of my arm; why shouldn't the regularity-state-ments, "When I wish to hand someone an ashtray my arm moves in such-

and-such a way" and "When such-and-such an electrochemical event takes place in my brain my arm moves in such-and-such a way" both be true? ("How can two different events *both* bring about the motion of my arm?" is only a confused question on the Hume-Ayer view.)

Imagine now that someone misinterprets a sense-quale on a particular occasion. I myself once referred to a sweater as "blue" several times before someone pointed out that it was green. And it *was* green—it didn't even *look* blue; it's just that I persisted in calling it blue. I didn't even notice that I was using "blue" for green (or whatever was really going on) until another person corrected me. According to Ayer such events don't matter; I still "recognized" the quale *green* even if I referred to it as "blue." What is this act of "primary recognition" that connects my mind to a universal?

According to Berkeley and Hume I do not have such a thing as an "abstract idea" or a "general idea" of green. When a particular token—be it a green color-patch or a token of the word "green"—occurs in my mind, and is used as a symbol for the whole class of green sense-data, all that happens is that the token is associated with a certain class of other tokens to which it is similar or which are similar to one another. Ayer and Russell depart from Berkeley and Hume on this point—and with good reason. For they see that if I can think of a *particular* relation of "similarity," then I am able to recognize at least one universal. Thus universals cannot really be avoided in the way Berkeley and Hume wanted to do.

But a naturalistic theory of the mind must try to analyze "primary recognition" into something scientifically more intelligible—say, into straightforward causal processes. Here is where the trouble starts.

If a class A of events is highly statistically correlated with another class B of events (with, say, a correlation coefficient of .97), then any class A′ of events which has almost the same members as A will also be correlated very highly with B. Thus there is no such thing as *the* class A of events with which a given class B is correlated. If the relation between occurrences of a sign, say the words "green sense-datum," and events (occurrences of a green patch in my visual field) were merely statistical correlation, then those words would be correlated with many different—at least slightly different—classes of events. There would be no such thing as *the* class of events associated with "green sense-datum," and no basis for saying that a particular event (imagine I utter the words "green sense-datum" when the sense-datum is really blue, and I fail to notice the slip) wasn't *really* associated with the words.

If one believes in non-Humean causation, then one can get around the problem by saying that the "right" class of events A is the class of events which exhibits whatever property objectively *brings about* utterances of the form "this is a green sense-datum" in the standard cases. Other classes A′ may have a high statistical correlation with the occurrence of an utterance of this type, but that is irrelevant if the correlation is not truly causal.

But in the empiricist view, events don't have objective, perspective-independent, "bringers-about." "Bringing about" is something we read into the world. "Bringing about" cannot be appealed to in explaining the nature of "primary recognition." On the other hand, mere statistical association is too weak a connection. The only remaining alternative is the one Russell and Ayer choose—to assume, or simply posit, a primitive, totally unanalyzed act of "primary recognition" which connects a sign directly to tokens that are not present to the mind performing the act (or, what comes to the same thing, connects the mind directly to one and only one "quality" of a token which is before it). This act of "primary recognition" is simply a mystery act, an occult sort of performance which establishes an intensional link between certain particulars and certain universals.

Perhaps it is no more of a mystery than Descartes' God, or Aristotle's Prime Mover (one needs *some* Archimedian point to avoid infinite regress, Ayer might claim), but a mystery nonetheless. For it has long been central to naturalistic psychology that the mind can interact with universals only through causal transactions involving instances of those universals, transactions which it is the business of psychology to analyze into elementary processes of a sort compatible with our scientific image of the world. But Ayer has no theory of the mind at all, nor is it clear that he has the building materials out of which such a theory—a theory of an organ with such capabilities as "primary recognition"—might be constructed. Is the mind supposed to be a collection of sense-qualia (as Hume thought)? Can a collection of sense-qualia engage in acts of primary recognition of universals? Ayer gives us nothing but matter and sense-qualia, and neither seems the sort of stuff that can perform such acts. It is strange that an empiricist and former positivist would feel so untroubled by the need to postulate a mysterious mental act.

Now that Ayer has become a realist about material objects, other problems occur which he does not notice, as well. The existence of material objects cannot really be a hypothesis which explains my sense-qualia, as Ayer thinks, unless I can *understand* this hypothesis. To explain how I can understand it I must solve the problem which so troubled Berkeley and Hume—I must succeed in somehow establishing a correspondence between the sign "material object," and something which is *not* a "sense-quale." Clearly, no act of "primary recognition" will help me here. Formerly Ayer would have been able to say that "material object" only stands for a set of logical constructions out of sense-qualia anyway; now that he has given up his positivism, he does not have this way out. Unfortunately, he does not appear to recognize the problem.

What is strange about this is that it was Russell (and the early Wittgenstein) who put this problem in the center of attention. Russell's theory of material objects as a species of logical construction, was part of a comprehensive attempt to speak to this very problem. The distinction between what one can "say" and what one can only "show" in Wittgenstein's *Tractatus* was an attempt to dissolve this problem by removing it to the realm of the ineffable. Ayer describes Russell's effort with loving care. But, after pointing out the many difficulties with Russell's solution, he simply opts for the idea that the existence of material objects is a causal hypothesis, without noticing that this idea speaks to a different problem altogether.

It is because Ayer has changed problems altogether that he now stresses the idea that philosophy is "theory of evidence." If the problem is *what is the evidence* that there is an external world in the causal realist's sense, a world of mind-independent and discourse-independent objects, and *not how can language or thought connect with what is outside the mind,* then we are, indeed, in the province of "theory of evidence" (if there is such a thing). But, as Russell and Wittgenstein saw, the latter problem is prior to the former. It looks as if, to solve the latter problem, one must either deny that material objects are "outside the mind" (perhaps by constructing both the "mind" and "material objects" our of something "neutral," which was another of Russell's ideas) or postulate a mysterious relation of "correspondence" between what is in the mind and what is outside. If you say, as Ayer in effect does, "Russell was wrong to treat material objects as logical constructions; so I will treat them as inferred entities," you ignore, rather than solve, the problem which made Russell *want* to treat them as logical constructions.

A way out, which Ayer ascribes to C. I. Lewis, is to say that the "criterion for the reality of an object is the confirmation of the hypothesis in which this reality is explicitly or implicitly affirmed." But, Ayer seems to be unwilling to go this far, although this is the sort of answer he himself gave in *Language, Truth, and Logic.* In any case, this answer, coupled wih the claim that the "evidence" for the existence of material objects consists entirely of sense-qualia, amounts to the claim that all talk about material objects is just highly indirect talk about sense-qualia. This is the world-view of Berkelian idealism, pure and simple.

But why should a theory which only a few philosophers have ever be-lieved, the theory that the only objects whose existence is not of a highly derived kind are sense-qualia—that sense-qualia are the Furniture of the Universe—be more credible than the worldview of science and common sense?

In sum, Ayer lands himself in the following predicament: either he must return to subjective idealism or he must face the problem which has al-ways been the nemesis of causal realism, the problem of the nature of the link between language and the world. (Even the nature of the link be-tween language and sense-data not immediately present to the mind is a problem, for Ayer's view. Postulating an act of "primary recognition" is not providing an analysis of this link at all.)

The materialists to whom Ayer refers have a view on these matters, but it is not mentioned in his book. (Only their view on the mind-body problem is discussed, and that view is misrepresented, as I mentioned.) The contemporary materialist view, for what it is worth, is that the cor-respondence between signs and their objects is established by "causal connection." The difficulty mentioned before—that there are too many regularities and too many statistical tendencies for reference to be a mat-ter of just regularities and/or statistical tendencies—is met by postulating that causality is more than a matter of regularities and statistical tenden-cies. Hume was just wrong; there are real "causal powers," real "abilities to produce" in the world, and these notions, these philosophers say, must be taken as primitive.

This view raises many problems, however, which I am sure Ayer would have pointed out had this issue been one he discussed. For one thing, the worldview of materialism is taken from fundamental physics—ignor-ing, however, the pervasive relativity of the state of a physical system to an "observer" which is characteristic of modern quantum mechanics. Ma-terialists think of the whole universe as a "closed" system, described as God might describe it if He were allowed to know about it clairvoyantly, but not allowed to interfere with it. The states of the closed system succeed one another; which state will follow which is determined by a system of equations, the Equations of Motion of the system. The claim that the states don't merely follow one another (as prescribed by the Equations of Motion), but actually "produce" the states which follow them, introduces an element which physicists have long rejected as a metaphysical addition to the content of physics itself.

Even if one is not bothered by this (or thinks that the physicists have been too influenced by empiricism), a relation of "producing" which applies only to "states" of the whole universe will hardly clarify the meaning of "causes" as in "John's wild gesture caused the vase to fall off the mantlepiece." To explain the idea that John's gesture "produced" the falling of the vase without going back to the Hume-Ayer account (causality as regularities plus statistical tendencies), some materialists bring in such recherché objects as possible worlds and a relation of "nearness" between possible worlds (a genuine causal regularity is supposed to hold not only in the actual world but in nonactual worlds "near" to the actual world), while others just take the idea that some events "explain" other events as primitive.

The fact is that the God's Eye View of the Universe as One Closed System—the metaphysical picture on which materialism is based—has no real room for "abilities to produce," a primitive relation of causation-as-explanation, or nearness-of-possible-worlds. This currently fashionable metaphysical talk is as incoherent from a consistent materialist view as it is from an empiricist view. On the other hand, the world of ordinary life—what Husserl called the "life-world" *(Lebenswelt)*—is full of objects which "produce effects" in other objects, of events which "explain" other events, of people who "recognize" things (and not only sense-qualia).

When the materialists get in trouble, what they do is forget their metaphysical picture and simply borrow whatever notions they need from the *Lebenswelt,* i.e., from spontaneous phenomenology. (That they then dress up these notions from spontaneous phenomenology in a language which comes from medieval philosophy is a curious aberration.) But the whole point of having a metaphysical picture—a picture of the Furniture of the Universe—was to analyze the notions of our spontaneous phenomenology. Just as Ayer ignores the fact that there is nothing in what he gives us to start with—Humean sense impressions under the new name "sense-qualia"—to give us minds (let alone an act of "primary recognition" to put those minds in direct contact with universals), so the materialists ignore the fact that there is nothing in what they give us to start with—

the closed system, its 'states," and the Equations of Motion—to give us "abilities to produce"; let alone a relation of "correspondence" between signs and objects.

In a way, Ayer's problem comes from Hume's project of analyzing causal talk into two parts: one part (the regularities) which is "objective," and one (the "necessity") which is nothing but a human projection (even if such projections are indispensible in practice). Both Ayer and the materialists are trying to carry out Hume's project of telling us what "really exists" (sense-qualia and their relations, in Ayer's view, until material objects got added on as a "causal hypothesis"; the closed system and its "states" in the materialist view), and what is only a "human projection." I want to suggest, as I think the later Wittgenstein was suggesting, that this project is now a total shambles. Analytic philosophy has great accomplishments, to be sure; but those accomplishments are negative. Like logical positivism (itself just one species of analytic philosophy), analytic philosophy has succeeded in destroying the very problem with which it started. Each of the efforts to solve that problem, or even to say exactly what could *count* as a solution to that problem, has failed.

This "deconstruction" is no mean intellectual accomplishment. We have learned an enormous amount about our concepts and our lives by seeing that the grand projects of discovering the Furniture of the Universe have all failed. But analytic philosophy pretends today not to be just one great movement in the history of philosophy—which it certainly was—but to be philosophy itself. This self-description *forces* analytic philsophers (even if they reject Ayer's particular views) to keep coming up with new "solutions" to the problem of the Furniture of the Universe—solutions which become more and more bizarre, and which have lost all interest outside of the philosophical community. Thus we have a paradox: at the very moment when analytical philosophy is recognized as the "dominant movement" in world philosophy, analytical philosophy has come to the end of its own project—the dead end, not the completion.

I now want to suggest that there is another way of reading the history of "philosophy in the twentieth century." In Ayer's reading, it all went somehow berserk after philosophers stopped talking about sense-data and about how sense-data are the "evidence" for everything we know. (Ayer professes to be optimistic, but on his description of the scene it is impossible to see why one should be.) I suggest that two things have happened. The first, which the first half of Ayer's book describes, consisted of a series of heroic attempts to solve the problems of traditional metaphysics. These attempts by Frege, Russell, Carnap, and the early Wittgenstein were called "attacks on metaphysics," but in fact they were among the most ingenious, profound, and technically brilliant constructions of metaphysical systems ever achieved. Even if they failed, modern symbolic logic, a good deal of modern language theory, and a part of contemporary cognitive science were all offshoots of these attempts.

The second thing that happened is almost unrecognized, even today. Beginning in the last decade of the nineteenth century, certain philosophers began to reject Hume's project—not just Hume's project with respect to causation, but the entire enterprise of dividing mundane "reality" into the Furniture of the World and our "projections." These philosophers have in common a rejection—a total root-and-branch rejection—of the enterprise mentioned, and a concern with the quotidian, with the *Lebenswelt*, with what a philosophy free of the search for a 'true world' (Nietzsche's phrase!) might look like. I myself see Husserl as such a philosopher (Ayer's treatment of Merleau-Ponty, whom he chooses as his representative of phenomenology, is rendered worthless by Ayer's failure to understand that Merleau-Ponty rejects Ayer's entire problematique.) Wittgenstein and Austin were such philosophers. Nelson Goodman is such a philosopher. Ayer does treat this last figure with a proper respect, but even here he cannot see quite *why* Goodman wants to be such a relativist—because Ayer has not seen the emptiness of his own resolution of the words-world problem.

The beginning of a philosophical movement which does not seek to divide our *Lebenswelt* into Furniture and Projections may itself only be a fashion, to be sure. But if it is the direction philosophical thought is going to take—and I rather hope that it is, because the old project deserves at least a respite, if not a permanent burial—then this is bound to affect the way in which the culture generally views almost all questions of general intellectual procedure. Much of our discussion—the discussion whether values are "objective" or "subjective" for example—is still trapped in the categories fixed by Hume. Stanley Cavell suggests that a less distanced attitude towards the life-world (the only world we have, after all), may be a matter of some lasting moral importance. (He connects this with a way of reading Emerson and Thoreau.) Nelson Goodman has suggested that a rejection of the question "is it the world itself or is it only a version?" may free us from "flat footed philosophy." He is not suggesting, as I understand it, that philosophers construct "worlds of worlds" irresponsibly; but he is suggesting that a recognition that philosophy is construction and not description of things-in-themselves, is compatible with recognizing that the philosopher is responsible to evolving but genuine requirements of objectivity—requirements of "fit" wth respect to his subject matter, and with respect to the self that he is both constructing and expressing.

What Ayer's book lacks is any sense of the way in which philosophy (like the arts) has become agonized, tormented by the weight of its past, burdened by predecessors whom it cannot escape. His tone is progressive throughout. But the fact that the key moves in Ayer's philosophy—postulating a primitive act of "primary recognition," and reviving causal realism (or more accurately, equivocating between causal realism and subjective idealism)—were in vogue before Kant even started to write the first *Critique,* explodes this particular conception of "progress." The authors that Ayer discusses in the second half of his book have almost all, in one way or another, undermined these moves. If few of these authors ever come quite into focus, it is because he has to fit their work into his own picture of philosophical "progress." And he cannot, for they are all in another world.

[3]
Subjective and Objective

THOMAS NAGEL

THERE IS a problem that emerges in several areas of philosophy whose connection with one another is not obvious. I believe that it can be given a general form, and that some treatment of it is possible in abstraction from its particular instances—with results that can be applied to the instances eventually. This discussion is a preliminary sketch for what I intend to treat more thoroughly in the future.

The problem is one of opposition between subjective and objective points of view. There is a tendency to seek an objective account of everything before admitting its reality. But often what appears to a more subjective point of view cannot be accounted for in this way. So either the objective conception of the world is incomplete, or the subjective involves illusions that should be rejected.

Instead of trying to define these terms at the outset, I shall begin with some examples, drawn from ethics and metaphysics. The parallels between them should emerge as I proceed.

Consider first a problem about the meaning of life. There is a way of considering human pursuits from within life, which allows justification of some activities in terms of others, but does not permit us to question the significance of the whole thing, unless we are asking, from within life, whether the allocation of energy or attention to different segments of it makes sense in virtue of their relative importance. This view comes under challenge from a position that regards life in detachment from specific or general human purposes. People, and oneself in particular, are perceived

Reprinted by permission from *Mortal Questions* (Cambridge: Cambridge University Press, 1979).

as having no significance, and absurd because they seem to accord their lives great importance in action, even though they can also appreciate a broader point of view from which they have no importance.

Each of the two points of view claims priority. The internal view asks, what is the importance for individual life of insignificance from an external point of view? Life is lived from inside, and issues of significance are significant only if they can be raised from inside. It therefore does not matter that from a point of view outside my life, my life does not matter.

The external view, on the other hand, comprehends within its scope of observation all the aims and commitments by reference to which internal significance is measured. It presents itself as the *right* way for the individual to look at the world and his place in it: the big picture. He develops this kind of detachment naturally, to counter the egocentric distortion of a purely internal view, and to correct the parochialism engendered by the contingencies of his overspecific nature and circumstances. But it is not merely corrective. It claims a position of dominance, as the only complete conception of how things really are. This dominance is not imposed from outside, but derives from the intrinsic appeal of impersonality to individual reflection. Life seems absurd because it seems absurd to *oneself*, taking up a point of view that is both natural and appealing.

The second example to consider is the problem of free will. This problem arises initially in the form of a threat to free agency from the hypothesis that actions are determined by antecedent circumstances. There have been many attempts to analyze agency in terms compatible with determinism—by reference to intentions, motives, second-order volitions, capacities, absence of obstacles, or coercion. Real advances have been made in specifying necessary conditions of agency, but the possibility that these conditions are themselves determined seems still to present a threat to some element of the ordinary concept of action.[1] They may be necessary, but they do not seem sufficient.

The next step, however, is the discovery that free agency is not implied by the *absence* of determinism, even though it appears to be threatened by the presence of determinism. Uncaused acts are no more attributable to the agent than those caused by antecedent circumstances. One is therefore led to wonder what further factor, in addition to the absence of determinism, is required for free agency, and whether this further factor might not be sufficient for freedom by itself. The most dificult problem of free will is saying what the problem is, which seems to survive every attempt to specify sufficient conditions for free action.

The recent attempt to analyze action in terms of *agent* causation rather than event causation is instructive because it reveals the true source of discomfort with determinism.[2] The problem is that when one views an action as an event causally connected with other events, there is no room in the picture for someone's *doing* it. But it turns out that there is no room for someone's *doing* it if it is an event causally *un*connected with other events, either. Hence some philosophers have tried to capture this aspect by making an agent, rather than an event, the cause. I do not find the concept of agent causation intelligible, but I think I understand its motivation. While its positive content is obscure, its negative implications are clear. It removes action from the causal sequence of events by denying that it is caused by antecedent circumstances; and by substituting an agent as the cause, it avoids the alternative that action is something that just *happens*. It is a doomed attempt to capture the *doing* of the action in a new kind of causation.

But the problem is not that the idea of agency clashes with this or that particular conception of what happens in action, viewed externally as a type of event. It is not predictability that creates the problem, for I make many choices and do many things that are completely predictable. It is just that when I pick the shiny apple instead of the rotten one, it is *my doing*—and there is no room for this in an external account of the event, deterministic or not. The real problem stems from a clash between the view of action from inside and *any* view of it from outside. Any external view of an act as something that happens, with or without causal antecedents, seems to omit the doing of it.

Even if an action is described in terms of motives, reasons, abilities, absence of impediments, or coercion, this does not capture the agent's own idea of himself as its source. His actions appear to him different from other things that happen in the world, but not merely a different kind of happening, with different causes or none at all. They seem in some indescribable way not to *happen* at all (unless they are quite out of his control), though things happen when he does them. And if he sees others as agents too, their actions will seem to have the same quality. The tendency to express this conception of agency in terms of freedom from antecedent causes is a mistake, but an understandable one. When the act is viewed under the aspect of determination by antecedents, its status as an event becomes prominent. But as appears upon further investigation, no account of it as an event is satisfactory from the internal viewpoint of the agent doing it.

The connection of this problem with moral responsibility is that when we view actions, our own or others, merely as part of the general course of events, it seems impossible to attribute them to individuals in a way that makes sense of the attitudes we take toward someone we regard as the source of an action. Certain attitudes toward the agent, rather than just about him, lose their footing. If an individual is destructive enough we may think it would be better if he did not exist; but if he is just a disastrous part of the world, blame directed at him or guilt he directs at himself make no sense, however, causally or indeterministically complex his behavior and motives are.

The true nature of the third problem I want to mention—that of personal identity—is also hidden in many discussions. The problem is usually presented as a search for the conditions that must obtain if two experiential episodes separated in time are to belong to a single person. Various types of continuity and similarity—physical, mental, causal, emotional—have been considered and they all seem to leave an aspect of personal identity unaccounted for. Given that any proposed set of conditions is met, there still seems to be a further question as to whether the same *subject* or *self* is preserved under these conditions. This further question can be raised by imagining that you have the first of two experiences and asking about the other (which bears the candidate relation to it), "Yes, but will it be *mine?*" As with free will, the real problem seems to be to identify the problem that always remains no matter how ingenious a solution has been proposed.

It may seem that this further question involves the assumption of a metaphysical ego which preserves personal identity. But this would be a mistake, for the ego, if it is a continuing individual with its own identity over time, would be just one more thing about which the same problem could be raised (will *that* ego still be me?). If on the other hand its *only* identity over time is that of still being me, then it cannot be the individual whose persistence *preserves* personal identity. For its identity would then simply consist in the fact that experiences had by it were all mine; and that cannot explain what makes them all mine.

The problem seems unreal when persons are viewed as beings in the world, whether physical or mental. They persist and change through time, and those are the terms in which they must be described. But as with the problem of free will, the persistent dissatisfaction with candidate analyses of this form derives from a submerged internal aspect of the problem which is left untouched by all external treatments. From the point of view of the person himself, the question of his identity or nonidentity with someone undergoing some experience in the future appears to have a content that cannot be exhausted by any account in terms of memory, similarity of character, or physical continuity. Such analyses are never sufficient, and from this point of view they may appear not even to supply necessary conditions for identity.

When someone poses inwardly the question whether a past or future experience was or will be *his,* he has the sensation of picking out something whose identity over time is well-defined, just by concentrating on his present experience and specifying the temporal extension of *its subject.* The concept of the self is a psychological one, and it is characteristic of such concepts to give rise to the philosophical idea that their subjective essence, expressed most clearly in first-person applications, is detachable from objective accompaniments and even to a considerable extent from necessary connection with other psychological phenomena. (Another example: the conviction that it is a perfectly well-defined but in principle unanswerable question whether sugar tastes like *this* to other people.) This may be an illusion. It may have no sense to speak of "the same self as this one" in complete detachment from all external conditions. But it is still the internal idea of the self that gives rise to the problem of personal identity. Any attempt to conceive persons completely as a kind of thing in the world persisting through time will come up against this obstacle. The self that appears to the subjects seems to disappear under external analysis.

My fourth example is the mind-body problem. A particularly difficult aspect of that problem comes from the subjective character of experience. So long as mental states are looked at objectively, in their causal relations to stimuli and behavior, no special issues arise which do not arise about the physical analysis of other natural phenomena. Even problems of intentionality may seem to be soluble if one puts aside their subjective aspect, for then one may be able to describe certain kinds of computers as intentional systems. What seems impossible is to include in a physical conception of the world the facts about what mental states are like for the creature having them. The creature and his states seem to belong to a world that can be viewed impersonally and externally. Yet subjective aspects of the mental can be apprehended only from the point of view of the creature itself (perhaps taken up by someone else), whereas what is physical is simply there, and can be externally apprehended from more than one point of view. Is there any way of including mental phenomena in the world as well, as part of what is simply *there*?

Here too the idea of impersonally comprehensible reality asserts its claim to dominance. We are not faced only with the problem of the relation between mind and body, or the inclusion of the mental in the physical world. The broader issues between personal and impersonal, or subjective and objective, arise also for a dualist theory of mind. The question of how one can include in the objective world a mental substance having subjective properties is as acute as the question how a physical substance can have subjective properties.

The physical is an ideal representative for the objective in general; therefore much obscurity has been shed on the problem by faulty analogies between the mental-physical relation and relations between the physical and other objective aspects of reality. As determinism is a substitute for externality or objectivity in posing the problem of free will, so the physical is a substitute for objectivity in posing the mind-body problem. All the disputes over causal role, theoretical identification, and functional realization, while of interest in themselves, fail to give expression to the central issue that makes the mind-body problem so hard. And as with free will and personal identity, the internal element remains, even if ignored, as the true source of persistent dissatisfaction with all physical or other external theories of the mind. At the same time, the idea that persons (along with everything about them) must be parts of objective reality continues to exert its powerful appeal. Objectivity is naturally linked with reality; it is easy to feel that anything has to be located in the objective world in order to qualify as real, and that it must have as its real nature some character which, whether physical or not, can be regarded impersonally and externally.

The final example I want to discuss comes from ethics, and concerns the difference between consequentialist and more agent-centered views of right and wrong. A familiar type of objection to utilitarianism and other consequentialist views charges them with unjustifiably making questions about what to do subordinate to questions about what would be best overall. Such criticisms assert that an ethical theory should leave some room for each individual to pursue his own life without having to consider at every point how he is serving more comprehensive goals; or else they urge the need for certain restrictions or requirements on action that are not justified by their contribution to the general good. In other words, both what is permitted and what is required of a person can sometimes deviate from what would be best. I group these two rather different exceptions to consequentialism together because, while they can also be opposed to each other, they deviate from the consequentialist viewpoint in the same direcion. This is clear in the case of permission to pursue one's own life, less clear in the case of general requirements or restrictions on action, whatever the goal.

Utilitarianism, or any purely consequentialist view, is very demanding. It requires you to justify the pursuit of your own personal life and interests only as components of the general good, and does not permit reasons for action to *end* with a reference to what you want or are devoted to. Those considerations are completely encompassed by an impersonal point of view which accords you no special position, unless it can be impersonally justified. Resistance comes, naturally enough, from the point of view of the individual, who may be willing to accord impersonal considerations some weight, but who is also powerfully motivated by the independent claims of his own life—of the view from where he is in the world. But this does not remain a conflict between impersonal values and mere individual interest, because the resistance can be generalized. Someone who regards consequentialist requirements as unacceptable because of their claim to dominance over his own point of view will naturally extend this objection to others. He will gravitate toward a *general* exception to consequentialism in favor of the personal viewpoint, and this will constitute an alternative ethic, rather than merely a resistance to ethics. Such an ethic need be no less universal than utilitarianism, but it will be subjective in a way that consequentialist positions are not. Each person will be permitted, within limits, to concentrate on the pursuit of *his* life, and there will not be a single, objectively describable end by reference to which everyone's actions must be justified.

In this sense the deontological requirements that resist a consequentialist account are also subjective. Constraints against murder, lying, betrayal, assault, or coercion, though intended to apply universally, oppose the agent's specific relations to other people to the conception of a single end that everyone should exclusively promote. They are agent-centered, but in a different way. The real source of these restrictions, unlike that of the agent-centered permissions, is not the agent but the potential victim whose rights are protected. But the wrongness of violating those rights implies a constraint on each person against violating them, rather than a requirement that he try to minimize their overall violation (even if this means committing a few himself). Deontological requirements are agent-centered because they instruct each person to determine the rightness or wrongness of his acts solely from the point of view of his position in the world and his direct relation to others. The very idea that the basic moral concepts are right and wrong rather than good and bad entails that the character of one's actions rather than the world as a whole must be one's primary concern.[3]

If there is a difference in point of view between the two types of exception to consequentialism, it is that the first derives simply from the standpoint of the individual agent, whereas the second emerges when he considers in a certain way his own point of view together with those of the persons to whom he is directly related in action. Deonological constraints are intermediate between purely individual motives and completely impersonal values.

There are familiar disputes about whether utilitarianism really does have the consequences attributed to it by anti-consequentialist critics—aspects of the wider dispute between radical and moderate interpretations of utilitarianism. Likewise there are disputes about the formulation of alternative views: how absolutist they are, whether they should be stated in terms of individual rights, or liberty, or self-realization, or interpersonal commitment. But the essence of the conflict is clearer than the exact nature of the alternatives. The issue is how the individual position of the agent should enter into a decision about what he should or may do.

Obviously it cannot fail to enter in certain ways. Even on a consequentialist view, what one should do will depend on what one is in a position to do, and on the relative desirability of the possible outcomes. Nevertheless, the consequentialist judgment that one should do something is essentially the judgment that it would be best if one did it—that it ought to *happen*. The right thing to do is to turn oneself as far as possible into an instrument for the realization of what is best *sub specie aeternitatis*.

Agent-centered views, on the other hand, detemine what is right, wrong, and permissible partly at least on the basis of the individual's life, his role in the world, and his relation with others. Agent-centered morality gives primacy to the question of what to do, a question asked by the individual agent, and does not assume that the only way to answer it is to say what it would be best if he did *sub specie aeternitatis*. It may also hold that the place for considerations of what would be best, in a decision about what to do, is not obvious and must be established by analysis of agent-centered choice and its grounds.

The real issue, therefore, is the relative priority, in regard to action, of two ways of looking at the world. On the one hand there is the position that one's decisions should be tested ultimately from an external point of view, to which one appears as just one person among others. The question then becomes, "What would be best? Which of the acts within my power would do the most good, considering matters from out here, impersonally?" This point of view claims priority by virtue of greater comprehensiveness. The agent's situation is supposedly given its due in a larger perspective.[4]

On the other hand there is the position that since an agent lives his life from where he is, even if he manages to achieve an impersonal view of his situation, whatever insights result from this detachment need to be made part of a personal view before they can influence decision and action. The pursuit of what seems impersonally best may be an important aspect of individual life, but its place in that life must be determined from a personal standpoint, because life is always the life of a particular person, and cannot be lived *sub specie aeternitatis.*[5]

The opposition looks like a stalemate because each of the points of view claims dominance over the other, by virtue of inclusion. The impersonal standpoint takes in a world that includes the individual and his personal views. The personal standpoint, on the other hand, regards the deliverances of impersonal reflection as only a part of any individual's total view of the world.

This list of problems could be extended. Obviously the difficulty of reconciling subjective and objective points of view arises with regard to space and time, death, and throughout the theory of knowledge. Perhaps the problem takes its purest form in a sense of incredulity that one should be anyone in particular, a specific individual of a particular species existing at a particular time and place in the universe. There is a pattern in these questions which justifies us in locating a common philosophical difficulty behind all of them, concealed by their diversity, and sometimes ignored in their treatment with unfortunate results. In what follows I shall discuss some strategies for dealing with the problem. But first I shall discuss the parallels among its different forms.

Although I shall speak of the subjective viewpoint and the objective viewpoint, this is just shorthand, for there are not two such viewpoints, nor even two such categories into which more particular viewpoints can be placed. Instead, there is a polarity. At one end is the point of view of a particular individual, having a specific constitution, situation, and relation to the rest of the world. From here the direction of movement toward greater objectivity involves, first, abstraction from the individual's specific spatial, temporal, and personal position in the world, then from the features that distinguish him from other humans, then gradually from the forms of perception and action characteristic of humans, and away from the narrow range of a human scale in space, time, and quantity, toward a conception of the world which as far as possible is not the view from anywhere within it. There is probably no end-point to this process, but its aim is to regard the world as centerless, with the viewer as just one of its contents.

The distinction between subjective and objective is relative. A general human point of view is more objective than the view from where you happen to be, but less objective than the viewpoint of physical science. The opposition between subjective and objective can arise at any place on the spectrum where one point of view claims dominance over another, more subjective one, and that claim is resisted. In the dispute over consequentialism in ethics, it appears in the clash between internal and external views of human life, both fully admitting the importance of human concerns and ends. In the mind-body problem, it appears in the clash between an internal human view of human beings and the external view of physical theory. In the problem of personal identity, it appears in the clash between the point of view of a particular individual toward his own past and future and the view that others may take of him as a continuing conscious being, characterized by bodily and psychological continuities.

Another point I wish to emphasize is this. What is more subjective is not necessarily more private. In general it is intersubjectively available. I assume that the subjective ideas of experience of action, and of the self are in some sense public or common property. That is why the problems of mind and body, free will, and personal identity are not just problems about one's own case.

I cannot here take up Wittgenstein's arguments about the publicity of rules and therefore of concepts.[6] I believe he is right, and that even our most subjective phenomenological concepts are public in a sense. But they are public in a very different way from that in which concepts used to describe the physical world are public. The coordination of the points of view of different individuals toward their own experiences is totally different from the coordination of their points of view toward the external world. Nothing in the former case corresponds to different individuals sharing a point of view toward the same object. Wittgenstein's position on sensations is that they just *are* appearances, so their properties are not the properties of objects which appear to whoever has them, and similarity in their properties is not similarity in the properties of such objects. Rather it is similarity in appearances. That is a similarity between irreducibly subjective phenomena. Only if we acknowledge their subjectivity—the fact that each is essentially an appearance *to* someone—can we understand the special way in which sensations are publicly comparable and not private. The private object or sense datum view is an instance of the false objectification of what is essentially subjective.

Since a kind of intersubjective agreement characterizes even what is most subjective, the transition to a more objective viewpoint is not accomplished merely through intersubjective agreement. Nor does it proceed by an increase of imaginative scope that provides access to many subjective points of view other than one's own. Its essential character, in all the examples cited, is externality of detachment. The attempt is made to view the world not from a place within it, or from the vantage point of a special type of life and awareness, but from nowhere in particular and no form of life in particular at all. The object is to discount for the features of our prereflective outlook that make things appear to us as they do, and thereby to reach an understanding of things as they really are. We flee the subjective under the pressure of an assumption that everything must be something not to any point of view, but in itself. To grasp this by detaching more and more from our own point of view is the unreachable ideal at which the pursuit of objectivity aims.

Some version of this polarity can be found in relation to most subject matter—ethical, epistemological, metaphysical. The relative subjectivity or objectivity of different appearances is a matter of degree, but the same pressures toward a more external viewpoint are to be found everywhere. It is recognized that one's own point of view can be distorted as a result of contingencies of one's makeup or situation. To compensate for these distortions it is necessary either to reduce dependence on those forms of perception or judgment in which they are most marked, or to analyze the mechanisms of distortion and discount for them explicitly. The subjective comes to be defined by contrast with this development of objectivity.

Problems arise because the same individual is the occupant of both viewpoints. In trying to understand and discount for the distorting influences of his specific nature he must rely on certain influence. He examines himself and his interactions with the world, using a specially selected part of himself for the purpose. That part may subsequently be scrutinized in turn, and there may be no end to the process. But obviously the selection of trustworthy subparts presents a problem.

The selection of what to rely on is based partly on the idea that the less an appearance depends on contingencies of this particular self, the more it is capable of being arrived at from a variety of points of view. If there is a way things really are, which explains their diverse appearances to differently constituted and situated observers, then it is most accurately apprehended by methods not specific to particular types of observers. That is why scientific measurement interposes between us and the world instruments whose interactions with the world are of a kind that could be detected by a creature not sharing the human senses. Objectivity requires not only a departure from one's individual viewpoint, but also, so far as possible, departure from a specifically human or even mammalian viewpoint. The idea is that if one can still maintain some view when one relies less and less on what is specific to one's position or form, it will be truer to reality. The respects in which the results of various viewpoints are incompatible with each other represent distortions of the way matters really are. And if there is such a thing as the correct view, it is certainly not going to be the unedited view from wherever one happens to be in the world. It must be a view that includes oneself, with all one's contingencies of constitution and circumstance, among the things viewed, without according it any special centrality. And it must accord the same detached treatment to the type of which one is an instance. The true view of things can no more be the way they naturally appear to human beings than the way they look from here.

The pursuit of objectivity therefore involves a transcendence of the self, in two ways: a transcendence of particularity and a transcendence of one's type. It must be distinguished from a different kind of transcendence by which one enters imaginatively into other subjective points of view, and tries to see how things appear from other specific standpoints. Objective transcendence aims at a representation of what is external to each specific point of view: what is there or what is of value in itself, rather than *for* anyone. Though it employs whatever point of view is available as the representational vehicle—humans typically use visual diagrams and notation in thinking about physics—the aim is to represent how things are, not *for* anyone or any type of being. And the enterprise assumes that what is represented is detachable from the mode of representation, so that the same laws of physics could be represented by creatures sharing none of our sensory modalities.

While there are problems about how to achieve this kind of transcendence, it is certainly one of the important ways of advancing our understanding. We cannot help wanting to extend it farther and farther, and to bring more and more of life and the world within its range. But the consistent pursuit of greater objectivity runs into trouble, and gives rise to the philosophical problems I have described, when it is turned back on the self, as it must be to pursue its comprehensive ambitions.

The trouble occurs when the objective view encounters something, revealed subjectively, that it cannot accommodate. Its claims to comprehensiveness will then be threatened. The indigestible lump may be either a fact or a value. The problems of personal identity and mind-body arise because certain subjectively apparent facts about the self seem to vanish as one ascends to a more objective standpoint. The problems about consequentialism and the meaning of life arise from a corresponding disappearance of certain personal values with the ascent to a more and more detached and impersonal point of view. The problem of free will combines both effects.

In either case it appears that something must give way, for two natural and necessary ways of thinking lead to a collision and cannot without adjustment be accommodated in a single view of how things are. But even allowing for adjustments, the options seem to be limited and unpalatable. If one wishes to insist that everything real must be brought under an objective description there seem to be three courses available with respect to any recalcitrant subjective aspect: reduction, elimination, and annexation.

First, reduction: one may try to save the appearances as much as possible, by accommodating them under an objective interpretation. Thus one might offer a consequentialist account of rights or special obligations or the allowable forms of self-interest. Or one might analyze experience in terms of behavioral criteria, or agency in terms of certain kinds of causes, or personal identity in terms of physical or mental continuity.

Secondly, elimination: if no reduction seems plausible one may dismiss the deliverance of a subjective viewpoint as an illusion, perhaps offering an explanation of how it arises. For example, one might say there is no such thing as pure personal identity, or free agency. One might even say that there is no such thing as the subjective character of experience, that experiences can be adequately characterized by their causal roles and do not possess phenomenological properties in addition. And one might dismiss deontological requirements and other nonconsequentialist ethical intuitions as superstitious, selfish, or rule-bound.

Thirdly, annexation: if one fails to reduce the subjective to familiar objective terms, and is unwilling to deny its reality outright, one may invent a new element of objective reality especially for the purpose of including this recalcitrant element: the will, the ego, the soul, or perhaps the command of God. Such metaphysical inventions, however, can seem to serve the purpose for which they were designed only because their obscurity prevents it from being obvious that the same problems of subjectivity will arise with regard to them, if they really belong to objective reality. It is no good trying to amplify our conception of the objective world to include whatever is revealed subjectively, for the problem is not that something has been left out. An objective conception of space and time cannot be faulted for *leaving out* the identification of the here and now. Any conception that included it would not be objective, and any objective realization would fail to capture it. This applies also to the prediction that mental phenomena will eventually come to be counted as physical, once we understand them systematically—even if they are not reduced to terms already admitted as physical.[7] We cannot solve these problems by simply annexing to the objective (or even physical) world everything that is not already in it.

The only alternative to these unsatisfactory moves is to resist the voracity of the objective appetite, and stop assuming that understanding of the world and our position in it can always be advanced by detaching from that position and subsuming whatever appears from there under a single more comprehensive conception. Perhaps the best or truest view is not obtained by transcending oneself as far as possible. Perhaps reality should not be identified with objective reality. The problem is to explain why objectivity is inadequate as a comprehensive ideal of understanding, without faulting it for not including subjective elements it could not possibly include. There is always room for improvement in our objective understanding of things, naturally, but the proposal I am considering is not that the objective picture is incomplete, but rather that it is, in essence, only partial.

This proposal is harder to accept than it may seem, for it implies that there is no single way things are in themselves. Even if one admits to the world facts or values involving a particular point of view, it is tempting to assume that something's being so from a particular point of view must consist in something else's being the case from no point of view. (The something else may of course involve some objective relations.) Those who believe there are no objective values may try to analyze the existence of subjective values in terms of objective facts about the individuals for whom they are values. Others have analyzed apparently subjective values in terms of objective ones.[8] And the philosophy of mind is full of refusals to admit that there may be no objective fact that is what *really* obtains when something looks red to someone.

The idealist tradition, including contemporary phenomenology, has of course admitted subjective points of view as basic, and has gone to the opposite length of denying an irreducible objective reality. I have concentrated on the tendency to resolve the conflict by objectifying everything because it has dominated recent analytic philosophy in spite of Wittgenstein. But I find the idealist solution unacceptable for the same reason: objective reality cannot be analyzed or shut out of existence any more than subjective reality can. Even if not everything is something from no point of view, some things are.

The deep source of both idealism and its objectifying opposite is the same: a conviction that a single world cannot contain both irreducible points of view and irreducible objective reality—that one of them must be what there *really* is and the other somehow reducible to or dependent on it. This is a very powerful idea. To deny it is in a sense to deny that there is a single world.

We must admit that the move toward objectivity reveals what things are like in themselves as opposed to how they appear; not just how they appear to one, relatively austere point of view as opposed to others. Therefore when the objective gaze is turned on human beings and other experiencing creatures, who are undeniably parts of the world, it can reveal only what they are like in themselves. And if the way things are for these subjects is not part of the way things are in themselves, an objective account, whatever it shows, will omit something. So reality is not just objective reality, and the pursuit of objectivity is not an equally effective method of reaching the truth about everything.

It is conceivable that everything has *some* objective properties. I do not know whether it makes sense to attribute physical and phenomenological properties to the same thing, but perhaps even experiences are events that can be in part described objectively, perhaps physically. But the properties that make them experiences exist only from the point of view of the types of beings who have them.

Since we are not the only creatures in the universe, a general conception of reality would require a general conception of experience which admitted our own subjective viewpoint as a special case. This is completely beyond us and will probably remain so for as long as human beings continue to exist.

It makes objectivity attractive by comparison. We can pursue a unified if very etiolated conception of reality by detaching progressively from our own point of view. We just have to keep in mind what we are leaving behind, and not be fooled into thinking we have made it disappear. This is particularly important in connection with philosophical problems about free will, personal identity, agent-centered morality, or mind and body, which cannot be dealt with in detachment from the subjective point of view on which they depend for their existence.

The power of the impulse to transcend oneself and one's species is so great, and its rewards so substantial, that it is not likely to be seriously baffled by the admission that objectivity has its limits. While I am arguing for a form of romanticism, I am not an extremist. The task of accepting the polarity without allowing either of its terms to swallow the other should be a creative one. It is the aim of eventual unification that I think is misplaced, both in our thoughts about how to live and in our conception of what there is. The coexistence of conflicting points of view, varying in detachment from the contingent self, is not just a practically necessary illusion but an irreducible fact of life.

NOTES

1. The literature on this subject is enormous. Three of the best recent articles are P. F. Strawson, "Freedom and Resentment," *Proceedings of the British Academy (1962);* Harry G. Frankfurt, "Freedom of the Will and the Concept of a Person," *Journal of Philosophy* (January 14, 1971), 63:5–20; Gary Watson, "Free Agency," *Journal of Philosophy,* (April 24, 1975), 62:209–220.

2. Roderick M. Chisholm, "Freedom and Action," in Keith Lehrer, ed., *Freedom and Determinism* (New York: Random House, 1966).

3. A moral theory of this type is developed by Charles Fried in *Right and Wrong* (Cambridge: Harvard University Press, 1978). An intermediate view has been put forward by Samuel Scheffler, in "Agents and Outcomes," Ph.D. dissertation, Princeton University, 1977: he defends agent-centered permissions but rejects agent-centered requirements as having no intelligible basis.

4. In Thomas Nagel, *The Possibility of Altruism* (Oxford: Oxford University Press, 1970), I defended a version of this position.

5. This position is persuasively presented by Bernard Williams in "A Critique of Utilitarianism," in J. J. C. Smart and Bernard Williams, *Utilitarianism: For and Against* (Cambridge: Cambridge University Press, 1973). See also Bernard Williams, "Persons, Character, and Morality," in Amelia Rorty, ed., *The Identities of Persons* (Berkeley: University of California Press, 1976), where he presses the claims not only of the view from within one's own life but of the view from the present time. This tendency of a subjective viewpoint to shrink into the present moment has been noted by Derek Parfit in his skeptical work on prudence (not yet published).

6. Ludwig Wittgenstein, *Philosophical Investigations* (Oxford: Blackwell, 1953).

7. See Noam Chomsky, *Language and Mind* (New York: Harcourt, Brace & World, 1968), pp. 83–84.

8. For example, G. E. More in *Principia Ethica* (Cambridge: Cambridge University Press, 1903), p. 99.

[4]

Dewey, Democracy: The Task Ahead of Us

RICHARD J. BERNSTEIN

A man's vision is the great fact about him.

William James

IN 1939, at a conference celebrating the eightieth birthday of John Dewey, he gave a talk entitled "Creative Democracy—The Task Before Us." The title and the occasion are significant for several reasons. As Dewey pointed out, his own life had already spanned a period of more than half the national life of the country in which "events of the utmost significance for the destiny" of democracy had occurred. (Dewey continued to be active until his death in 1952.) It was characteristic of Dewey to return once again to the theme—democracy—that had been his life-long preoccupation, and to emphasize that it was still a task before us. For democracy was not simply one topic among others that he explored. It stood at the center of his being and his intellectual endeavors. His words and deeds always emanated from his concern with the process and precarious fate of democracy. His articulation of his vision of democracy in 1939 has a special poignancy, not only because of the ominous rise of fascism and the growing attacks on the very idea of democracy, but for another less well known reason.

Two years earlier Dewey had agreed to serve as chairman of the Commission of Inquiry which was formed to hear and evaluate the charges made against Trotsky at the Moscow trials. Although attacked and villified by communists and liberals sympathetic with the Soviet Union, and despite threats of violence and pleas by family and friends, Dewey made the arduous trip to Mexico City where the inquiry was held in April 1937, and Trotsky testified. It was an opportunity to investigate the charges made against Trotsky and his son, and publically to expose the terrors and horrors of the Moscow purges. Dewey's willingness to set aside his intellectual work and serve as chairman of the commission was thoroughly consistent with his basic convictions, for he not only wrote about the unity of thought and action, he practiced it throughout his life. When Dewey had visited the Soviet Union in 1928, he was enthusiastic and optimistic about the prospects of freedom and education, but he now expressed his "bitter disillusionment." Reflecting on what he had learned from the inquiry and his encounter with Trotsky, he wrote:

> the great lesson for all American radicals and for all sympathizers with the U.S.S.R. is that they must go back and reconsider the whole question of the means of bringing about social changes and of truly democratic methods of approach to social progress. . . . The dictatorship of the proletariat had led and, I am convinced always must lead to a dictatorship over the proletariat and over the party. I see no reason to believe that something similar would not happen in every country in which an attempt is made to establish a Communist government.[1]

Democracy was threatened not only by the rise of fascism and Stalinism, but, as we shall see, Dewey came to believe that the most serious danger for democracy was an internal one—that there was an erosion and distortion of the very conditions required for the flourishing of democracy. What then did Dewey mean by democracy and what was central to his vision of democracy?

His 1939 talk provides a clue, for he focused on democracy as a *moral ideal,* a personal way of life to be concretely embodied in everyday practices. Democracy for Dewey was not primarily a set of institutions, formal procedures, or even legal guarantees. It is the culture and practice of democracy in day-to-day life that Dewey stresses. Democracy is a reflective faith in the capacity of all human beings for intelligent judgment, deliberation, and action if the proper conditions are furnished.

> Democracy as compared with other ways of life is the sole way of living which believes wholeheartedly in the process of experience as end and as means; as that which is capable of generating the science which is the sole dependable authority for the direction of further experience and which releases emotions, needs, and desires so as to call into being the things that have not existed in the past. For every way of life that fails in its democracy limits the contacts, the exchanges, the communications, the

interactions by which experience is steadied while it is enlarged and enriched. The task of this release and enrichment is one that has to be carried on day by day. Since it is one that can have no end till experience itself comes to an end, the task of democracy is forever that of creation of a freer and more humane experience in which all share and to which all contribute.[2]

If we are to grasp what Dewey is saying here— his linkage of democracy and science, his distinctive meaning of experience and the process of experience as end and as means, his emphasis on communication, interaction and sharing, then we need to explore how his understanding of democracy is related to his larger vision.

Dewey's interests span the entire range of human affairs and culture including education, psychology, the natural and social disciplines, art, religious experience, as well as the political and economic events of his time, but he was trained and primarily thought of himself as a philosopher. Dewey strongly advocated and sought to bring about a reconstruction of philosophy where philosophy would no longer be thought of as a rarified discipline exclusively concerned with the technical problems of philosophy. He was deeply skeptical and critical of what he took to be outmoded and misguided conceptions of philosophy—as some sort of super science, as *the* foundational discipline of culture, or as a discipline that has access to some special realm of transcendental truth. He sought to uncover, expose, and exorcise what he believed to be a central impulse of much of traditional philosophy—the quest for certainty. He thought of philosophy as having more to do with vision, imagination, and meaning (rather than Truth), with gaining a critical perspective on the deepest problems and conflicts in society and culture, and with projecting ideals for achieving a more desirable future. He characterized philosophy as the "criticism of criticisms," and criticism is "discriminating judgment and careful appraisal." He believed that much of modern philosophy had gotten itself into a rut, that in its obsession with epistemology, philosophy had even lost touch with the ways in which inquiry, especially scientific inquiry, is actually practiced. He attacked what he called the "spectator theory of knowledge," and the "idea of an invidiously real reality." He was suspicious of the dualisms, dichotomies, and binary oppositions that loomed so large in modern philosophy—whether they be mind/body; subject/object; reason/experience; fact/value; individual/social; or nature/culture. Distinctions and differences are important for all philosophic thinking, but Dewey sought to unmask the tendency of philosophers to reify and hypostasize changing, fluid, functional distinctions into metaphysical and epistemological dichotomies.

Dewey's critics have frequently criticized him for his alleged anti-intellectualism—and his irreverent treatment of the history of philosophy certainly offended many of his professional colleagues. But the charge of anti-intellectualism is a gross slander. Dewey was steeped in the history of philosophy and typically he would approach almost every problem by reviewing and evaluating differing philosophic approaches. But he was always seeking critically to appropriate what was still viable in the traditions that have shaped us. Viewed as a quest for certainty, or as the search for some final and definitive Truth, the history of philosophy had to be judged a failure, but understood as imaginative attempts to gain critical perspective, to locate, specify, and clarify human problems, as attempts to provide orientation and guidance, philosophy takes on a much more vital and dramatic significance. What Dewey feared—and to a great extent he was prophetic—is that as philosophy becomes more academic and professional, and as philosophers become more nervous and defensive about protecting their turf, the entire discipline would become more marginal and irrelevant to the "problems of men." In *opposition* to what he took to be the strong anti-intellectual tendencies in American life, Dewey wrote:

> As far as any plea is implicit in what has been said, it is, then, a plea for casting off of that intellectual timidity which hampers the wings of imagination, a plea for speculative audacity, for more faith in ideas, sloughing off a cowardly reliance upon those partial ideas to which we are wont to give the name facts. I have given to philosophy a more humble function than that which is often assigned to it. But modesty as to its final place is not incompatible with boldness in the maintenance of that function, humble as it may be. A combination of such modesty and courage affords the only way I know of in which the philosopher can look his fellowmen in the face with frankness and humanity.[3]

If philosophy is the "criticism of criticisms," if the "distinctive office, problems, and subject matter of philosophy grow out of stresses and strains . . . in community life," what did Dewey take to be the most urgent problem of his (and our) time? Although he gave a variety of formulations, the key problem is the character of our moral and political lives. It is the problem of human practice, in the sense of "practice" characterized by Aristotle when he spoke of *praxis* as the distinctive form of human activity. The question that Dewey took to be most central is the question of the moral character of "community life" itself. And democracy "is the idea of community life itself." More specifically, Dewey was concerned with the split and divorce between science and *praxis*. Despite the enormous success of the natural sciences, Dewey argued that the "spirit of scientific inquiry" had not yet adequately informed our moral and social practices. He was well aware of the growth of scientism, subjectivism, relativism, narcissism, and of the ever increasing power of science and technology to shape our lives. Dewey was not an innocent champion of the Enlightenment tradition. He was relentlessly critical of all philosophies of history that claimed that there is an ineluctable logic working itself out behind the backs of human beings leading inevitably to the realization of freedom—or to barbarism and global disaster. He wrote that "it is no longer possible to hold the simple faith of the Enlightenment that assured advance of science will produce free institutions by dispelling ignorance and superstition:—the sources of human servitude and the pillars of oppressive government."[4]

It is certainly true that at times "science" and "scientific method" seem to serve as Dewey's "god terms." But it is crucial to look and see what he meant by "scientific method" and what he sought to appropriate from his understanding of experimental science. He did not mean a set of formal decision procedures or rules for advancing and justifying scientific hypotheses and theories. He was not advocating what Sheldon Wolin has characterized as the *vita methodi*—a shaping of the human mind which under the guise of objectivity and value neutrality avoids fundamental criticism and commitment. He conceived of science as a set of interlocking practices in the sense of "practice" recently characterized by Alasdair MacIntyre—social practices which have their own internal standards of excellence which require and presuppose characteristic *virtues*.[5] It is the openness of scientific inquiry, the imagination required for its successful practice, the willingness to submit hypotheses to public test and criticism, the intrinsic communal and cooperative character of scientific inquiry that Dewey highlighted when he spoke of "scientific method." If we are to dedicate ourselves to the task of the concrete realization of "creative democracy," then, it is these virtues that must be cultivated and nurtured in our everyday moral and political lives.

If the philosopher has the responsibility of not only projecting and rationally defending ideals for the achievement of a more desirable future, but also must clarify the means by which they are to be embodied, then we can ask how did Dewey think such an end-in-view could be achieved? From this perspective we can best understand Dewey's lifelong involvement in the theory and practice of education in a democratic society. The way in which Dewey conceives of the educative process contributes to and is affected by his understanding of human experience.

Dewey sought to appropriate the spirit of experimental science as a self-corrective activity, but he was also profoundly influenced by the lessons of the new biology. (Dewey was born in 1859, the year when Darwin's *Origin of Species* appeared.) Dewey's early infatuation with Hegelianism predisposed him to the influence of Darwin. In a revealing autobiographical sketch written in 1930, Dewey spoke of the "subjective reasons" for the appeal of Hegel's thought.

> It supplied a demand for unification that was doubtless an intense emotional craving, and yet was a hunger that only an intellectualized subject matter could satisfy. It is more than difficult, it is impossible, to recover that early mood. But the sense of divisions and separations that were, I suppose, borne in upon me as a consequence of a heritage of New England culture, divisions by way of isolation of self from the world, of soul from body, of nature from God, brought a painful oppression—or, rather, they were an inward laceration. . . . Hegel's synthesis of subject and object, matter and spirit, the divine and the human, was, however, no mere intellectual formula; it operated as an immense release, a liberation. Hegel's treatment of human culture, of institutions and the arts, involved the same dissolution of hard-and-fast dividing walls, and had a special attraction for me.[6]

The same "subjective" considerations that attracted the young Dewey to Hegel were the reasons why he "drifted away from Hegelianism," even though Dewey confessed that "acquaintance with Hegel has left a permanent deposit in my thinking."

Dewey came to believe that Darwin and the new biology supplied a more concrete and richer perspective on human experience. It was not the popular Social Darwinism of the day that appealed to Dewey. He saw through this as pseudoscience and ideology. Nor was he interested in the battles between science and religion provoked by Darwin's work. It is the understanding of life and experience as process, as change, as organic interaction that Dewey emphasized. We are neither beings with a fixed human nature which unfolds in the course of time nor are we infinitely plastic and perfectible. Human beings are continuous with the rest of nature but have the capacity to develop those habits, dispositions, sensitivities and virtues that Dewey called "reflective intelligence." Experience itself involves undergoing, suffering, activity, and consummations. In sharp contrast to the thin, emasculated, subjectivistically tinged conceptions of experience that had become entrenched in modern epistemology, he elaborated a thicker, richer, situational notion of experience, whereby experience is capable of being funded with meaning and emotion and is given direction. What emerges from Dewey is a distinctive image of human beings and human experience. We are always *in media res,* there are no absolute beginnings or finalities. We are always in the process of being shaped by and shaping our history and our traditions. We are eminently fallible. We never escape from the precariousness and contingency of existence. We become fools of history if we believe that we can achieve total control by expert knowledge, or if we think we can collectively impose our wills and completely determine our destinies.

Dewey had little patience with those who succumb to a nostalgia or longing for a "golden era" that never really existed, or with the type of utopian thinking that seeks to make a total break with existing realities. Both of these modes of thinking all too easily lead to despair. It was not adjustment to the status quo that Dewey advocated, but the constant challenging task of reconstruction. He was scornful of what he called "moralism"—the belief that social change can be effected by calls for moral reform. In this respect, he was close in spirit to the tradition of practical philosophy that has its roots in Aristotle's *Ethics* where leading the good life and becoming virtuous requires that we constantly seek to develop the habits, dispositions, judgment *(phronesis),* and character that can only be cultivated in a proper communal life. But the Greek *polis,* for all its glory, could no longer serve as an adequate model for communal life in advanced industrial societies.

Dewey did have enormous faith in what education and schooling could achieve in a democratic society. In all his writings on education and from his practical involvement with the founding of the Laboratory School at the University of Chicago, he stressed the role of the school as a social institution and as providing a model of community life. There is still a popular myth that Dewey, the so-called father of progressive education, advocated a child-centered conception of education that sentimentalizes and idealizes the child's development. This is one of the extremes that he opposes. "Doing as one pleases signifies a release from truly *intellectual* initiative and independence." When unlimited free expression is allowed, children "gradually tend to become listless and finally bored, while there is an absence of cumulative, progressive development of power and actual achievement in results."[7] But Dewey objected just as strongly to the theory of education that presupposes that the child is naturally recalcitrant and must have discipline forced upon him or her. It is directed, cumulative, ordered reconstruction of experience that is central to Dewey's understanding of the educative process. And in "My Pedagogic Creed" published in 1887, Dewey returns over and over again to the theme of the school as a form of community life: "Much of present education fails because it neglects this fundamental principle of the school as a form of community life."[8] But what precisely does Dewey mean by community life?

Recently, Michael J. Sandel has suggested a classification of three conceptions of community that is helpful for pinpointing the strong sense of community that Dewey has in mind. Sandel distinguishes an instrumental, sentimental, and constitutive conception of community. The first conceives of community as a social union "where individuals regard social arrangements as a necessary burden and cooperate only for the sake of pursuing their private ends." The second—the sentimental conception—assumes "the antecedent individuation of the subjects of cooperation, whose actual motivations may include benevolent aims as well as selfish ones." To the extent that there are shared values and sentiments, these are shared in the sense that each individual distributively has these values and sentiments. But the third—the constitutive or strong sense of community—questions the presupposition of the antecedent individuation of the subject; it claims on the contrary that what an individual is and the type of individuality manifested is not something that comes temporally or logically prior to community life, but is in part constituted by the type of community within which one participates. "On this strong view, to say that the members of a society are bound by a sense of community is not to say that a great many of them profess communitarian sentiments and pursue communitarian aims, but rather that they conceive their identity—the subject and not just the object of their feelings and aspirations—as defined to some extent by the community of which they are a part."[9]

All of Dewey's intellectual pathways lead to a defense of this strong sense of community. This is why he was so suspicious of the dichotomy of the individual and the social, and why he thought that individualism versus collectivism was such a misleading contrast. It is also the reason why he was so critical of classical forms of liberalism and individualism (what he called the "old liberalism" and the "old individualism"). For whether classical forms of liberalism take benign or malignant forms, they implicitly or explicitly assume that it makes sense to speak of human individuals existing apart or independently of their social relationships. Genuine individualism is not a given or a starting point, it is only an *achievement*—an achievement that Dewey claimed could be realized in and through democratic communal life. Dewey stressed this strong sense of community for both philosophical and practical reasons. Our task now is "to re-create by deliberate and determined endeavor the kind of democracy which in its origin . . . was largely the product of a fortunate combination of men and circumstances."

Jefferson was always one of Dewey's heroes because his own formulation of democracy "is moral through and through: in its foundations, its methods, and its ends." Dewey did think that Jefferson was right in discerning a serious threat to the moral character of democracy in the coming industrialization of America. But it was not "industrialization" that Dewey took to be the main problem: but rather the resulting "dislocation and unsettlement of local communities." Dewey was sharply critical of a laissez faire ideology, which under the pretense of an appeal to an older liberalism and individualism "legitimized" practices that undermined and manipulated communal life. The "tragedy" of what Dewey called the "lost individual" is due to the fact that while individuals are now caught up into a vast complex of associations, "there is no harmonious and coherent reflection of the import of these connections into the imaginative and emotional outlook on life." But increasingly Dewey came to see that the most poignant problem in the United States, and the most serious threat to democracy, was to be found in the rise and spread of the "corporate mentality":

> the business mind, having its own conversation and language, its own interests, its own intimate groupings in which men of this mind, in their collective capacity, determine the tone of society at large as well as the government of industrial society. . . . we now have, although without formal or legal status, a mental and moral corporateness for which history affords no parallel.[10]

This growing corporateness and the mentality that it fosters is the most serious threat to the type of communal life that Dewey took to be the lifeblood of a creative democracy.

In the *Public and Its Problems,* which was written in part as a response to the beginnings of elitist conceptions of democracy, Dewey called for a radicalization of democracy, for a reconstruction of local communities, for a revitalization of public life. In Arendt's phrase, he called for the cultivation of those "public spaces" where "debate, discussion and persuasion" would become manifest. Dewey spoke of the search for the Great Community, but he did not mean a single undifferentiated community in which all individuality is submerged. Rather his vision was that of a community of communities, but he realized that this makes no sense unless we begin with local, face-to-face communal life.

> Unless local communal life can be restored, the public cannot adequately solve its most urgent problem; to find and identify itself. But if it be reestablished, it will manifest a fullness, variety and freedom of possession and enjoyment of meanings and goods unknown in the contiguous associations of the past. For it will be alive and flexible as well as stable, responsive to the complex and world-wide scene in which it is emeshed. While local, it will not be isolated.[11]

It has become fashionable and all too facile to attack Dewey from a variety of perspectives. The sad truth is that many professional philosophers barely take him seriously today. The reconstruction of philosophy that Dewey sought to bring about has not only failed to occur, but many professional philosophers have become more and more obsessed with the "problems of philosophy." It is true that Dewey, for all his talk about being concrete and specific, could be incredibly vague. In his desire to soften all dichotomies, distinctions, and dualisms, at times, he seems to deprive us of the analytic tools needed for advancing our understanding. Social theorists who are sympathetic with Dewey tend at times to take a patronizing attitude toward him. His vision of democracy which did inspire many of his contemporaries can now strike us as flat. Even if we credit him with being sensitive to the problems that continue to plague us—the eclipse of public life, the breakdown of local communities, the distortions of social life effected by the growth of corporateness—it may be said that Dewey provides little guidance about how to meet and solve these problems.

Dewey did call for a radical transformation of economic and political institutions, but does not seem to address the issues of what this concretely means or how it is to be achieved. We may also feel that even after a sympathetic reading of Dewey's understanding of "scientific method," he does not sufficiently help us to understand the crucial differences between scientific and democratic communities, or how instrumental rationality and scientism can deform the deliberation and judgment required for the practice of democracy. Witnessing the way in which our educational institutions, from elementary schools to institutions of higher learning, are deformed by the imperatives of a corporate society, it is difficult to see how they might become the beacons for democratic communal life that Dewey saw as their primary function. There is a genuine need to engage in the type of criticism of his own philosophy that Dewey took to be the mark of all philosophy.

But there is a danger of "overkill"—of forgetting how much in Dewey endures and has special relevance for us. Once again there is a growing uneasiness in philosophy. It is not accidental that a philosopher like Richard Rorty who has brilliantly criticized much of the sterility and irrelevance of recent philosophy cites Dewey as one of the most important philosophers of the twentieth century and calls for a return to the spirit of Dewey's pragmatism.[12] It is instructive, that despite recent attempts to articulate and defend a variety of classical versions of liberalism, many of these doctrines founder because they do not do justice to the strong constitutive sense of community that defines our moral and political identities. Sometimes it seems as if we are living through a rage against modernity, a total disenchantment with the hopes and aspirations of what is best in our own democratic heritage, and with the type of fallibilistic humanism that Dewey advocated. But perhaps, after the dialectic of fashionable forms of relativism and domesticated nihilism work themselves out, we may return to the spirit of Dewey. For what is most enduring in Dewey is his sanity and his courage, his refusal to submit to despair. Dewey did emphasize the projective and future-oriented dimension of all thinking, and he was aware of the ways in which history and tradition are always effectively shaping what we are in the process of becoming. But his central focus was with the living present, with facing our present conflicts and problems with honesty and imagination, and with finding the concrete ways in which we can reconstruct experience where free communication, public debate, rational persuasion, and genuine sharing are integrated into our everyday practices. Creative—radical—democracy is still "the task before us."

NOTES

1. *Washington Post,* December 19, 1937.

2. John Dewey, "Creative Democracy—The Task Before Us," reprinted in Fisch, ed, *Classic American Philosophers* (New York: Appleton-Century-Crofts, 1951), p. 394.

3. John Dewey, "Philosophy and Civilization," in *Philosophy and Civilization* (New York: Minton, Balch, 1931), p. 12.

4. John Dewey, *Freedom and Culture* (New York: Putnam, 1939), p. 131.

5. See Alasdair MacIntyre, *After Virtue* (Notre Dame: University of Notre Dame Press), pp. 175ff.

6. "From Absolutism to Experimentalism," reprinted in Richard J. Bernstein, *John Dewey: On Experience, Nature, and Freedom* (New York: Liberal Arts Press, 1960), p. 10.

7. John Dewey, *Construction and Criticism* (New York: Columbia University Press, 1930), p. 11; "Individuality and Experience," *Journal of the Barnes Foundation* (1926), 2:1.

8. "My Pedagogic Creed," reprinted in McDermott, *The Philosophy of John Dewey* (Chicago: University of Chicago Press, 1981), p. 446.

9. Michael J. Sandel, *Liberalism and the Limits of Justice* (Cambridge: Cambridge University Press, 1982), pp. 147ff.

10. John Dewey, *Individualism: Old and New* (New York: Minton, Balch, 1930), p. 41.

11. John Dewey, *The Public and Its Problems* (New York: Henry Holt, 1927), p. 216.

12. See Richard Rorty, *Consequences of Pragmatism* (Minneapolis: University of Minnesota Press, 1982).

TWO
LITERARY CULTURE

[5]

Philosophy as/and/of Literature

ARTHUR C. DANTO

> *By displaying what is subjective, the work, in its whole presentation, reveals its purpose as existing for* the subject, for the spectator and not on its own account. The spectator is, as it were, in it from the beginning, is counted in with it, and the work exists only for this point, i.e., for the individual apprehending it.
>
> G. W. F. Hegel, *Aesthetik*

OUR DISCIPLINE seems so singular a crossbreed of art and science that it is somewhat surprising that only lately has it seemed imperative to some that philosophy be viewed as literature—surprising and somewhat alarming. Of course so much has been enfranchised as literature in recent times that it would have been inevitable that literary theorists should have turned from the comic strip, the movie magazine, the disposable romance—from science fiction, pornography, and graffiti—to the texts of philosophy, this in virtue of a vastly widened conception of the text which enables us to apply the strategies of hermeneutical interpretation to bus tickets and baggage checks, want ads and weather reports, laundry lists and postage cancellations, savings certificates and address books, medical prescriptions, pastry recipes, olive oil cans and cognac labels—so why *not* meditations, examinations, and critiques? Admittedly this is not the exalted sense of literature we have in mind in speaking of philosophy as an art, but even if we retain the normative connotations of the term, there is something disturbing in the fact that this particular face of philosophy should have now become visible enough

Presidential Address delivered before the Eightieth Annual Eastern Meeting of the American Philosophical Association, in Boston, December 28, 1983.

that we should have been enjoined to treat its texts as a particular literary genre. For after all the imperatives which have governed the transformation of philosophy into a profession have stressed our community with the sciences. Were a kind of semiotic egalitarianism to direct us to regard as so many texts the papers which regularly appear in *Physical Review,* their literary dimension must seem deeply secondary, as ours has always seemed to us to be: so to treat it suddenly as primary has to be unsettling.

Philosophy-as-literature carries implications in excess of the claim that philosophical texts have at times a degree of literary merit. We take a remote satisfaction that some of us—Strawson, Ryle, or Quine—let alone Santayana, Russell, and James—write distinguished prose, and we would all regard as astute a teacher of English who took pages from any of these as compositional paradigms. Still, our tendency is to regard style, save to the degree that it enhances perspicuity, as adventitious and superfluous to that for the sake of which we finally address these texts: as mere *Farbung,* to use Frege's dismissive term. So to rotate these texts in such a way that the secondary facets catch the light of intellectual concern puts what we regard as the primary facets in shadow; and to acquiesce in the concept of philosophy-as-literature just now seems tacitly to acquiesce in the view that the austere imperatives of philosophy-as-science have lost their energy. Considering what has been happening to texts when treated in recent times, our canon seems suddenly fragile, and it pains the heart to think of them enduring the frivolous sadism of the deconstructionist. But the perspective of philosophy-as-literature is an uncomfortable one for us to occupy, quite apart from these unedifying violations.

Consider the comparable perspective of the Bible-as-literature. Certainly it can be read as such, its poetry and narrative responded to as poetry and narrative, its images appreciated for their power and its moral representations as a kind of drama. But to treat it so is to put at an important distance the Bible considered as a body of revelations, of saving truths and ethical certitudes; a text of which a thinker like Philo could believe that everything in it and nothing outside of it is true. So some fundamental relationship to the book will have changed when it sustains transfer to the curriculum as "living literature." Of course some aspect of its style has from the beginning of its historical importance played a role in biblical epistemology. The language of the Koran is said so to transcend in its beauty the powers of human expressiveness as virtually to guarantee its own claim to have been dictated by an angel and to be, not even metaphorically, the word of God; so its style is taken to be the best evidence for its truth. Biblical writing, by contrast, was taken to be the record of human witnesses, and much of it was so offensive to literary taste that it had to be true. A second century apologist writes: "When I was giving my most earnest attention to discover the truth I happened to meet with certain barbaric writings . . . and I was led to put faith in these by the unpretending cast of the language." Origen, admitting the stylistic inferiority of Scripture by specific comparison with Plato, finds in this evidence that it is exactly the word of God, since if written by men it would be classier; its rudeness is a further weapon for confounding the wise. "However roughly, as regards mere authorship, my book should be got up," Poe has his fictional hero write in the arch forward to *The Narrative of Arthur Gordon Pym*, "its very uncouthness, if there were any, would give it all the better chance of being received as truth."

That plain prose has a better chance of being received true is a stylistic maxim not unknown in adopting a philosophical diction—think of Moore—but my point is only that there is a profound contrast between taking the Bible as literature and viewing it as the Word, and I would suspect disjoint classes of passages to become prominent depending on which view we take. The remaining music of the Bible must count as small compensation when the truth-claims made on its behalf are no longer felt to be compelling, and something like this contrast arises with philosophy-as-literature set against philosophy-as-truth. On the other hand, it provides an occasion to reflect, as I shall briefly, on how philosophical truth has been regarded if we approach philosophy for the moment as though it were a genre of literature; it enables us to see how we construed truth when we hadn't thought of ourselves as producing literature. And so we may reflect on the ways in which the dimensions of our professional being are connected.

For a period roughly coeval with that in which philosophy attained professionalization, the canonical literary format has been the professional philosophy paper. Our practice as philosophers consists in reading and in writing such papers, in training our students to read and write them, in inviting others to come read us a paper, to which we respond by posing questions which in effect are editorial recommendations, typically incorporated and acknowledged in the first or last footnote of the paper, in which we are exempted from such errors and infelicities as may remain, and thanked for our helpful suggestions. The journals in which these papers finally are printed, whatever incidental features useful to the profession at large they may carry, are not otherwise terribly distinct from one another, any more than the papers themselves characteristically are. If, under the constraints of blind review, we black out name and institutional affiliation, there will be no internal evidence of authorial presence, but only a unit of pure philosophy, to the presentation of which the author will have sacrificed all identity. This implies a noble vision of ourselves as vehicles for the transmission of an utterly impersonal philosophical truth, and it implies a vision of philosophical reality as constituted of insolable, difficult, but not finally intractable problems, which if not altogether soluble in fifteen pages more or less, can be brought closer to resolution in that many pages. The paper is then an impersonal report of limited results for a severely restricted readership, consisting of those who have some use for that result since they are engaged with the writers of the papers in a collaborative enterprise, building the edifice of philosophical knowledge.

It is perfectly plain that the implied vision of philosophical reality, as well as of the form of live evolved to discover it and the form of literature in which it is suitable to represent it, are closely modeled on the view of reality, life, and literature which compose what Thomas Kuhn has instructed us to think of as normal science. Mastery of the literary form is the key to success in the form of life, bringing tenure and the kind of recognition which consists in being invited to read papers widely and perhaps the presidency of one or another division of the American Philosophical Association. These practical benefits aside, no one could conceivably be interested in participating in the form of life defined by the literary form in issue, were it not believed that this is the avenue to philosophical truth. It is less obviously a matter of agreement that philosophical truth is defined by this being believed to be the way to find it.

It is not my purpose here to criticize a form of life in which I after all participate, nor to criticize the format of speech and writing which, after all, reinforces the virtues of clarity, brevity, and competence in those compelled to use it.

I only mean to emphasize that the concept of philosophical truth and the form of philosophical expression are internally enough related that we may want to recognize that when we turn to other forms we may also be turning to other conceptions of philosophical truth. Consider the way in which we address our predecessors, for example. A lot of what I have read on Plato reads much as though he to whom the whole of subsequent philosophy since is said to be so many footnotes, were in effect a footnote to himself, and being coached to get a paper accepted by *The*

Philosophical Review. And a good bit of the writing on Descartes is by way of chivying his argumentation into notations we are certain he would have adopted had he lived to appreciate their advantages, since it is now so clear where he went wrong. But in both cases it might at least have been asked whether what either writer is up to can that easily be separated from forms it may have seemed inevitable it be presented in, so that the dialogue or meditation flattened into conventional periodical prose might not in the process have lost something central to those ways of writing. The form in which the truth as they understood it must be grasped just might require a form of reading, hence a kind of relationship to those texts, altogether different from that appropriate to a paper, or to what we sometimes refer to as a "contribution." And this because something is intended to happen to the reader other than, or in addition to, being informed. It is after all not simply that the texts may lose something when flattened into papers: life may have lost something when philosophy is flattened out to the production and transmission of papers, noble as the correlative vision is. So addressing philosophy as literature is not meant to stultify the aspiration to philosophical truth so much as to propose a caveat against a reduced concept of reading, just because we realize that more is involved even in contemporary, even analytical, philosophy than merely stating the truth; to get at that kind of truth involves some kind of transformation of the audience, and the acquiescence in a certain form of initiation and life.

I cannot think of a field of writing as fertile as philosophy has been in generating forms of literary expression, for ours has been—to use a partial list I once attempted—a history of dialogues, lecture notes, fragments, poems, examinations, essays, aphorisms, meditations, discourses, hymns, critiques, letters, summae, encyclopedias, testaments, commentaries, investigations, tractatuses, *Vorlesungen, Aufbauen,* prolegomena, parerga, pensees, sermons, supplements, confessions, sententiae, inquiries, diaries, outlines, sketches, commonplace books, and, to be self-referential, addresses, and innumerable forms which have no generic identity or which themselves constitute distinct genres: *Holzwege,* Grammatologies, Unscientific Postscripts, Geneologies, Natural Histories, Phenomenologies, and whatever the *World as Will and Idea* may be or the posthumous corpus of Husserl, or the later writings of Derrida, and forgetting the standard sorts of literary forms, e.g., novels, plays, and the like, which philosophers have turned to when gifted those ways. One has to ask what cognitive significance is conveyed by the fact that the classic texts of China are typically composed of conversational bits, a question brought home vividly to me when a scholar I respect, complained that it is terribly hard to get any propositions out of Chuang Tzu; for this may be the beginning of an understanding of how that elusive sage is to be addressed, and what it means to read him. Responding to a review of *The Realm of Truth* by his amenuensis, Santayana wrote: "It is well that now you can take a holiday: which doesn't exclude the possibility of returning to them with freshness of judgement and apperception. Perhaps then you might not deprecate my purple passages, and might see, which is the historical fact, that they are not applied ornaments but natural growths and *realizations* of the thought moving previously in a limbo of verbal abstractions."

It is arguable that the professional philosophical paper is an evolutionary product, emerging by natural selection from a wild profusion of forms Darwinized into oblivion through maladaptation, stages in the advance of philosophy toward consciousness of its true identity, a rockier road than most. But it is equally arguable that philosophers with really new thoughts have simply had to invent new forms to convey them with, and that it may be possible that from the perspective of the standard format no way into these other forms, hence no way into these systems or structures of thought can be found. This claim may be supported, perhaps, by the consideration that pretty much the only way in which literature of the nonphilosophical kind has impinged upon philosophical awareness has been from the perspective of truth-or-falsity. The philosopher would cheerfully consign the entirety of fiction to the domain of falsehood but for the nagging concern that a difference is to be marked between sentences which miss the mark and sentences which have no mark to miss and are threatened, in consequence of prevailing theories of meaning, with meaninglessness. Some way must therefore be found for them to have meaning before they can be dismissed as false, and pretty much the entirety of the analytical—and I may as well add the phenomenological—corpus has been massively addressed to the question of fictive reference. Literature sets up obstacles to the passage of semantical theories which would go through a great deal more easily if literature did not exist. By assessing it against the concept of reference, literature derives what intellectual dignity philosophy can bestow, with the incidental benefit that if literature is merely a matter of relating words to the world, well, if philosophy is literature it is meaningful, providing it can only show how. And philosophy's way of relating literature to reality may make philosophy-as-literature one with philosophy-as-truth.

This is scarcely the place to tell the chilling tale of fictional reference, in part because it seems not to have reached an end, there being no accepted theory of how it works. But if there ever was an argument for philosophy as a kind of literature, it might be found in the extravagant ontological imagination of semantical theorists in proposing things for fictive terms to designate. Since *Don Quixote* is meaningful "Don Quixote" must refer—not, to be sure, to some specific addled Spaniard in La Mancha, but to Don Quixote himself, a subsistant entity, which *Don Quixote* can now be about in just the way it would if he were indeed an addled Spaniard in La Mancha. How such subsistant entities confer meaning, or at least how they explain the fact that we grasp it, was never particularly explained, causal transactions between the domain of subsistant entities and existent entities such as we, being surely ruled out of question. This problem is aggravated when we purge the universe of fictive beings by waving a Quinian wand which changes names into predicates, Don Quixote becoming the x that quixotizes all over the y that lamanchas. The prodigality complained of in manufacturing entities to order is evidently unnoticed when it comes to manufacturing predicates to order, and the change from *Gegestande* to *Gedanke* leaves the question of meaning and its being grasped about as dark as ever—nor is the matter especially mitigated when we allow *Don Quixote* to pick a possible world to be about, for the relationship of it to ours and finally to us remains as obscure as that between Don Quixote and us when he was a homeless wraithe, an ontological ghost wandering in worlds undreamt of by poets.

From this point of view Professor Goodman's elegant theory of secondary extensions is particularly welcome, first from the perspective of ontology, since secondary extensions are comprised of things we can put our hands on, like inscriptions, and secondly from the point of view of epistemology, since pictures play a prominant part in the secondary extension of a term and we in fact begin our adventures into literature with picture books. It does on the other hand throw an immense semantical burden on illustrated editions and the like; and tangles us in puzzles of its own since the set of pictures ostensibly *of* the same thing may look so little alike that we may have severe doubts as to what their subject would look like if it existed, while pictures of altogether different subjects may look so alike that we could not tell them apart were they to be real. Whether we must ascend to tertiary extensions and beyond, and how these would solve our further problems, are matters not to be taken up here. For the question I want to raise is why, whichever of these theories is true, we, as readers, should have the slightest interest in *Don Quixote* if what it is about is an unactualized thin man in a region of being I would have no reason to know about save for the interventions of semantical theory: or if it were about the x that quixotizes (there being none) or a set of possible worlds other than my own, or primarily about nothing but secondarily about such things as a set of engravings by Gustave Doré?

I raise the question because literature, certainly in its greatest exemplars, seems to have something important to do with our lives, important enough that the study of it should form an essential part of our educational program, and this is utterly unexplained if its meaning is a matter of its reference, and its candidate referenda are as bizarre a menagery of imaginabilia as the fancy of man has framed. And it may be that when we show the kind of connection there is, there will not be a problem of the sort to which semantical theory has been so elaborate a response. Well, it may be said, this might simply remove literature from the sphere of philosophical concern, a welcome enough removal but for the fact that it might remove philosophy itself from the domain of philosophical concern if philosophy itself is literature. And my insinuation has been that the sorts of things philosophy has laid down to connect literature in order to give it meaning—Gegenstånde, intensions, fictive worlds—are themselves as much in need of ontological redemption as the beings to whose rescue they were enlisted: Don Quixote, Mr. Pickwick, Gandolf the Grey. To believe we can save fiction by means of fiction is one of the endearing innocences of a discipline that takes pride in what it likes to think is its skeptical circumspection.

Semantical theory does the best it can in striving to connect literature to the world through what, after all, are the only kinds of connections it understands: reference, truth, instantiation, exemplification, satisfaction, and the like. And if this means distorting the universe in order that it can *receive* literary representations, well, this has never been reckoned a heavy price for philosophy to pay—has not been reckoned a price at all but a creative opportunity—and it remains to the credit of this enterprise that it at least believes *some* connection between literature and the world is required. In this it contrasts with literary theory as currently practiced, which impugns philosophical preoccupations with sematical ligatures as but a further instance of what one leading theoretician dismisses as the Referential Fallacy. Literature does not refer at all to reality, according to this view, but at best to other literature, and a concept of *intertextuality* is advanced according to which a literary work is to be understood, so far as referentiality facilitates understanding, only in terms of other works a given work refers to, so that no one equipped with less than the literary culture of the writer of a work up for interpretation can be certain of having understood the work at all. There is certainly something to this view if Northrop Frye is correct in claiming, of Blake's line "O Earth, O Earth return" that "though it contains only five words and only three different words"—five tokens and three types as we might more briskly say— "it contains also about seven direct allusions to the Bible." The author of the Referential Fallacy, a practitioner of literary criticism whom I prefer for somewhat complex reasons to refer to simply as R—he after all speaks for his profession—assures us that "the poetic text is self-sufficient." But "If there is external reference, it is not to reality—far from it! Any such reference is to other texts." This extreme view merits some examination if only for its vivid opposition to the standard philosophical view.

Consider one of his examples, the last line of Wordsworth's poem *Written in March,* which goes: "Small clouds are sailing,/ Blue skies prevailing,/ The rain is over and done." This line, together with the title, might lead the reader to suppose that the poem refers to the end of winter and expresses the poet's gratitude that Spring has come at last—but this easy reading is, according to R, quite seriously and fallaciously wrong: it refers in fact to *The Song of Songs,* from which Wordsworth's line is taken verbatim, and is in fact a fragment of the biblical line which begins "For lo! The winter is past . . ." Now it hardly can be doubted that Wordsworth knew *The Song of Songs,* and it is certain that literary scholarship, in explaining the sources of the poem, will refer to it as an ultimate source for the last line. Perhaps every line, or every phrase in a poem may be explained with reference to something in the literary culture of the writer. But not every literary effect necessarily *refers* to its causes, and there is a considerable difference between understanding a poem, which may require understanding its references when it makes them, and understanding the provenances of a poem, which is quite another matter: it is specialist knowledge, and likely incidental to understanding a poem.

Let me offer an illustration from another art, in part to make my argument more general, in part to confirm a claim about pictorial semantics. Raphael's beautiful *Madonna della sedia* is composed within a circular frame—a *tondo*—not, as Gombrich points out, because Raphael one day seized a handy barrelhead in order to paint up an innkeeper's daugh-

ter who charmed him, together with her pretty child, as Madonna and
Infant, which is the tour guide's lovely explanation; but rather because,
like many of his contemporaries, Raphael was excited by some recently
exhibited drawings of Leonardo, among them some circular compositions. Every painter in the region would have known about those drawings, and hence the provenance of Raphael's painting, but for all that,
Raphael was not referring to the drawings which inspired him. By contrast, the American painter Benjamin West did a portrait of his wife and
son in *tondo* form, her garment the garment of Raphael's Madonna, not
as a copy of but in *reference to* Raphael's painting. It was an exceedingly
pretentious reference, depicting his wife as Madonna, his child as the Baby
Jesus, *his* painting as the *Madonna della sedia,* and himself as Raphael.
But to understand the painting is to understand those allusions, for he is
representing his family *as* the Holy Pair *as* depicted by Raphael, and a
very self-exalting metaphor is being transacted. (What a humiliation to
have had this hopeful vision deaccessioned by the Reynolds' collection in
exchange for a merely typical Thomas Cole!)

It was a triumph of art-historical scholarship to demonstrate the un-
mistakable use made by Manet of an arrangement of figures in an engraving by Marcantonio Raimondi in setting the figures in his *Dejeuner
sur l'herbe*. This by no means excludes the possibility, or rather the fact,
that Manet was representing friends of his, wits and demimondaines, en-
joying an elegant outing. Of course it is a different painting depending
upon whether he was referring to or merely using Raimondi's work. If
he was referring to it, then his subject is *that* outing *as* a feast of the
gods, which is the subject of the original engraving. Raimondi was the
most famous engraver of his age (as well as a notorious forger), but in
Manet's world he was doubtless too obscure for such an allusion to be
made, by contrast perhaps with biblical references in Wordsworth's world;
and probably obviousness is a condition of allusion as banality is a condition of validity in the enthymeme. But even so, Manet's use of that engraving must be distinguished from a use made by the American painter,
John Trumbull, in his famous portrait of General Washington with his
horse, of a certain preexisting form of horse representation. Far from being
the finely observed depiction of Washington's elegant steed, Washington's horse, as shown, is but one in a long historical sequence of similar
horses which Leo Steinberg has traced back to a Roman cameo, and which
probably could be traced even further. Still, it is Washington with his
horse that is being referred to, and not any member of this series, each

of which but conforms to a pattern. The pattern, which may be an example of what Gombrich speaks of as a schema, is a very satisfactory way of representing horses which are, as we know, very difficult to observe (until Muybridge nobody knew whether all four legs were altogether off the ground in gallop) and yields up a kind of representational a priori of a sort whose narrative and lyrical counterparts may be found in literature and, though this is not my topic, there may be profound similarities with scientific representations as well.

In all these cases and countless others, reference to the world works together with references to other art, when there are such references, to make a complex representation; so why should or must it be different in the case of Wordsworth? R writes thus: "The key word—*winter*—absent from Wordsworth, is the matrix penetrating every Spring detail in the poem . . . now perceived as the converse of an image that has been effaced, so that the poem is not a direct depiction of reality, but a negative version of a latent text on the opposite of Spring." This is the kind of hermeneutic contortion that earns interpreters of literature distinguished chairs in universities—the kind who argue, for example, that *Hamlet* is a negative version of a latent text about Fortinbras, the *true* hero of the play, perceived now as comedy rather than tragedy since the hero is alive at the end, and making Shakespeare a clever forerunner of Tom Stoppard. But my concern is not to argue with the interpretation but with the "so" to which R is not entitled: a proper interpretation would have to show why Wordsworth referred to the season through the medium of a biblical allusion if in fact it was an allusion and not a cliché of the sort that has simply entered language the way so much of *Hamlet* has that a student is said to have criticized it for being too full of clichés, though a pretty exciting story. And what of *The Song of Songs* itself, if poetry: is *it* about winter, or, to use the other option offered us, altogether self-contained?

In a famous letter to his mistress, Louise Collet, Flaubert lays out his own ideal as an artist: "What I should like to write is a book about nothing, a book dependent upon nothing external, which would be held together by the internal strength of its style, just as the earth, suspended in the void, depends upon nothing external for its support: a book which would have almost no subject, or at least in which the subject would be invisible, if such a thing is possible." Flaubert's astronomy is appalling, and if R is right he could not have failed of his purpose, all literature, just so far as it is literature, being about nothing. Or at best, being about other literature, work holding work in referential orbit, to give Flaubert a happier physical metaphor, but basically untethered to reality. The question is what considerations recommend the guaranteed irrelevancy of literature to life?

"In everyday language," the author of The Referential Fallacy writes, "words seem to refer vertically, each to the reality it seems to render, like the labels on a barrelhead, each a semantic unit. While in literature the unit of meaning is the text itself. The reciprocal effects of its words on one another, as members of a finite network, replaces the vertical semantical relationship with a lateral one, forged along the written line, tending to cancel the dictionary meanings of the words."

Now I want to applaud the concept of a text as a network of reciprocal effects. Not original with R, of course, it has entered our world from European sources, making an immense impact upon literary theorists while leaving philosophy so far untouched. I feel that were the concept of the text to become as central in analytical philosophy as the sentence has been since Frege gave it primacy, or as the term has been since Aristotle, a vast world for philosophical research will have opened up. For the concept of the text is considerably wider than literary texts alone. It applies to musical compositions and to architectural structures, art forms whose referentiality has been in occasional question, and to personalities, whole lives in the biographical sense of the term, families, villages, cultures, things for which the question of referentiality has hardly been raised at all. And the expression "a network of reciprocal effects" will come to be exchanged for a class of relationships as various as, and perhaps as important as, those which bind sentences into arguments, and which have been so massively explored in contemporary philosophical thought. Even so, it is altogether compatible with being united through a network of reciprocal effects that a literary work should refer, as it were, extratextually—though the reference may be complicated as much by intra- as by intertextual references. The prelude and finale of *Middlemarch* refer reciprocally, as well as to the novel they frame, and both refer or allude to Saint Teresa, herself not a text save in so wide a sense as to make R's theory timid and disappointing. They refer to her to provide a metaphor for Dorothea Brooks—Miss Brooks as erotic ascetic perhaps—proving that her character has remained constant through two marriages, and saying finally something deep about the narrow space there after all is for being different from what we are.

But this goes well beyond what philosophers have wanted to say in supposing *Middlemarch* refers, say, to a world of its own or to some fleshless subsistant woman, Dorothea Brooks. And it goes well beyond what R will allow, who leaves us with the same question that philosophical discussions of fictional reference did, namely why should we be interested in *Middlemarch*? Why, since not ourselves literary scholars, should we concern ourselves with these intricate networks of reciprocal effects? "Because they are there" was not even a good reason for climbing mountains, but I am struck by the fact that philosophers seem only to understand vertical and literary theorists, if R is right, only horizontal references. On this coordinate scheme it is difficult to locate literature in the plane of human concern at all. Clearly we need a z-coordinate, we must open a dimension of reference neither vertical nor horizontal reference quite reveal, if we are to get an answer. In what remains of this paper, that is what I shall begin to do.

"The distinction between historian and poet is not in the one writing prose and the other verse," Aristotle writes, helpfully as always. "You might put the work of Heroditus into verse and it would still be a species of history." Though he neglects the reverse possibility, I take Aristotle to mean that one ought to be unable to tell by mere examination of a text whether it is poetry or something else, which gives my own question an immediate philosophical structure. The form of a philosophical question is given—I would venture to say always, but lack an immediate proof—when indiscriminate pairs with nevertheless distinct ontological locations may be found or imagined found, and we then must make plain in what the difference consists or could consist. The classical case is matching dream experience with waking experience in such a way that, as Descartes required, nothing internal to either mode of experience will serve as differentiating criterion. So whatever internal criterion we in fact, and, as it happens, preanalytically employ will be irrelevant to the solution of the problem, e.g., that dreams are vague and incoherent: for dreams may be imagined, and possibly had, which are as like waking experience as we require to void the criterion. So the difference must come in at right angles to the plane of what we experience, and philosophy here consists in saying what it can be. Kant discovers the same thing in moral theory, since he imagines it possible that a set of actions should perfectly conform to principle and yet have no moral worth, since that requires a different relationship to those principles than mere conformity, and outward observation cannot settle the matter. And Adeimanthus furnishes the stunning example which generates the *Republic,* of a perfectly just man whose behavior is indiscriminable from that of a man perfectly unjust: the example requires that justice be orthogonal to conduct, and entails as uniquely possible the kind of theory Plato gives us.

Other examples lie ready to hand. The present state of the world is compatible with the world being any age at all, including five minutes old, and nothing on the surface of the world will arbitrate without begging the question. A mere bodily movement and a basic action might appear exactly alike, just as what we take to be an expression of a feeling may be but a kind of rictus. Nothing open to observation discriminates a pair of connected events, to use Hume's distinction, from a pair merely conjoined. And in my own investigations into the philosophy of art, I have benefited immensely from Duchamp's discovery that nothing the eye can reveal will arbitrate the difference between a work of art and a mere real thing which resembles it in every outward particular. So any proposed distinction based upon perceptual differences, even in the visual arts, will have proved, as with the Linnaean system in botany, to be artificial, however useful in practice. Duchamp consigned all past theories to oblivion by proving that the problem was philosophical. And here is Aristotle, telling us that the differences between poetry and history do not lie on the surface of texts, and that distinguishing them is not an ordinary matter of classification but a philosophical matter of explanation.

It is indeed not at all difficult to imagine two quite sustained pieces of writing which belong to relevantly distinct genres, without there being so much difference as a semicolon. I once imagined a pair of indiscriminable texts, one a novel, one a piece of history. My colleague Stern, suppose, comes across an archive containing the papers of a Polish noblewoman of the last century, who died characteristically in a convent. Incredibly, she was the mistress of Talleyrand, of Metternich, of the young Garibaldi, of Jeremy Bentham, Eugène Delacroix, of Frederic Chopin, and Czar Nicholas of Russia, though the great loves of her life were George Sand and the nubile Sarah Bernhardt. Published by Viking, it wins the Pulitzer prize in history in the same year as a novel with exactly the same name is published—*Maria Mazurka, Mistress to Genius*—written by Erica Jong, who was inspired to invent a heroine who dies appropriately in a convent, but who in her time had been the mistress of Talleyrand, Metternich, the younger Garibaldi, of Jeremy Bentham, Eugène Delacroix, of Frederic Chopin, and Czar Nicholas of Russia, though the great loves of her life were George Sand and the nubile Sarah Bernhardt. Jong's novel, unfortunately, is too improbable, has too many characters, sprawls all over the place, as Jong is wont to do these days—and it bears critical comparison with Stern's marvelous book which manages to keep track of all its characters, is tightly regimented given the diversity of materials, and contains not a fact in excess. So Jong's book, to the despair of the author and Random House, is soon remaindered, and for $2.98 you can get a lot of pages which cannot be told apart from Stern's book—on special at $19.99 through the History Book Club—though none of Stern's readers would be caught dead reading a mere novel. Stern's book, of course, refers vertically, while Jong's, being a novel, is a network of reciprocal effects, and self-sustained or nearly so, characterized only by horizontal reference. I realize I am slipping out of philosophy into literature: but the point is that whatever is to mark the difference must survive examples such as these.

Aristotle's famous suggestion, of course, is that "poetry is something more philosophical and of graver import than history, since its statements are of the nature of universals, whereas those of history are singular." It is plain that this difference is not registered grammatically or syntactically, if the example just constructed is possible and in the Aristotelian spirit. So there must be a way in which Jong's book, for all its failings is universal, and in which Stern's book, splendid as it is as historiography, remains for just that reason singular—about that specific woman in just those steamy liaisons. On the other hand, there must be some way in which Jong's book, if universal and hence more philosophical than Stern's, is not quite so philosophical as philosophy itself is— otherwise the problem of construing philosophy as a form of literature would be solved at the cost of so widening philosophy, since nothing could be more philosophical than it, as to compass whatever Aristotle would consider poetry. In whatever way philosophy is to be literature, if it is to be literature at all, it must respect whatever differences there may be with literature which is not philosophy, however necessarily philosophical it has to be in order to be distinguished from mere history.

My own view is that philosophy wants to be more than universal; it wants necessity as well: truth for all the worlds that are possible. In this respect it contrasts with history, or for that matter with science, which is concerned with the truths of just this particular, uniquely actual world, and happy if it can achieve that much. My contention here has been that philosophical semantics renders literature true of possible worlds, to lapse into vernacular, in such a way that it would be history for any of them if actual instead of ours. As *Gulliver's Travels* would just be anthropology for a world in which there were Lilliputians instead of Melanesians. This, I am afraid, is very close to Aristotle's own view, history dealing, according to him, with the thing that has been while poetry deals with "a kind of thing that might be." And that sounds too much like being true of a possible world to be comfortable with as an analysis. I nevertheless believe there is a kind of universality to literature worth considering, different from this, and I shall now try to say what it is in my own way, recognizing that if philosophy is also literature, it might have to be universal and possibly even necessary in two kinds of ways.

The thought I want to advance is that literature is not universal in the sense of being about every possible world insofar as possible, as philosophy in its nonliterary dimension aspires to be, nor about what may happen to be the case in just this particular world, as history taken in this respect in exemplificatory science aspires to be, but rather about each reader who experiences it. It is not, of course, about its readers as a book about reading is, which happens incidentally to be about its readers just as a subclass of its subject, but rather in the way in which, though you will look for him in vain, Benjamin West's pretentious family portrait is about him. He does not show himself in the manner of Velasquez in *Las Meninas,* but still, the painting is about Benjamin West *as* Raphael *as* painter of the Holy Family, through an allusive and metaphoric identification: he informs the work as a kind of *dieu caché.* Well, I want to say that a literary work is about its readers in this metaphoric and allusive way, in an exact mirror image of the way West's painting is about him: in Hegel's wonderful thought, the work exists for the spectator and not on its own account; it exists, as he says, only for the individual apprehending it, so that the apprehension completes the work and gives it final substance. The difficult claim I am making can be put somewhat formally as follows: the usual analysis of universality is that $(x)Fx$ is via the mechanisms of natural deduction equivalent to a conjunction of all the values on x, true in the event each is F. The universality of literary reference is only that it is about each individual that reads the text at the moment that individual reads it, and it contains an implied indexical: each work is about the "I" that reads the text, identifying himself not with the implied reader for whom the implied narrator writes, but with the actual subject of the text in such a way that each work becomes a metaphor for each reader— perhaps the same metaphor for each.

A metaphor, of course, in part because it is literally false that I am Achilles or Leopold Bloom or Anna or Oedipus or King Lear or Hyacinth Robinson or Strether or Lady Glencora; or a man hounded by an abstract bureaucracy because of an unspecified or suspected accusation, or the sexual slave O, or the raft-rider responsible to a moral being that an unspeakable nation refuses to countenance as a man, or the obsessive narrator of the violence of my ancestors which is my own violence since their story is in the end of my story, or one who stands to Jay Gatsby as Jay Gatz stood to the same dream as mine of "love, accomplishment, beauty, elegance, wealth" (which is a list I just found in a marvelous story by Gail Godwin). It is literature when, for each reader I, I is the subject of the story. The work finds it subject only when read.

Because of this immediacy of identification, it is natural to think, as theorists from Hamlet upwards have done, of literature as a kind of mirror, not simply in the sense of rendering up an external reality, but as giving me to myself for each self peering into it, showing each of us something inaccessible without mirrors, namely that each has an external aspect and what that external aspect is. Each work of literature shows in this sense an aspect we would not know were ours without benefit of that mirror: each discovers, in the eighteenth-century meaning of the term, an unguessed dimension of the self. It is a mirror less in passively returning an image than in transforming the self-consciousness of the reader who in virtue of identifying with the image recognizes what he is. Literature is in this sense transfigurative, and in a way which cuts across the distinction between fiction and truth. There are metaphors for every life in Herodotus and Gibbon.

The great paradigm for such transfiguration must be Don Quixote, Cervantes having to be credited not only with the invention of the novel but with discovering the perversion of its philosophy. Quixote is transformed, through reading romances, into an errant knight while his world is transformed into one of knightly opportunities, wenches turning into virgins and innkeepers into kings, nags into steeds and windmills into monsters. Yet it is a perversion of the relationship between reader and romance because Quixote's own sense of his identity was so antecedently weak that he failed to retain it through the transformation, and his own sense of reality was so weak that he lost his grip on the difference between literature and life. Or he read poetry as though it were history, poetry becoming not philosophical but particular. He would be like those who, through reading Descartes, seriously come to believe that "they are kings while they are paupers, that they are clothed in gold and purple while they are naked; or imagine that their head is made of clay or that they are gourds, or that their bodies are glass." Or that there is an Evil Genius, or that there is no world, or that the belief in material objects is misguided. These are failures to distinguish philosophy from life, whose counterpart in Cervantes induces an illusion so powerful that the distinction is lost: which may be a formula for happiness—living in an illusion—making *Don Quixote* genuinely comic.

I have encountered the tragic obverse of this, where one's sense of self is strong but one's sense of reality has become desperate through literature having thrown a bitter discrepancy into the relationship between the two. I knew a lady who discovered the truth from Proust's novel that she really was the Duchess of Guermantes, as unavailing, in her case, unfortunately, as the Prince's knowledge of who he really is, when a spell has nevertheless required that he live in the investitures of a frog. *Her* land was Combray and the Faubourg Saint-Germain, an air of wit and exquisite behavior and perfect taste—not the Upper West Side, falling plaster, children with colds, a distracted husband, never enough money, and nobody who understood. Her moments of happiness came when reality on occasion agreed to cooperate with metaphor, when she could coincide with an alien grace, too ephemeral alas, leaving her with the dishes to clear and the bills to pay and a terrible exhaustion. Unlike Quixote, her illusions never were strong enough to swamp reality, only in a sense to poison it; and while she maintained that her greatest happiness consisted in reading Proust, in truth he only caused her anguish.

I should like to place the theorist R alongside these two readers of fiction, Don Quixote and my acquaintance, one of whom happens to be in fiction as well, since R himself, like Quixote, could be a fictional being and "The Referential Fallacy" a fiction within a fiction, both of them created by me. In fact both the theorist and article are real. R is a man of great pride and passion, who has lived through times of extremity and has known, as much as anyone I know has known, the defining tribulations of the full human life. Surely he cannot have been drawn to literature simply to be a reader of literature through literature to literature, unless, like the professor in Mann's *Disorder and Early Sorrow,* he meant to draw a circle in order to exclude life. If it were a piece of literature, "The Referential Fallacy" would offer a metaphor of extreme dislocation, putting life as a whole beyond the range of reference, displaying an existence lived out in an infinite windowless library, where book sends us to book in a network of reciprocal relationships the reader can inhabit like a spider. Imagine that it had been written by Borges, whose life is almost like that, and included in *Ficciones!* But it in fact is by R and it gives us a misanalysis rather than a metaphor, it refers vertically to readers whose relationship to texts it gets wrong, rather than to the reader of the text whose life it metaphorically depicts. If this address were art, it would be a mirror only for R, who seeing his own image reflected back, might find his consciousness entrapped and mend his thought.

R's text, which I have sought to view once as literature and once as science, illustrates, since it is about reading, the two ways in which a text might refer to readers, and with these two modes of reference in mind, we may return to *philosophy* as literature, not by way of treating philosophical texts as literature, which would be merely a conceit if they were not that, as R's text is not that, but by way rather of displaying one of the ways in which philosophy really does relate to life. *One* of the ways. There is a celebrated deconstructionist text which holds that philosophy must be treated as a genre of literature because it is ineluctably metaphoric, when in fact it only becomes interestingly metaphoric when it is decided to treat it as literature, and that deconstructionist text begs just the question it has been taken by its enthusiasts to have settled. Metaphors have in common with texts, as such, that they do not necessarily wear their metaphoricity on their surfaces, and what looks like an image may really be a structural hypothesis as to how a reality we heretofore lack words for is to be understood. One mark of metaphors is their ineliminability, a feature which makes them para-intensional if not fully intensional. But in philosophical as in scientific writing, what looks like a metaphor in the beginning ends as a fact, and it may be eliminated in favor of a technical term, as Locke begins with the natural light—with "the candle within us"—and ends with the technical term *intuition*. So what appears to be metaphors, what have been taken by deconstructionists to be metaphors, belong to philosophy as science, rather than to philosophy as literature.

There is a view abroad, credited to Nietzsche, that in metaphor we have the growing edge of language, assimilating by its means the unknown to the known, where the latter must originally have been metaphor now grown cold and dessicated and taken for fact. It is difficult to understand how, on its own view, this process got started, but I think it must be appreciated as a transvaluational and necessarily paradoxical view, like saying that the first shall be last or that the meek shall inherit the earth, giving poetry the place science has presumed was its own. But it is a view lent credibility by the fact that structural hypotheses look enough like metaphors to be taken for metaphors by theorists resolved to view an activity like philosophy as largely if not altogether metaphorical. It is my own thought that philosophical texts are kept alive as metaphors when they have long since stopped seeming plausible as structural hypotheses, a tribute to their vivacity and power, their status as literature being a consolation prize for failing to be true. But this is to overlook the way in which philosophy just functions as literature does, not in the sense of extravagant verbal artifacts, but as engaging with readers in search of that sort of universality I have supposed to characterize literary reference: as being about the reader at the moment of reading through the process of reading. We read them as literature in this sense because, in Hegel's stunning thought, they exist for the reader who is "in them from the beginning." The texts require the act of reading in order to be complete, and it is as readers of a certain type that philosophical texts address us all. The wild variety of philosophical texts implies a correspondingly wild variety of possible kinds of readers, and hence of theories of what we are in the dimension of the reading. And each such text finds a kind of ontological proof of its claims through the fact that it can be read in the way it requires.

The most conspicuous example of such a text is obliged to be the *Meditations,* where the reader is forced to co-meditate with the writer, and to discover in the act of co-meditation his philosophical identity: he must be the kind of individual the text requires if he can read it, and the text must be true if it can be read. He finds himself there since he was in it from the beginning. How astonishing I find it that precisely those who insist that philosophy is merely a genre of literature offer readings of Descartes so external that the possibility of their being universal in the way literature demands is excluded from the outset. To treat philosophical texts after the manner of Derrida, simply as networks of reciprocal relationships, is precisely to put them at a distance from their readers so intraversable as to make it impossible that they be about us in the way literature requires, if my conjecture is correct. They become simply artifacts made of words, with no references save internal ones or incidental ones. And reading them becomes external, as though they had nothing to do with us, were merely there, intricately wrought composites of logical lacework, puzzling and pretty and pointless. The history of philosophy is then like a museum of costumes we forget were meant to be worn.

The variety of philosophical texts, then, subtend a variety of philosophical anthropologies, and though each text is about the reader of it and so is a piece of literature by that criterion, it does not offer a metaphor but a truth internally related to the reading of it. Even now when textual innovativeness has abated in philosophy and all texts are pretty much alike, so much so that the address to the reader has thinned almost to nothingness, the reader in the act of reading exercises some control over what the text says, since what the text says must be compatible with its being read. A text, thus, which set out to prove the impossibility of reading would have a paradox of sorts on its hands. Less flagrantly, there are texts in philosophy, current reading among us, which if true would entail their own logical illegibility. And it is inconceivable that philosophers would have fallen into such incoherences if they had not, as it were, forgotten that their texts, in addition to being representations of a kind of reality, were things to be *read*. We pay a price for forgetting this in the current style of writing, since it enables us to depict worlds in which readers cannot fit. The propensity to overlook the reader goes hand in hand with the propensity to leave beings of the sort readers exemplify outside the world the text describes.

Contemporary philosophies of mind, language, humanity may be striking examples of an oversight which is encouraged by a view of philosophical writing which makes the reader ontologically weightless: like some disembodied professional conscience. Science, often and perhaps typically, can get away with this, largely because, even when about its readers, is not about them as readers, and so lacks the internal connection philosophical texts demand, being about their readers *as* readers. So philosophy is literature in that among its truth conditions are those connected with being read, and reading those texts is supposed then to reveal us for what we are in virtue of our reading. Really to reveal us, however, not metaphorically, which is why, I think, I cannot finally acquiesce in the thought that philosophy is literature. It continues to aim at truth, but when false, seriously false, it is often also so fascinatingly false as to retain a kind of perpetual vitality as a metaphor. It is this which makes our history so impossible to relinquish, since the power is always there, and the texts engage us when we read them vitally as readers whose philosophical portraits materialize about us as we enter that place that awaited us from the beginning.

[6]

Emerson, Coleridge, Kant

STANLEY CAVELL

THE SUBJECT of this essay grows out of my book *The Claim of Reason,* roughly the first half of which contains, among other things, an interpretation of Wittgenstein's *Philosophical Investigations* which focuses on its linked notions of criteria and of grammar and which argues that while Wittgenstein's work is written as a continuous response to the threat of skepticism, it does not, and is not meant to, constitute a refutation of philosophical skepticism. By skepticism I mean directly that radical doubt, or anxiety, as expressed in Descrates and in Hume, and in Kant's determination to transcend them, about whether we can know that the world exists, and I and others in it. The idea that the *Investigations* does, and was meant to, constitute such a refutation was, so far as I knew, the unchallenged, received wisdom of professional philosophy, motivating either a philosopher's liking or deploring of that book. My argument depends on coming to understand that this temptation to refutation itself constitutes skepticism's fundamental victory.

Several strands from my general discussion of the "quest for the ordinary" will be carried forward, more or less inexplicitly, here. (1) An idea that Romanticism is understandable in part as an effort to overcome both skepticism and philosophy's responses to skepticism. (2) An idea that our everyday lives are understandable as expressing the working of skepticism, our lives as characterized by the likes of Thoreau when he speaks of our quiet desperation, of Emerson when he speaks of our silent mel-

This paper is a version of the second of a sequence of four lectures given at Berkeley in February 1983 as the Mrs. William Beckman Lectures, under the sponsorship of the Department of English of the University of California. Reprinted by permission from *Raritan* (Fall 1983).

ancholy, of Wordsworth and Coleridge when they define our despondency, of Wittgenstein and of Heidegger in their notations of our cravings both to escape and to attain the common, hence a quest and an inquest of the ordinary. (3) A thought of philosophy as an endless responsibility for one's own discourse, for not resting with words you do not happily mean. The thought takes this responsibility to be discharged less in argumentation than in a mode of reading, you may say interpretation, which makes problematic, or thematic, the knowledge of when and how to go on philosophizing, and when and how to stop. This conception of philosophy derives, in my case, principally from my reading of Wittgenstein and of Heidegger, whose visions of philosophy I find to intersect, among other places, at a study of the obvious, hence of the obscure, where each of these studies concerns ideas of the ordinary or the everyday. On this conception the issue arises as to how the spirit or aspiration of philosophy is to be distinguished from that of poetry, an issue distressed by the professional willingness not to distinguish the spirit and aspiration of philosophy from that of science. A respect for the entanglements of philosophy with poetry (call this the Romantic entanglement) leads directly to an assessment of Romanticism's traffic in animism. (4) This conception of philosophy feeds, and is fed by, my desire to inherit Emerson and Thoreau as philosophers, who are, I claim, repressed as thinkers by the culture of thinking they have formed. It is to begin specifying what is involved in the idea of our repression of our founding thinkers that the ensuing reading of Emerson's "Fate" is above all designed.

I take it for granted that Emerson and Thoreau are unknown to the culture whose thinking they worked to found (I mean culturally unpossessed, unassumable among those who care for books, however possessed by shifting bands of individuals), in a way it would not be thinkable for Kant and Schiller and Goethe to be unknown to the culture of Germany, or Descartes and Rousseau to France, or Locke and Hume and John Stuart Mill to England. While I have been variously questioned about what this means, and what it betokens, I am not yet prepared to describe the mechanisms that have made it possible and necessary. But since I rather imply that the repression of these thinkers is linked with their authority as founders, I should at least note the preparation of their repression by their self-repressions.

Founders generally sacrifice something (call this Isaac, or call this Dido), and teach us to sacrifice or repress something. And they may themselves be victimized by what they originate. I take such matters to be in play in the way Emerson and Thoreau write in and from obscurity, as if to obscure themselves is the way to gain the kind of standing they require of their fellow citizens. As if to demonstrate their self-repression, hence their powers to undo this repression, were to educate us in self-liberation, and first of all to teach us that self-liberation is what we require of ourselves. That this is within our (American) grasp means that to achieve it we have above all to desire it sufficiently. This achievement of desire is equally an intellectual and a spiritual, or say passionate, exercise. In "Thinking of Emerson" (added to *The Senses of Walden*), I characterize the thinking Emerson preaches and practices in terms of abandonment, abandonment of something, by something, and to something. Those who stay with the entering gentilities of Emerson's prose will naturally take his reputed optimism as a sign of his superficiality and accommodation; it is an understandable stance, because to follow his affirmations to their exits of desire is to be exposed to the intransigent demands they place upon his reader, his society.

Heidegger's idea of the attraction to thinking is exactly not something he expects to be of interest to his fellow citizens, but at best is to single out further thinkers. A thinker is one drawn, you may say seduced, by the authority of thinking, that is, drawn to the origin of thinking (say in Parmenides) that philosophy has obscured, or repressed in establishing itself, or say founding, itself. But in the way I conceive of Emerson and of Thoreau it is as if they play Parmenides to their own Plato, Dido to their own Aeneas, Holderlin to their own Heidegger. (I am not here speaking of comparative quality but of comparative structure, although without my conviction in the soundness of the Americans' quality, I do not know that I would be interested in their structure.) Even in the absence of an understanding of how it is that the repressed performs its own repression, one may surmise that a thinker would wish to acquire the authority of thinking in this way in order to teach the authority whose acquisition consists in its relinquishment. I think of this as philosophical authority.

If something like this in an intelligible and practical background to bring to Emerson and Thoreau, the advantage, to it and to them, is that it can be investigated with as it were, one's own hands, and in open air; as if the origins of philosophy were hardly different in age from the origins of movies. Someone my age will have had a teacher whose teacher could have heard Emerson. So that the philosophical waltz of obviousness and obscurity is—most obviously, if *therefore* most obscurely—of one's own calling.

It is habitually said, I suppose correctly, that what we think of as Romanticism is a function of how we conceive the philosophical settlement proposed in the achievement of Kant. Since what we think about any view of the relation of the mental and the material, so to speak, is bound to be some such function (that is, since Kant's achievement is part of how we think) this is not a very specific claim. In this essay I specify what I understand a certain force of the Kantian function to be. That I confine myself to working this out only relative to a reading of one essay of Emerson's and of a few passages from Coleridge's autobiographical prose will naturally require various justifications, not to say excuses. The fact that these texts do not undertake to quote and refute particular passages from Kant's writing would not for me be enough to show that, on a reasonable view of argument, they are not in argument with his philosophy. This too depends on what you understand Kant to have accomplished (what you think the name "Kant," means) and on what you understand to be the cause of the kind of writing in which Romantics have expressed themselves. That it is not what we may expect of philosophical prose would hardly take such writers by surprise, as if they wrote as they did inadvertently, or in ignorance of the sound of philosophy. Consider that they were attacking philosophy in the name of redeeming it. Should professional philosophers, now or ever, care about that? It is true that philosophy habitually presents itself as redeeming itself, hence struggling for its name, famously in the modern period, since Bacon, Locke, and Descartes. But can philosophy be redeemed *this way*, this Romantic way? To consider further what that way is, is a motive for taking up the texts in question here.

To prepare for them I had better set out some version of what can be said to be Kant's accomplishment. Or let Kant say it for us, in two summary paragraphs from his *Prolegomena to Any Future Metaphysics*.

> Since the oldest days of philosophy inquirers into pure reason have conceived, besides the things of sense, or appearances (phenomena), which make up the sensible world, certain creations of the understanding, called noumena, which should constitute an intelligible world. And as appearances and illusion were by those men identified (a thing which we may well excuse in an undeveloped epoch), actuality was only conceded to the creations of thought.
>
> And we indeed, rightly considering objects of sense as mere appearances, confess thereby that they are based upon a thing in itself, though we know not this thing in its internal constitution, but only know its appearances, viz., the way in which our senses are affected by this un-

known something. The understanding therefore, by assuming appearances, grants the existence of things in themselves also, and so far we may say, that the representation of such things as form the basis of phenomena, consequently of mere creations of the understanding, is not only admissible, but unavoidable.

You can take these paragraphs as constituting the whole argument of the *Critique of Pure Reason,* in four or five lines: (1) Experience is constituted by appearances. (2) Appearances are of something else, which accordingly cannot itself appear. (3) All and only functions of experience can be known; these are our categories of the understanding. (4) It follows that the something else—that of which appearances are appearances, whose existence we must grant—cannot be known. In discovering this limitation of reason, reason proves its power to itself, over itself. (5) Moreover, since it is unavoidable for our reason to be drawn to think about this unknowable ground of appearance, reason reveals itself to itself in this necessity also.

Then why do we need the rest of the 800-plus pages of the *Critique of Pure Reason?* They can be said to be divided between those that set up or fill in the pictures or structures necessary to get this argument compellingly clear (clear, you might say, of the trucks that are invited to drive through it), and those pages that set out the implications of the argument for human nature, hence for our moral and aesthetic and scientific and religious aspirations. I am prepared to call all of these pages pages of philosophy. What I claim is that if you are not at some stage gripped by a little argument very like the one I just drew out, your interest in those 800-plus pages will be, let me say, literary. The question would still remain whether you are seriously interested in that argument—interested more than, let me say, academically—if you are *not* interested in those 800 pages. A good answer, I think, and sufficient for my purposes, is Yes and No. I am going to focus here on the Yes side.

What would the argument, supposing it is convincing, accomplish? Kant had described his philosophical settlement as limiting knowledge in order to make room for faith. This is a somewhat one-sided way of describing his effort concerning knowledge since what he meant by "limiting" it was something that also secured it, against the threat of skepticism and powers of dogmatism. It can accordingly be seen as one in the ancient and mighty line of philosophical efforts to strike a bargain between the respective claims upon human nature of knowledge or science and of morality and religion. Kant's seems to be the most stable philosophical settlement in the modern period; subsequent settlements have not displaced it, or rather they have only displaced it. I take this stability, for the purposes of the story I have to tell, as a function of the balance Kant gives to the claims of knowledge of the world to be what you may call subjective and objective, or say to the claims of knowledge to be dependent on or independent of the specific endowments—sensual and intellectual—of the human being. The texts I am using as examples of Romanticism I understand as monitoring the stability of this settlement—both our satisfaction in the justice of it and our dissatisfaction with this justice.

The dissatisfaction with such a settlement as Kant's is relatively easy to state. To settle with skepticism (and dogmatism, or fanaticism, but I won't try to keep including that in the balance), to assure us that we do know the existence of the world, or rather, that what we understand as knowledge is *of* the world, the price Kant asks us to pay is to cede any claim to know the thing-in-itself, to grant that human knowledge is not of things as they are in themselves (things as things, Heidegger will come to say). You don't—do you?—have to be a Romantic to feel sometimes about that settlement: Thanks for nothing.

The companion satisfaction with the settlement is harder to state. It is expressed in Kant's portrait of the human being as living in two worlds, in one of them determined, in the other free, one of which is necessary to the satisfaction of human Understanding, the other to the satisfaction of human Reason. One Romantic use for this idea of two worlds lies in its accounting for the human being's dissatisfaction with, as it were, itself. It appreciates the ambivalence in Kant's central idea of limitation, that we simultaneously crave its comfort and crave escape from its comfort, that we want unappeasably to be lawfully wedded to the world and at the same time illicitly intimate with it, as if the one stance produced the wish for the other, as if the best proof of human existence were its power to yearn, as if for its better, or other, existence. Another Romantic use for this idea of our two worlds is its offer of a formulation of our ambivalence toward Kant's ambivalent settlement, or a further insight into whatever that settlement was a settlement of—an insight that the human being now lives in *neither* world, that we are, as it is said, between worlds.

Emerson and Thoreau joke about this from time to time. "Our moods do not believe in each other," Emerson says in "Circles"; "I am God in nature; I am a weed by the wall." And Thoreau identifies his readers as, for example, those "who are said to *live* in New England." That Wittgenstein and Heidegger can be understood to share this Romantic perception of human doubleness I dare say helps account for my finding its problematic unavoidable—Wittgenstein perceiving our craving to *escape* our commonness with others, even when we recognize the commonness of the craving; Heidegger perceiving our pull to *remain* absorbed in the common, perhaps in the very way we push to escape it.

About our worldlessness or homelessness, the deadness to us of worlds we still see but, as it were, do not recollect (as if we cannot quite place the world)—about this Wordsworth and Coleridge do not joke (though they can be funny), as though they hadn't quite the American confidence that world-changing change would come, or that they could help it happen. When Wordsworth dedicated his poetry, in his preface to *Lyrical Ballads,* to arousing men in a particular way from a "torpor," the way he sought was "to make the incidents of common life interesting," as if he saw us as having withdrawn our interest, or investment, from whatever worlds we have in common, say this one or the next. This seems to me a reasonable description at once of skepticism and of melancholia, as if the human race had suffered some calamity and were now entering, at best, a period of convalescence. The most familiar interpretation of this calamity has seen it as the aftermath of the French Revolution; Nietzsche will say the death of God. However this calamitous break with the past is envisioned, its cure will require a revolution of the spirit, or say the conversion of the world. Wittgenstein accounted for his appearance by saying that history has a kink in it. I am not interested here in comparing Romantic writers in terms of whether they saw redemptive possibilities in politics, or in religion, or in poetry. My subject is rather how such an idea may pressure philosophy to think about its own redemption.

Since those who are said to live in New England, or for that matter in England, are after all alive, a vision such as that expressed in *The Ancient Mariner* has recourse to the idea of the living dead, or rather of death-in-life, for example, of animated corpses. Here the relation to Kant's worlds is, as I read it, all but explicit, as is the idea that the place we inhabit, in which we are neither free nor natural, is itself a world, as it were a third world of the spirit, so that our consciousness is not double, but triple.

Of course all such notions of worlds, and being between them and dead to them and living in them, seeing them but not knowing them, as if no longer knowing them, as it were not remembering them, haunted by them, are at most a sheaf of pictures. How seriously one takes them is a matter of how impressed one is by the precision and comprehension of their expression. To test this is a purpose of the texts under discussion here.

Emerson's fluctuating reputation is a gaudy expression of the tendency of Romantic writing to go dead for one periodically, perhaps perma-

nently, as if in obedience both to its perception of our capacity to reab-
sorb our investment in the world, and of our capacity, or nerve, to ask,
and sometimes to get, a melodramatic exaggeration of one's life in response to it. I have had occasion to say how long it took me to forgive
Emerson, so to speak, for his nerve, and to follow my sense of his precision and depth. The essay "Fate" is also useful here because of its pretty
explicit association with Kantian perplexities. "The bulk of mankind believe in two Gods," it declares, having established the two Gods, or poles
of the essay, as Freedom and Fate (or say determinism, or nature). It would
be Emerson's reputation as much as his sound that makes it hard for one
to credit him with the philosophical stamina to take on Kant and his
worlds, and I pause before that essay in part to make that reputation one
more feature of the problem Emerson makes for one who acknowledges
him as a thinker.

Of all the moments in the history of what I am calling the repression
of Emerson in American philosophy, none seems to me more decisive,
apart from the professionalization of philosophy itself, than Santayana's
marking of him as a pillar of the Genteel Tradition. (This moment of the
professionalization of philosophy is gone into at somewhat greater length
in an essay entitled "Politics as Opposed to What?" in *Critical Inquiry,*
Spring 1982.) It is hard for me, coming from the Harvard Philosophy
Department to lecture at Berkeley on subjects in Romanticism and skepticism, to put aside a discussion of Santayana's fantastically influential essay named, and naming, "The Genteel Tradition in American Philosophy," delivered at Berkeley a little over seventy years ago, written by a
man who was living in Boston during the last ten years of Emerson's life,
and who at Harvard had been the most glamorous teacher of one who
would be my glamorous teacher of *Walden* when I was an undergraduate
at Berkeley halfway back those seventy-odd years. Particularly hard since
Santayana remains, I believe, the figure most likely to occur to an American intellectual who hears that someone is proposing, or remembering,
some confrontation of philosophy and poetry by one another. For some,
Santayana will represent the last serious writer in America in whose work
such a confrontation was undertaken, for others a warning that such an
undertaking is doomed to posturing; if infectious for a while, in the end
ineffectual. I hope that both representations are wrong, but I will not
argue against them now. What interests me here is that when in "The
Genteel Tradition" Santayana describes Emerson as "a cheery, childlike
soul, impervious to the evidence of evil" he shows, neither there nor anywhere else I know that he mentions Emerson, any better understanding

of Emerson's so-called optimism than, say, his contemporary H. L. Mencken shows of Nietzsche's so-called pessimism—he merely retails, beautifully of course, but essentially without refinement, the most whole-sale view there is of him.

In recent years this charge of cheeriness has been under attack, by among others Stephen Whicher and Harold Bloom, and a more sophisticated picture has emerged according to which Emerson's early optimism is tempered by a mature or more realistic acceptance of life's limits and rav-ages, signaled most perfectly in "Fate," the opening essay of *The Conduct of Life,* published some twenty years after his first volume of essays. But in what is the new maturity in "Fate" supposed to reside? It strikes me that people who talk about Emerson on the whole quote him (if they do—Santayana, so far as I know, harps on him without quoting one line of his prose) as they would quote a writer of incessant public celebra-tions, as though he wears all he means that way. Whereas an essay such as "Fate" seems to me excruciatingly difficult to come to terms with, pre-senting writing that is as indirect and devious as, say, Thoreau's is, but more treacherous because of its care to maintain a more genteel surface.

I guess the new maturity is supposed to be announced in sentences like the following:

> The book of Nature is the book of Fate. . . . Nature is what you may do. There is much you may not. We have two things,—the circum-stance, and the life. Once we thought positive power was all. Now we learn that negative power, or circumstance, is half. Nature is the tyran-nous circumstance, the thick skull, the sheathed snake, the ponderous, rock-like jaw; necessitated activity; violent direction; the conditions of a tool, like the locomotive, strong enough on its track, but which can do nothing but mischief off of it. . . .

Is the change in this marked by "Once we thought . . . Now we learn"? But why take this as sheer autobiography? It would be more like Emer-son to be speaking of the human race, or human maturation, generally. As for himself personally, he says somewhere, I seem to remember, that he was born old.

In any case, if this is the sort of thing that is supposed to show a new maturity, our new respect for it is bound in turn to fade. In 1930 the historian James Truslow Adams published in the *Atlantic Monthly* a piece called "Emerson Reread" (Stephen Whicher cites it as perhaps one of the two most intelligent anti-Emerson statements), in which Adams finds

Emerson, who had been for him, as he was for so many others, an inspiration when a youth, no longer able to sustain the man of fifty. Adams has the grace to ask whether this is his or Emerson's fault; but not for long; he knows the answer. Emerson fails because he does not know about evil—about war, disease, misfortunes of every kind. As far as I can tell these evils are the very sort of circumstances Emerson is summarizing when he says, halfway through "Fate," drawing a breath for a new response, "No picture of life can have any veracity that does not admit the odious facts." He had listed some facts earlier in the essay in a well-remembered pair of sentences: "The way of Providence is a little rude. The habit of snake and spider, the snap of the tiger and other leapers and bloody jumpers, the crackle of the bones of his prey in the coil of the anaconda,—these are in the system, and our habits are like theirs." But these are lists of matters no less obvious than "The heart-ache and the thousand natural shocks / That flesh is heir to. . . ." What could it mean to suppose that Emerson, in his early writing, had not known of their existence? That he mostly does not mention them, early or late, is surely more plausibly to be attributed to his finding them too obvious to mention than too obscure to have noticed.

But I think I know by now what the man of fifty finds distasteful that made the boy of sixteen or seventeen ecstatic. It is an idea that Emerson and any Romantic would be lost without, that the world could be—or could have been—so remade, or I in it, that I could *want* it, as it would be, or I in it. In time the idea is apt to become maddening if kept green (certainly it makes one's grown-up acquaintances impatient), a continuous rebuke to the way we live, compared to which a settled despair of the world, or cynicism, is luxurious. This dual perspective, of hope and of despair, proves to be internal to the argument of the essay on Fate, which I might summarize as the overcoming of Kant's two worlds by diagnosing them, or resolving them, as perspectives, as a function of what Emerson calls "polarity." It is as if Emerson's present essay is prophesying the fate of his reputation when it says: "In youth we clothe ourselves with rainbows and go as brave as the zodiac. In age we put out another perspiration—gout, fever, rheumatism, caprice, doubt, fretting and avarice."

Yet there is, I agree, a departure in the essay "Fate," a steady awareness that may present itself as a new maturity or realism. I find it contained in the statement: "In the history of the individual is always an account of his condition, and he knows himself to be party to his present estate"—

as if we are conspirators either for or against ourselves. The departure, or advance, shows in comparing this with a remark from "Self-Reliance": "Society everywhere is in conspiracy against the manhood of every one of its members." Now, in "Fate" it emerges that we, in so to speak taking our place in the world, are joining the conspiracy, and we may join it to our harm or to our benefit. "If Fate follows and limits Power [elsewhere called will], Power attends and antagonizes Fate. . . . [Man is] a stupendous antagonism, a dragging together of the poles of the Universe."

Living this antagonism (as relentless as electricity), we are either the victims or the victors of Fate (which is a remark about Fate as much as about us, the sort of thing Wittgenstein calls a grammatical remark); the remark above all means that Fate is not a foreign bondage; human life is not invaded, either by chance or by necessities not of its own making. "The secret of the world is the tie between person and event. . . . He thinks his fate alien, because the copula is hidden." Freud and Marx say no less. (I think here of a remark from the *Investigations:* "It is in language that an expectation and its fulfillment make contact.")

Of course this is all, if you like, mythology, and as such cannot philosophically constitute what Emerson claims for it; namely "One key, one solution to the old knots of fate, freedom, and foreknowledge." But suppose I emphasize, on his behalf, that he is offering his solution *merely* as a key; and, as Pascal had put it, a key is not a hook—a key has just what Pascal calls the *aperitive* virtue, that is, it only opens, it does not further invite, or provide. Whether you find Emerson entitled to such a gloss will depend on who you think Emerson is, something I am trying to leave, or to get, open. It would be, to my mind, key enough if Emerson's thought here opens to us the thought, or opens us to the thought, that our past solutions to these mysteries, however philosophical in aspect, are themselves mythology, or as we might more readily say today, products of our intuitions, and hence can progress no further until we have assessed which of our intuitions are satisfied, and which thwarted, by the various dramas of concepts or figures like fate, and freedom, and foreknowledge, and will. Disagreements over such matters do not arise (as they do not arise in skepticism) from one of us knowing facts another does not know, but, so Emerson is saying, from how it is one aligns the facts, facts any of us must have at our disposal, with ideas of victimization, together with whatever its opposites are. (One of Emerson's favorite words for its opposite is Lordship.) Something you might call philosophy would consist in tracing out the source of our sense of our lives as alien to us, for only then is there the *problem* of Fate. This looks vaguely like the project to trace out the source of our sense of the world as independent of us, for only then is skepticism a problem.

Even someone willing to suspend disbelief this far might insist that Emerson's writing maintains itself solely at the level of what I was calling mythology. So I must hope to indicate the level at which I understand the provision of philosophy, or its entry beyond its opening, to take place.

One key to Emerson's "Fate" is the phrase "the mysteries of human condition." I take the hint from the awkwardness of the phrase. I assume, that is, that it is not an error for "the mysteries of *the* human condition," as if Emerson were calling attention to mysteries of something which itself has well-known attributes. One attribute of what is called *the* human condition may be said to be that man must earn his bread by the sweat of his brow, another that the spirit is willing but the flesh is weak, another that we are subject to Fate. Such are not Emerson's bread, but his grist. The hint the phrase "the mysteries of human condition" calls attention to is that there is nothing Emerson will call *the* human condition, that there is something mysterious about condition as such in human life, something which leads us back to the idea that "in the history of the individual is always an account of his condition," and that this has to do with his "[knowing] himself to be a party to his present estate." "Condition" is a key word of Emerson's "Fate," as it is of the *Critique of Pure Reason*, as both are centrally about limitation. In the *Critique:* "Concepts of objects in general thus underlie all empirical knowledge as its a priori conditions." I am taking it that Emerson is turning the *Critique* upon itself and asking: What are the conditions in human thinking underlying the concept of condition, the sense that our existence is, so to speak, had on condition? (Descartes pivotally interpreted an intuition of conditionality, or limitation, or finitude, as the dependence of human nature on the fact and on the idea of God, from which followed a proof of God's existence. Nietzsche reinterpreted such an interpretation of dependence as an excuse for our passiveness, or self-punishment, our fear of autonomy, hence as a cover for our vengefulness, from which follows the killing of God.)

It is as if in Emerson's writing (not in his alone, but in his first in America) Kant's pride in what he called his Copernican Revolution for philosophy, understanding the behavior of the world by understanding the behavior of our concepts of the world, is to be radicalized, so that not just twelve categories of the understanding are to be deduced, but every word in the language—not as a matter of psychological fact, but as a matter of, say, psychological necessity. Where Kant speaks of rules or laws brought to knowledge of the world by Reason, a philosopher like Wittgenstein speaks of bringing to light our criteria, our agreements (sometimes they will seem conspiracies). Starting out in philosophical life a quarter of a century ago, I claimed in "The Availability of Wittgenstein's Later Philosophy" that what Wittgenstein means by grammar in his grammatical investigations—as revealed by our system of ordinary language—is an inheritor of what Kant means by Transcendental Logic; that more particularly when Wittgenstein says "Our investigation . . . is directed not towards phenomena but, as one might say, towards the 'possibilities' of phenomena" (paragraph 90) he is to be understood as citing the concept of possibility as Kant does in saying "The term 'transcendental' . . . signifies [only] such knowledge as concerns the a priori possibility of knowledge, or its a priori employment." Here I am, still at it.

Whatever the conditions are in human thinking controlling the concept of condition they will be the conditions of "the old knots of fate, freedom, and foreknowledge," immediately because these words, like every other in the language, are knots of agreement (or conspiracy) which philosophy is to unravel; but more particularly because the idea of condition is internal to the idea of limitation, which is a principal expression of an intuition Emerson finds knotted in the concept of Fate. His first way of expressing Fate is to speak of "irresistible dictation"—we do with our lives what some power dominating our lives knows or reveals them to be, enacting old scripts. The problem has famously arisen with respect to God, and with God's or nature's laws. Emerson adds the new science of statistics to the sources of our sense of subjection to dictation, as if to read tables concerning tendencies of those like me in circumstances like mine—Emerson spoke of circumstances as "tyrannous"—were to read my future; as if the new science provides a new realization of the old idea that Fate is a book, a text, an idea Emerson repeatedly invokes. Then further expressions of the concept of condition are traced by the rest of the budget of ways Emerson hits off shades of our intuition of Fate, for example as predetermination, providence, calculation, predisposition, fortune, laws of the world, necessity; and in the introductory poem to the essay he expresses it in notions of prevision, foresight, and omens.

Emerson's initial claim on the subject (and it may as well be his final) is this: "But if there be irresistible dictation, this dictation understands itself. If we must accept Fate, we are not less compelled to affirm liberty, the significance of the individual, the grandeur of duty, the power of character." This sounds like a nice little bale of genteel sentiments. Perhaps we can now begin to unpack it.

Dictation, like *condition*, has something to do with language—dictation with talking, especially with commanding or prescribing (which equally has to do with writing), condition with talking together, with the public, the objective. "Talking together" is what the word *con-dition*, or its derivation, says. Add to this that conditions are also terms, stipulations that define the nature and limits of an agreement, or the relations between parties, persons, or groups, and that the term *term* is another repetition in Emerson's essay. Then it sounds as though the irresistible dictation that constitutes Fate, that sets conditions on our knowledge and our conduct, is our language, every word we utter. Is this sound attributable to chance? I mean is the weaving of language here captured by (the conditions, or criteria of) our concept of chance?

"This dictation understands itself," Emerson says; but the essay sets this understanding as our task. And he says: "A man's fortunes are the fruit of his character." The genteel version of this familiarly runs, 'Character is fate," and it familiarly proposes anything from a tragic to a rueful acquiescence in our frailties. But to speak of the fruit of one's character is to suggest that our character is under cultivation by us, and Emerson says of it, in line with a line of his from "Self-Reliance," that it constantly "emits" something, that it is "betrayed," betrays itself, to anyone who can "read [its] possibility." (In that earlier essay, which I claim is about communication, and specifically writing, he had said, unnervingly: "Character teaches above our wills. Men imagine that they communicate their virtue or vice only by overt actions, and do not see that virtue or vice emit a breath every moment.") He emphasizes that this reading is a trivial, daily matter: "The gross lines are legible to the dull." And now add that by "character," associated with ideas of being read, and with communicating itself, Emerson is again, as in "Self-Reliance," proposing us as texts; that what we are is written all over us, or branded; but here especially the other way around, that our language contains our character, that we brand the world, as for example with the concept of Fate; and then listen again to such an idea as that one's character is one's fate.

Now it says openly that language is our fate. It means hence that not exactly prediction, but diction, is what puts us in bonds, that with each word we utter we emit stipulations, agreements we do not know and do not want to know we have entered, agreements we were always in, that were in effect before our participation in them. Our relation to our language—to the fact that we are subject to expression and comprehension, victims of meaning—is accordingly a key to our sense of our distance from our lives, of our sense of the alien, of ourselves as alien to ourselves, thus alienated.

"Intellect annuls Fate. So far as a man thinks, he is free." This apparently genteel thought now turns out to mean that we have a say in what we mean, that our antagonism to fate, to which we are fated, and in which our freedom resides, is as a struggle with the language we emit, of our character with itself. By the way, "annul" here, I feel sure, alludes to the Hegelian term for upending antitheses *(aufheben),* or what Emerson calls our polarity, our aptness to think in opposites, say in pitting together Fate and Freedom. "Annul" also joins a circle of economic terms in Emerson's essay, e.g., interest, fortunes, balances, belongings, as well as terms and conditions themselves; and in its connection with legislation, in the idea of voiding a law, it relates to the theme of the essay that "We are lawgivers." The terms of our language are economic and political powers, and they are to be positioned in cancelling the debts and convictions that are imposed upon us by ourselves; and first by antagonizing our conditions of polarity, of antagonism.

In putting aside Emerson's essay for the moment, I note that this last idea of us as lawgivers suggests that the essay is built on a kind of philosophical joke, a terrible one. Philosophy, as in Kant and as in Rousseau, has taken human freedom as our capacity to give law to ourselves, to be autonomous. Emersons essay shows that fate is the exercise of this same capacity, so that fate is at once the promise and the refusal of freedom. Then on what does a decision between them depend? I think this is bound up with another question that must occur to Emerson's readers: Why, if what I have been saying is getting at what Emerson is driving at, does he write that way? That he shows himself undermining or undoing a dictation would clearly enough show that his writing is meant to enact its subject, that it is a struggle against itself, hence of language with itself, for its freedom. Thus is writing thinking, or abandonment. Still the question remains why it is a genteel surface that he works at once to provide and to crack.

I turn to Coleridge, the figure from whom the American transcendentalists would have learned most of what they knew about Kant, and about

German philosophy generally, and from whom Emerson would have been preceded in his emphasis on polarity in human thinking.

While I had opened the *Biographia Literaria* many times, increasingly in the past few years, recognizing in its mode of obsession at once with the existence of the external world and with German philosophy a fore-running of my own excitements in linking transcendentalism, both in Kant and later in Emerson and Thoreau, with ordinary language-philosophy's confrontation of skepticism, I had never been able to stay with it for longer than a chapter, and maybe half of the next, before closing the book with fear and frustration—both at the hopelessness in its ambitions for recon-stituting the history of thought, by means, for example, of its elated ob-scurities as it translates Schelling on the task of something called uniting subject and object; and at its oscillation of astounding intelligence and generosity together with its dull and withholding treatment of Words-worth's sense in claiming for poetry the language of the rustic and the low. I do not know that anything short of my growing sense of its per-vasive bearings on the issues I have recently found myself involved with would have taken me all the way through it. The pain in it mounts the more one feels the hatred in Colridge's ambivalent address toward Wordsworth, praising his power and promise in terms reserved for the heroes of language, but cursing him, no doubt in the profoundly frien-dliest way, for not doing what it was given to him to do, for failing his power and breaking his promise.

I do not see how one can fail to sense projection in this; but of course the claim could still—could it not?—be true. Then, has it been con-sidered that it may also be false, or worse, that whatever Coleridge had in mind in demanding of Wordsworth "the first genuine philosophic poem" *(Biographia,* chapter 22), it was something Wordsworth had already pro-duced, and not just massively in *The Prelude* but fully in, for example, the "Intimations Ode"—that, so to speak, such achievements are all Cole-ridge could have *meant* in his prophecies? That it was critical for him to deny these achievements in this light, to project the achievements back into promises, is proven for me in the very incessance of his brilliance about them.

Since it was Coleridge who defined what most of us mean by literary criticism, he is, I assume, beyond praise in this regard. But in what he actually says, in the *Biographia,* when at last he gets around to mention-ing the intellectual drive of a work like the "Intimations Ode," while it is as brilliant as his technical discussions of poems and of what poetry should be, he is as dismissive and supercilious as anything he felt in the poisonous critics he so bravely and tirelessly defends his friends against. He dismisses thinking about what Wordsworth may have meant in invoking Plato's notion of Recollection, beyond saying that he cannot have meant it literally (then why insinuate that perhaps he did?), and he concludes that by describing the child as a philosopher Wordsworth can have meant nothing sensible whatever. It is this sudden—when Wordsworth flies his philosophical colors—that Coleridge's seemingly limitless capacity for sympathetic understanding toward other writers he thought genuine, is stripped away, his tolerance for mysticism and his contempt for reductive empiricisms forgotten; and he starts firing at will. I don't deny that Wordsworth is in trouble when he talks philosophy. But we are speaking of what one is to expect of Coleridge.

I propose one day—even alerted to the folly in being, or remaining, promising—to write something about this book based on the assumption that it is composed essentially without digression. May I remind you how perverse a claim that must seem, as if contesting with the perverseness of the book itself, which cannot be foreign to its permanence. Its fourth chapter opens with the remark, "I have wandered far from the object in view," when he has described no such object; the tenth chapter explicitly summarizes itself in its headnote as "A chapter of digressions and anecdotes, as an interlude preceding that on the nature and genesis of the imagination . . ." but the chapter it precedes—the eleventh—is not about imagination, but, as its headnote describes it, is "An affectionate exhortation to those who in early life feel themselves disposed to become authors," and that chapter opens with a sentence whose second clause is fully worthy to be considered the title of an essay of Montaigne's: "It was a favorite remark of Mr. Whitbread's, that no man does any thing from a single motive." The next chapter, twelve, describes itself as "A Chapter of requests and premonitions concerning the perusal or omission of the chapter that follows," and what follows, chapter 13, which actually entitles itself "On the imagination," consists mostly of its absence; more specifically it consists largely of the printing of a letter the author says he received—a letter in prose self-evidently identical with the prose which we have all along been treated to—which he says persuaded him not to print the chapter, on the ground that it really belongs with that major work he has been (and will be forever) promising. The last sentence of that chapter refers the reader, for further amplification, to an essay said to be prefixed to a new edition of *The Ancient Mariner,* an essay which turns out also to be nonexistent. Thus ends the first volume of the *Biographia Literaria*.

To say that the book is composed without digression means accordingly that it has some end the approach to which it follows in as straightforward a path as the terrain permits. This suggests that the end is, or requires, continuous self-interruption. But then this will be a way of drawing the consequence of philosophy's self-description as a discourse bearing endless responsibility for itself. And this could be further interpreted as a matter of endless responsiveness to itself—which might look to be exactly irresponsible.

The end is indicated by the surface of the book's concern to preserve or redeem genuine poetry from its detractors and its impersonations, in a world that, as he demonstrates, cannot read; and to demonstrate that this preservation is bound up with the preservation or redemption of genuine philosophy, where the preservation of poetry and philosophy by one another presents itself as the necessity of recovering or replacing religion. This contesting of philosophy and poetry and religion (and I guess of politics) with one another, for one another, together with the disreputable sense that the fate of the contest is bound up in one's own writing, and moreover with the conviction that the autobiographical is a method of thought wherein such a contest can find a useful field, and in which the stakes appear sometimes as the loss or gain of our common human nature, sometimes as the loss or gain of nature itself, as if the world were no more than one's own—some such statement represents the general idea I have of what constitutes serious Romanticism's self-appointed mission, the idea with which I seek its figures. Our current humanist appeals to the interdisciplinary would be traces of such contests.

From where is such an intellectual ambition to gain backing? Having repudiated the English and the French philosophical traditions because of their basis in the occurrence to the mind of ideas construed as representations and subject to laws, Coleridge turns for inspiration—and teaches us to turn—to German philosophy, both to the religious and mystical Germans who preceded Kant and to the idealists, preeminently Schelling, who thought to overcome Kant's limitations. And an essential preparation for the success of the ambition is the diagnosis of the fear and hatred of those who oppose such writing as he is undertaking and championing, as though an understanding of the hatred and the fear of poetry and of philosophy is internal to (grammatically related to) an understanding of what those aspirations are. No wonder Coleridge remarks, "Great indeed are the obstacles which an English metaphysician has to encounter." I take it as to Coleridge's philosophical credit that he finds the initial obstacle, perhaps therefore the greatest, the image of all the rest, to be the finding of a place to begin, undigressively. Such is a cost of refusing to identify the vocation to philosophy with the vocation to science, enviable, glamorous, as that may be.

The Kantian pressure upon the *Biographia* is conveniently measured in taking it as the key to a Kantian reading of *The Ancient Mariner*. For this purpose we can expose the issue by breaking in on a moment of the *Biographia* in which Coleridge is struggling with two of his main obsessions: his particular, engulfing sense of indebtedness to the work of others, and his tendency to deal in shady regions of learning.

The moment is occupied by a pair of sentences in which he is expressing his gratitude, his debt, to the writings of mystics, the boon he has received from them in "[preventing my] mind from being imprisoned within the outline of any single dogmatic system. They contributed to keep alive the *heart* in the *head;* gave me an indistinct, yet stirring, and working presentiment, that all the products of the mere *reflective* faculty partook of DEATH." It is they, he goes on to say, who "during my wanderings through the wilderness of doubt . . . enabled me to skirt, without crossing, the sandy deserts of unbelief." Now since it is of objects, or what he calls "objects as objects," that Coleridge otherwise speaks of as "dead, fixed" in contrast to the will or to imagination, and since he speaks of "the writings of the illustrious sage of Königsberg" as having "[taken] possession of me as with a giant's hand," I interpret the death, of which the reflective faculty partakes, as of the world made in our image, or rather through our categories, by Kant's faculty of the Understanding, namely that very world which was meant to remove the skeptic's anxieties about the existence of objects outside us.

Here is extreme testimony that what both the world and the faculty of the world need redeeming from is felt to be at once skepticism and the answer to skepticism provided in the *Critique of Pure Reason*. And I think the feeling or intuition can be expressed by saying: since the categories of the understanding are ours, we can be understood as carrying the death of the world in us, in our very requirement of creating it, as if it does not yet exist.

Naturally it may be imagined that someone will profess not to understand how the world could die. But then there will also be those who will profess not to understand how the existence of the world may be doubted. A difference between these cases is that a philosopher might undertake to provide you with skeptical considerations that lead you to the possibility he or she has in mind, whereas a Romantic will want you to see that his vision expresses the way you are living now. Both may fail in their demands. No one wants to be a skeptic; to be gripped by its threat is to wish to overcome it. And for each one who wants to be a Romantic, there is someone else who wishes him to outgrow it.

Against a vision of the death of the world, the Romantic calling for poetry, or quest for it, the urgency of it, would be sensible; and the sense that the redemption of philosophy is bound up with the redemption of poetry would be understandable: the calling of poetry is to give the world back, to bring it back, as to life. Hence Romantics seem to involve themselves in what look to us to be superstititious, discredited mysteries of animism, sometimes in the form of what is called the pathetic fallacy.

Now this quest of poetry for the recovery of the world (which I am interpreting as the recovery of, or from, the thing-in-itself), this way of joining or paralleling the philosophical effort to recover from skepticism, will look to poetry very like the quest for poetry, as if the cause of poetry has become its own survival. For what is poetry without a world—I mean, what is a fuller expression of the Romantics' sense of the death of the world than a sense of the death of the poetry of the world? But then again, how can the loss of poetry be mourned *in poetry*? (If it is gone, it is gone.) Which I take as the twin of the question: How can philosophy be ended *in philosophy*? (If it is here, it is here.) Yet ending philosophy is something a creative philosophy seems habitually to undertake.

I recognize certain of these recent formulations concerning Romanticism as under the influence at once of a decisive indebtedness to what I have so far read on these subjects by M. H. Abrams, Harold Bloom, Geoffrey Hartman, and Paul de Man; and at the same time of an uneasiness with those readings. For all their differences, they seem to share (in the writings in question) an assumption, as Bloom has expressed it in *Romanticism and Consciousness,* "that the central spiritual problem of Romanticism is the difficult relation between nature and consciousness." Of course I do not think this assumption is wrong, and its receipts have been rich; but I find that I do not know how to assess the price of so fundamental a stake in the concept of consciousness. By its price I mean two matters primarily; that the concept takes in train a philosophical machinery of self-consciousness, subjectivity, and imagination, of post-Kantian-ism in general, that for me runs out of control; and that it closes out a possible question as to whether what is thought as fundamental to Ro-manticism, especially to what any of its critics will feel as its sense of es-trangement, is first of all the relation of consciousness and nature, or first of all say, of knowledge and the world; whether accordingly self-con-sciousness is the cause or the effect of skepticism, or whether they are simultaneous, or whether one or other of these possibilities leads from and to one or another version or notion of Romanticism.

Provisionally take skepticism as fundamental, or anyway more under my control, I will propose *The Ancient Mariner* as a study of the issue of Kant's two worlds, in the following way. I begin with the prose argu-ment that prefaced its first printing in 1798, which was replaced, to be amplified, by the running marginal prose gloss in 1817, the year of the *Biographia*.

> How a Ship having passed the line was driven by Storms to the cold Country towards the South Pole; . . . and of the strange things that befell; and in what manner the Ancient Mariner came back to his own Country.

(We are bound, I guess, to hear this as inviting us to pass, and warning us against passing, beyond and below the lines of poetry and prose. I am taking it as asking us to go beyond this way of taking it.) I note an im-plied image of a mental line to be crossed that is interpreted as a geo-graphical or terrestrial border, in the following passage early in chapter 12 of the *Biographia*.

> A [philosophical] system, the first principle of which is to render the mind intuitive of the *spiritual* in man (i.e., of that which lies *on the other side* of our natural consciousness) must needs have a greater obscurity for those who have never disciplined and strengthened this ulterior con-sciousness. It must in truth be a land of darkness, a perfect *Anti-Goshen,* for men to whom the noblest treasures of their own being are reported only through the imperfect translation of lifeless and sightless *notions* [i.e., for us drifters]. . . . No wonder, then, that he remains incomprehen-sible to himself as well as to others. No wonder, that, in the fearful de-sert of his consciousness, he wearies himself out with empty words, to which no friendly echo answers. . . .

Earlier in that paragraph Coleridge says of this "common consciousness" that it "will furnish proofs by its own direction, that it is connected with

master-currents below the surface." I will relate this to the Mariner's returning "Slowly and smoothly/ Moved onward from beneath" back toward the line, in particular moved onward by what the marginal gloss
calls "The Polar Spirit."

Later in the *Biographia* chapter, as he is announcing his philosophical
theses, Coleridge gives the geographical or civilian name of what the
Mariner's glosses only call "the line," and places that feature of the earth
as the center of thinking:

> For it must be remembered, that all these Theses refer solely to one of
> the two Polar Sciences, namely, to that which commences with, and rig-
> idly confines itself within, the subjective, leaving the objective (as far as
> it is exclusively objective) to natural philosophy, which is its opposite
> pole. . . . The result of both the sciences, or their equatorial point, would
> be the principle of a total and undivided philosophy. . . .

That Coleridge is part of a tradition obsessed with the polarity of human
thought needs no confirmation from me. (See, for instance, Thomas
McFarland, "Coleridge's Doctrine of Polarity and its European Contexts.") In the passage just cited I understand the very impossibility of
the idea of an "equatorial point," taken as an image or picture, to express
his diagnosis of the Mariner's curse—that in being drawn toward one pole
he is drawn away from the other, that is, that he is enchanted by a way
of thinking, an isolated Polar Science, one in which, let me say, a dia-
gram of the mind (as by a line below which knowledge cannot reach) is
not an allegory but a representation, as of a matching substance. So the
"Polar Spirit" with which the Mariner returns has yet to enter into the
"two Polar Sciences" which will institute an undivided philosophy.

I end here with two remarks about this proposal for reading *The Ancient Mariner*.

1. By 1798 Coleridge knew something about Kant, but scholars agree
that the giant's hand did not take hold of him until his return from Germany a few years later. Accordingly I am not saying that when he wrote
his poem he meant it to exemplify Kant's *Critique of Pure Reason,* merely
that it does so, and that there are passages in the *Biographia* where Coleridge is summarizing his hopes for philosophy in the form of post-Kantian idealism, primarily in Schelling, in which he virtually states as much.
Conviction in this idea obviously depends on how strongly or naturally
one envisions the first *Critique* as projecting a *line* below which, or a circle outside which, experience, hence knowledge, cannot, and must not

presume to, penetrate. Here I must appeal to the experience of those who have tried to explain Kant's work, if just to themselves; I mean to that moment at which, quite inevitably, one pictures its architectonic by actually drawing a line or circle, closing off the region of the thing-in-itself. I realize that I imply, in this appeal, not merely that such a gesture is not accidental, but that so apparently trivial a sketch can control, or express, one's thinking for a long lifetime, like a Fate. Then one profit in thinking through the Mariner's journey by means of the poem is to assess that Fate, to suggest, for example, that if the Mariner's experience *is* to be imagined or conceived as of the region below the line, showing that its structure can be mapped, then it is not an a priori limitation of reason that prohibits its penetration by knowledge, but some other power, less genteel; call it repression.

This cautions me to be explicit that the region of the thing-in-itself, below the line, underlies both the inner and the outer horizons of knowledge (using Kant's distinction), toward the self or mind as much as toward the world or nature. Here is a way I can understand something of Freud's contempt and fear of the standing of philosophy. One reason Freud gives for shunning philosophy is that it identifies the mental with consciousness, but this seems no truer of Kant than it does of Plato. Something like the reverse would be a cause to fear Kant. If Freud's unconscious is what is not available to knowledge (under, let us say, normal circumstances) then Kant's Reason projects a whole realm of the self or mind which is even more strongly unavailable to knowledge; but, as part of reason, it is surely mental! What Freud must object to, however, is Kant's ground for excluding this realm from knowledge, namely that this realm cannot be *experienced,* hence that there is something in the self that *logically* cannot be brought to knowledge. If this is the wisdom of reason, Freud *must* try to outdistance it, which is to say, to change the shape of reason. Here is a sense in which he was preceded by Romanticism.

2. I do not take this projected reading of *The Ancient Mariner* as in competition with the familiar reading of it as an allegory of the Fall. Rather on the contrary, I take it to provide an explanation of why it fits the Fall, that is, of what the Fall is itself an allegory of. Accordingly, I take the story in the poem to allegorize any spiritual transgression in which the first step is casual, as if, to borrow a phrase, always already taken, and the downward half of the journey—to the cold Country—is made "Driven by Storms," as if by natural, or conceivably logical, consequences. On this understanding the transgression fits what I understand the idea to come

to of the craving to speak, in Wittgenstein's phrase, "outside language games." (It had better fit, since I take that idea as itself an interpretation of the Kantian *Critique*.) For that description ("outside language games") from the *Philosophical Investigations* itself is hardly more than an allegory, or myth. I use it in *The Claim of Reason* to record the pervasive thought of that book that a mark of the natural in natural language is its capacity to repudiate itself, to find arbitrary, or merely conventional, the lines laid down for its words by our agreement in criteria, our attunement with one another (that is to say, in my lingo, the threat of skepticism is a natural or inevitable presentiment of the human mind). and the discovery that what presents itself upon a skeptical repudiation of this attunement is another definite, as it were, frozen, structure—one to which I habitually say (I now realize afresh) that we are "forced" or "driven."

But if the Fall is also to be read as an interpretation of this condition, it is no wonder that it seems a Romantic's birthright, not to say obligation, at some point to undertake an interpretation of the story of Eden. A dominant interpretation of it, as in Hegel, if I understand, is that the birth of knowledge is the origin of consciousness, hence self-consciousness, hence of guilt and shame, hence of human life as severed and estranged, from nature, from others, from itself. Hence the task of human life is of recovery, as of one's country, or health. I find myself winding up somewhat differently.

The explicit temptation of Eden is to knowledge, which above all means: to a denial that, as we stand, we know. There was hence from the beginning, no Eden, no place in which names are immune to skepticism. I note that the story in the Bible as told does not equate the knowledge of nakedness with being ashamed, or self-consciousness (however consequential such things will be), but with fear. "I was afraid, because I was naked; and I hid myself," Adam says. And when God thereupon asks him, "Who told thee that thou wast naked?" the very fantasticality of that question of course drives us to ask what nakedness is and what it is to learn it of oneself. The feature of the situation I emphasize is that its sense of exposure upon the birth of knowledge is both to one's vulnerability to knowledge, to being known (as if one's first reaction to the trauma of separation is to try to preserve it), but as well to the vulnerability of knowledge itself, to the realization that Eden is not the world, but that one had been living as within a circle or behind a line; because when God "drove out the man" the man was not surprised that there was an elsewhere.

[7]

The Pragmatics of Contemporary Jewish Culture

HAROLD BLOOM

"AMERICAN JEWISH CULTURE," considered merely as a phrase, is as problematic say as "Freudian Literary Criticism," which I recall once comparing to the Holy Roman Empire: not holy, not Roman, not an empire; not Freudian, not literary, not criticism. Much that is herded together under the rubric of American Jewish Culture is not American, not Jewish, not culture. Here I will take these terms backwards, starting with "culture," which began as a Roman concept, became European, has not quite yet become American, and never could be Jewish, if by Jewish we mean anything religious as all, since culture is a stubbornly secular concept. Whether we know what we mean by "Jewish" is so problematic that I will begin on "culture" with one of our enemies, since our enemies have known well enough what they meant. I will quote an eminent speculator upon culture, Carl Gustav Jung. Of course, he has his followers and apologists, but I will let him speak for himself, in an essay of 1934:

> The Jew as a relative nomad has never created, and presumably will never create, a cultural form of his own, for all his instincts and talents are dependent on a more or less civilized people. . . .

By the "cultural," Jung would appear to have meant his divinely creative Collective Unconscious, very fecund in Aryans, but lacking in Freudians, who to Jung were identical with all Jews. Culture, in some of

*Harold Bloom is Sterling Professor of the Humanities at Yale University and a Visiting University Professor in the Humanities at the New School for Social Research.

its Germanic overtones, rightly makes us a touch nervous, in consequence, when it is applied to Jewish matters. Yet we hardly can resign
the term to the conceptual contexts of anthropologists and sociologists.
We *were* a text-centered people, perhaps as much as any people ever has
been. If we still *are* a people, it can only be because we have some texts
in common. Culture in our context broadly must mean literary culture,
if by "literary" one means biblical and post-biblical *written* tradition. Even
our oral tradition was more text-oriented than not, since it too was com-
mentary upon the ultimate book.

Culture, in the sense expounded by the Matthew Arnold-Lionel Trilling tradition, essentially is the culture of the highly literate, an elite class
whose ideology is determined by a relationship between text and society,
rather than between folkways and society. Whether that sense of culture
still prevails is clearly dubious. Deep reading is a vanished phenomenon,
practiced now only at selected academies, where already it shows tokens
of decline. In some large sense, such reading was one of the residues of
Platonic tradition, since even the Hebraic emphasis upon study as salva-
tion was a Platonic importation, though we are uneasy at acknowledging
this. But I do not want to repeat here my melancholy prophecy in regard
to the cultural prospects of American Jewry, uttered in Jerusalem at an
American Jewish Congress dialogue a few years ago; since that essay is
now available in my book, *Agon*. Rather than speculate upon the proba-
ble further decline of American Jewish culture, I prefer here to ask whether
there ever *could* have been such a culture anyway, in the literary or Arnoldian sense of culture. What is truly problematic in the question has
little to do with definitions of culture, and everything to do with the difficult definition of being Jewish. "Culture" is a nagging term however,
even in its essentially literary sense, whether we seek its meaning in Arnold and Trilling, or in T. S. Eliot, or in a Marxist critic like Raymond
Williams. So, before abandoning it here, I want to start with its origins,
particularly as set forth by Hannah Arendt.

Arendt wrote an essay on the social and political significance of "The
Crisis in Culture," first published in 1960, and still available in what I
believe to be her most useful book, *Between Past and Future*. She gives
there a true starting point for our inquiry:

> Culture, word and concept, is Roman in origin. The word "culture" de-
> rives from *colere*—to cultivate, to dwell, to take care, to tend and pre-
> serve—and it relates primarily to the intercourse of man with nature in

the sense of cultivating and tending nature until it becomes fit for human habitation. . . .
The Greeks did not know what culture is because they did not cultivate
nature but rather tore from the womb of the earth. . . . Closely connected with this was that the great Roman reverence for the testimony
of the past as such, to which we owe not merely the preservation of the
Greek heritage but the very continuity of our tradition, was quite alien
to them. . . .

Arendt stresses the agricultural metaphor of loving care for the earth,
which by extension became loving care for the testimony of tradition. In
Matthew Arnold, these Roman concepts were broadened and modern-
ized into the most famous of all definitions of culture: "being a pursuit
of our total perfection by means of getting to know on all matters which
most concern us, the best which has been thought and said in the world."
T. S. Eliot's revision of Arnold, in a less than generous work called *Notes
Towards the Definition of Culture* emphasized the conflict between culture
and equalitarianism. Lionel Trilling, rather than Eliot, became the true
heir of Arnold by compounding Arnold with Freud:

> To make a coherent life, to confront the terrors of the outer and in-
> ner world, to establish the ritual and art, the pieties and duties which
> make possible the life of the group and the individual—these are cul-
> ture. . . .
> This intense conviction of the existence of the self apart from culture
> is, as culture well knows, its noblest and most generous achievement.
> . . . We can speak no greater praise of Freud than to say that he placed
> this idea at the very center of his thought.

We are left then, by Trilling, with what has become the Freudian or
normative notion of culture in American intellectual society. (The self
stands within yet beyond culture, culture being that ideology which helps
produce such a self: coherent, capable of standing apart, yet dutiful and
pious toward the force of the best which has been thought and said in
the past.) This noble idealization has become a shibboleth of what the
academy regards as its humanism, but it is already sadly dated, and truly
it does seem to me far more Arnoldian than Freudian. Not that our high
culture is less literary than it used to be; quite the contrary, as a darker
view of Freud and culture might show us. Freud thought that the prime
intellectual enemy of psychoanalysis was religion, with philosophy a kind
of poor third in the contest, and literature too harmless to compete. We
see now that Freud fought shadows; religion and philosophy alike no
longer inform our culture, and psychoanalysis, merged with our culture,

has been revealed as another branch of literature. The ideology of the Western world, whether sounded forth within or beyond the universities, depends upon a literary culture, which explains why teachers of literature, more than those of history or philosophy or politics, have become the secular clergy or clerisy of the West. A culture becomes literary when its conceptual modes have failed it, and when its folkways have been homogenized into a compost heap of ocular junk, nightly visible upon our television screens.

I think that this is the somber context in which the supposed achievement of any American Jewish culture has to be examined. Such an examination requires touchstones, and there seem to me only two candidates for greatness in modern Jewish cultural achievement: Freud and Kafka. But what is Jewish about the work of Freud and Kafka, rather than Austrian German or Czech German, respectively? Vienna and Prague are neither of them Jerusalem, and Freud and Kafka were not traditional or religious Jews, in any way crucially indebted to our normative tradition. I grant the apparent absurdity of touchstones for Jewish culture whose own Jewish culture was essentially so peripheral, but American Jewish culture is at best as much an oxymoronic phrase as German Jewish culture was, and without the conscious use of paradox there is no way into the dilemmas of my subject. (If American Jewish identity is a cultural puzzle, and it is, why then let us acknowledge also that all Jewish identity in the Diaspora is a permanent enigma.)

But I want now to go against traditional practice, and against all current Israeli polemic, by multiplying the enigma. There are three areas of Jewish identity today: Israel, the Diaspora, and the United States. I doubt that Israel, in its Western cultural and so non-normative Jewish aspects, is in much more continuity with Diaspora traditions than we are. As for our identity, well where shall I begin, how could I ever end? However we seem from the perspective of Jerusalem, we know that we are not in Exile. I am aware many German Jews had deluded themselves into a similar knowledge, but American Jewry is unlike any previous Jewry in supposed Exile, with the single possible exception being the Hellenized Jewry of Alexandria, from roughly the third century before the Common Era until the third century after. But everything that is problematic about our identity is capable of sustaining some illumination from my touchstones, so return to Freud and to Kafka. Why do we think of their cultural achievement as having been Jewish, and what about these idiosyncratic spirits *was* incontrovertibly Jewish?

Peter Gay, in his book, *Freud, Jews, and Other Germans,* has preceded me by arguing the opposite. His Freud is culturally a German, not a Jew, who "offered the world but German wisdom." Gay is one of the most distinguished of cultural historians, but I read and teach Freud constantly, and I do not acknowledge that I read and teach "German wisdom." Every close reader of Freud learns that "they" are the gentiles and "we" are the Jews. Freud perhaps came to trust a handful of gentiles, of whom Ernest Jones was foremost, but I can think of no other modern Jewish intellectual so remorseless in dividing off, socially and spiritually, Jews from gentiles, and so rigorous in choosing only his own people as companions. Kafka, who had a far gentler spirit, also chose Jews as his ambience. I do not think that I am citing a sociological element, an instance of defensive clannishness, or the simple reversal of Kafka's famous outburst in his 1914 diary: "What have I in common with Jews? I have hardly anything in common with myself and should stand very quietly in a corner, content that I can breathe." Seven years later, Kafka phrased this rather differently:

> In any case we Jews are not painters. We cannot depict things statically. We see them always in transition, in movement, as change. We are story-tellers. . . . A story-teller cannot talk about story-telling. He tells stories or is silent. That is all. His world begins to vibrate within him, or it sinks into silence. My world is dying away. I am burned out.

The *locus classicus* upon the vexation of what is Jewish in Kafka can be found in Robert Alter's *After the Tradition* where Alter confronts two antithetical truths. First: "No other Jew who has contributed so significantly to European literature appears so intensely, perhaps disturbingly, Jewish in the quality of his imagination as Kafka." But, second: "Kafka . . . addressed himself to the broadest questions of human nature and spiritual existence, working with images, actions, and situations that were by design universal in character." Following Alter I acknowledge the paradox and the mystery of Kafkan Jewishness as against Kafkan universality. But I have a curious suggestion as to the center of this Kafkan antithesis, and I quote the following Kafkan parable as proof-text:

> He is thirsty, and is cut off from a spring by a mere clump of bushes. But he is divided against himself: one part overlooks the whole, sees that he is standing here and that the spring is just beside him; but another part notices nothing, has at most a divination that the first part sees all. But as he notices nothing he cannot drink.

Is this a Jewish parable? It is called *The Spring* by its translator, which necessarily loses the German language overtone of "source" or "origin" that also is involved in the word "Quelle." I will assert that even if this was not a Jewish parable *when* Kafka wrote it, it certainly is one now, precisely because *Kafka* wrote it. In that assertion I am suggesting that Kafka, in at least some ways, was a strong enough writer to modify or change our prior notions of just what being Jewish meant. Since Freud, *in toto,* is an even stronger writer than Kafka, I thus assert that Freud's Jewishness, whatever it was or was not in relation to tradition, even more strongly now alters our notions of Jewish identity. I would like not to be too weakly misunderstood on this rather subtle point and so I will labor it for a space.

All origins or sources are arbitrary, yet if sufficient continuities issue forth from them, we learn to regard their teleologies as being inescapable. I once wrote something like that and added that we knew this truth best from what we so oxymoronically called our love lives. I would think now that this difficult notion of the brute facticity of tradition is best known by meditating upon the indescribable history of the Jews. The continuities of that history are its scandal, and constitute the fine absurdity of this occasion. I stand here, just past fifty years in age and worry out loud about the problematics of my identity, an identity inescapably determined for me by a continuity of ancestors stretched past at least 3,500 years, or seventy times my age. Jewish mothers have given birth to Jewish daughters and sons for perhaps one hundred and fifty generations, a facticity so overwhelming as to dwarf every conceptualization as to what Jewish identity might mean, *unless* it is to mean precisely what the Talmud wanted it to mean.

The authority of so immense and so somber a history must compel awe and at least some recognition in every sensitive consciousness exposed to that tradition. This awe tends to obscure a curious truth about Jewish identity, or perhaps of any people's identity; always changing, such identity conceals its changes under the masks of the normative. The authority of identity is not constancy-in-change, but the *originality* that usurps tradition and becomes a fresh authority, strangely in the name of continuity. Freud and Kafka already have usurped much of the image of Jewishness, by which I mean precisely the cultural image. A Western secular intellectual, searching for the elitist image of Jewishness, these days is likelier to come up with the names of Freud or Kafka or even Gershom Scholem than with those of Maimonides or Rashi or Moses Mendelsohn. Originality in this usurping and elitist sense includes the notion of profound difficulty. Whoever J was, J here meaning the Yahwist or first crucial author of the Torah, J was more idiosyncratic and difficult to interpret even than Freud or Kafka. Indeed, he still is, perhaps more than ever. It may have been quite arbitrary that nearly every other biblical writer took J as his point of origin. Once this had happened, J ceased to be arbitrary, and our relation to his work has been governed ever since by an inescapable contingency, however normative tradition may have misread it. We are imprisoned by a factuality that interpretations of J have imposed upon us, just as we are imprisoned by a Freudian factuality as well. In a high cultural sense, the Freudian images, and to a lesser extent the Kafkan ones, have invaded and by now contaminated the composite image of Jewish identity, at least for elitists. So the issue is no longer whether Freud or Kafka represent Jewish high culture, in the sense that a writer like Philip Roth can only resort to them as icons when he seeks images of that culture.

If my admittedly curious argument is at all suggestive, then it is simple enough to say why we do not yet have an American Jewish culture. Our writers and speculators just have not been original enough until now, and probably will not be for some time to come. Freud and Kafka came late in German language Jewish culture. There had been Heine of course, long before, and American Jewish culture, alas, has not produced any Heine either. We have some good novelists of the second rank, there is no Faulkner among them, let alone a Hawthorne or Melville or Henry James. We have a few good poets, still young enough to undergo interesting development, but they do not include a Wallace Stevens or Hart Crane, let alone a Whitman or a Dickinson. We have various speculators, scholars and critics, but none among us will turn out to have been an Emerson. The absence of overwhelming cultural achievement compels us to rely upon the cultural identity of the last phases of *Galut,* yet we, as I have said before, scarcely feel that we are in Exile.

Kafka, in a letter to Max Brod, wrote that the despair over the Jewish question was the inspiration of the German Jewish writers, and he remarked that this was "an inspiration as respectable as any other but fraught . . . with distressing pecularities." These peculiarities stemmed from the hideous distress that *their* problem was not a German one. We do not have despair over the Jewish question; it is not even clear that there *is* a Jewish question in the United States. America, like Hellenistic Alexandria and unlike Germany, is an eclectic culture, of which we are a part. The Jewish writer's problem here and now does not differ from the Hellenistic or American *belatedness,* from the anxiety that we may all of us just be too late. (Cultural belatedness makes the American literary culture problematic precisely as is American Jewish culture; this problem, ours, is truly American.) I think that is why Nathanael West, who was something of a Jewish anti-Semite, is still the most powerful writer that American Jewry has produced. His masterwork, *Miss Lonelyhearts,* marvelously rewrites Milton's *Paradise Regained* in American terms, though also in terms curiously less Jewish than Milton's own. West, like Heine, may have arrived a touch too soon. A deeper awareness that American culture and Jewish culture in America could not differ much might have saved West some self-hatred yet might also have weakened him as a writer.

No one now can prophesy the appearance of cultural genius, because we do have an oppressive sense of belatedness. I want therefore to turn the rest of this speculation not to a messianic longing for an American Freud or Kafka, but to the other paradox, which is the pragmatic ending in this country of the trope or myth of *Galut* which remains essential evidently, to and for Israeli culture. I recall vividly from that Jerusalem dialogue of a few years ago the troubled and hyperbolic eloquence of the Israeli writer A. B. Yehoshua, proclaiming his conviction that Israel had to break off all relations with American Jewry, in order to compel the saving remnant of that Jewry to forsake Exile and return geographically and nationally to Zion. My memories have been stirred anew by reading the novelist's just-translated polemic, *Between Right and Right.* Yehoshua is passionately sincere, but he is so far from American Jewish realities as to sound more ironic than he intended to be. He seems to offer only three alternatives: assimilate completely and thus forsake Jewish identity; perish in another Holocaust; live in Israel. All of us here reject the first two, and almost all of us reject the third as well. Yehoshua's logic is appalling: *Galut* caused the Holocaust and will cause it again. The Jew therefore must become either a gentile, or a corpse, or an Israeli.

Yet I would praise Yehoshua for provoking us, because such provocation leads back to the central question of American Jewish culture. What is the identity of the secular American Jew? The question returns us to what always has been most problematic about us: a religion that became a people, rather than a people that became a religion. The religion of Akiba is not dead, in America, Israel, and elsewhere, but it no longer dominates the lives of the majority among us; here, Israel, wherever. And since we also are no longer a text-obsessed people, whether in America or Israel or anywhere, we are in truer danger of vanishing from lack of real literacy than from lack of religion or lack of defense against another Holocaust. If we lose our identity it will be because, as I have warned elsewhere, there is no longer a textual difference between ourselves and the gentiles.

To ask just what a textual difference can be is to confront the truest question of Jewish cultural identity. The difference is not so much in a choice of texts, our Bible and Talmud against their Old Testament and New Testament structure, as it is in the relationship of a people to a text or texts. I go back to my earlier formulation: we were a religion become a people, and not a people become a religion. The parodies of our process are all American, the most successful in contemporary terms being the Mormons, very much now a religion become a people. But of course the Yankees of New England, once a religion, are now a people also. Except for the Fundamentalists, this has been the American Protestant pattern, and so Jews, Quakers, Congregationalists, and doubtless someday Mormons, very much now a religion become a people. But of course the Yankees of New England, once a religion, are now a people also. Except for the Fundamentalists, this has been the American Protestant pattern, and so Jews, Quakers, Congregationalists, and doubtless someday Mormons, truly melt together. The authentic American majority is not Moral but whatever you want to call the peoplehood that survives a religious origin.

The cultural consequences of this analogy between Jews without Judaism and Protestants without Christianity are larger than any mode of study has yet chronicled. But at the least Jews become no more in Exile than Quakers are, or Calvinists of all varieties. If we are survivors of an Election Theology, why then so are they. A contemporary Jewish poet tends to have the same untroubled relationship, or lack of relationship, to Judaism that Walt Whitman has to the Hicksite Quakerism of his boyhood. And, for similar reasons, poets as varied as Philip Levine, John Hollander, and Irving Feldman are no more in Exile in America than are say John Ashbery, James Merrill, and A. R. Ammons. The old formulae of *Galut* simply do not work in the diffuse cultural contexts of America.

I want now to draw together the two paradoxical arguments I have been exploring. When we speak of the relative failure of an American Jewish culture, what we mean pragmatically is our lack of strong figures like Freud and Kafka, because *their achievement has not redefined Jewish culture, even though we could hardly say what was Jewish about them if we approached them apart from the facticity or contingency they have imposed upon us. That is to say, they are Jewish cultural figures only when they are viewed retrospectively*. But now we come to the second paradox; they define for us the final Jewish cultural achievement of the *Galut*, yet we are not in Exile. They were cultural summits of a people, once a religion, in a hostile context. We are a people once a religion, in a diffuse context, in which hostility is less prevalent than is a variety of diffusenesses parallel to our own. What is culturally problematic about ourselves as a people is precisely what is culturally problematic about the other peoples of the American elite and establishment. But this too will only be seen clearly when it will be seen retrospectively.

Whatever the future American Jewish cultural achievement will be, it will become Jewish only *after* it has imposed itself as achievement. And because it will not bear the stigmata of *Galut*, it will be doubly hard for us to recognize it as Jewish, even after it has imposed itself. But by then it will be very difficult for us to recognize ourselves as Jewish anyway, unless an achievement will be there that revises us even as it imposes itself upon us.

What remains most problematic is the question of the normative Jewish religion. I cannot know what the religion of Moses was, let alone the religion of Abraham or of Jacob. It is clear to me when I read the first and greatest of Jewish writers, J or the Yahwist, that his religion (if he has one, in our sense) is not the religion of Akiba. The thousand years that intervened between the Yahwist and the *Pirke Aboth* were no more a continuity than the eighteen hundred years between *Aboth* and ourselves. What the masks of the normative conceal is the eclectric nature even of rabbinical Judaism. Philo obviously was more of a Platonist than (perhaps) he knew. Nothing, we think, coud be more Jewish than the idea of achieving holiness through learning, but the idea was Plato's and was adopted by the rabbis to their own profound purposes.

Judiasm has been Platonized several times since, and been brought closer to Aristotle by Maimonides, who is now another mask for the normative though widely denounced as heterodox by much of Jewry in his own time. The Judiasm of the Lurianic Kabbalah, still with us as transmuted into belated Hasidism, is another version of the normative, despite its Gnostic kernel. We know that Jewish culture *was*, but we cannot know what it now is, let alone what it will be. Everything called Judaism today essentially is antiquarianism, insofar as its intellectual content exists at all. Of course, that same sentence would be as valid if the word "Christianity" were substituted for "Judaism," and as valid again if the names of many academic disciplines were the substituted words.

Can the Jews survive, *as a people,* the waning of rabbinical Judaism? Have they not begun to survive it already? Jewish spirituality, in our literary culture, is hardly identical with the normative religion. Kafka, Freud, and Gershom Scholem already are larger figures in the ongoing tradition of Jewish spirituality than are say, Leo Baeck, Franz Rosenzweig and Martin Buber, and only because the former grouping far surpass the latter in *cultural* achievement. When I said precisely that, in the discussion after a talk, I gave much offense, but the offense or injustice belongs to the nature of a literary culture, and not merely to my opinions. A cultural canon, in an era when religion and philosophy have died, and science is dying, creates itself by the fierce laws of literary strength. I have written so many books and essays about the dialectics of literary usurpation, that I have no desire to resume an account of those dialectics here. But I refer whoever is skeptical to either *A Map of Misreading* or *Kabbalah and Criticism,* among my books, for evidence and argument on such matters. My concern in the rest of this essay is wholly pragmatic; what can we know about the elements in our culture that will help us to see, however retrospectively, that those elements indeed *were* somehow Jewish?

There is no Jewish aesthetic, and cannot be, because of the deep and permanent warfare between Yahweh and all idolatry whatsoever, and yet we cannot deny the aesthetic strength of the Hebrew Bible, since its spiritual authority is inseparable from its rhetorical power. Authority and power, in a literary sense, are peculiarly the attributes of J or the Yahwist, a writer whose originality and difficulty alike surpass these qualities in all others, even in Shakespeare. But we are in danger of losing all sense of the Yahwist, because of the endless work of normative revisionists, from Elohistic, Deuteronomistic, and Priestly redactors down through a long line of scholiasts, Jewish and Christian, of whom the most recent is that great homogenizer of literature, Northrop Frye, in his recent *Great Code of Art.* Emerson once observed that the Originals were not Original. Yes, but the Normatives were not Normative either, and the Yahwist is as close to an Original as ever we will have. After all, the Yahwist has Yahweh staging an unmerited murderous attack upon none less than Moses himself, and Akiba, as I have said, has his Platonic overtones. Gershom Scholem fiercely kept insisting that Kabbalah was nothing but Jewish, and indeed not so heretical as it might seem, yet Kabbalah is wholly an uneasy compound of Gnosticism and Neoplatonism, and all that these rival doctrines had in common was that each was a misprision or strong misreading of aspects of Platonism.

I want to illustrate the problematic element in Jewish literary culture, by briefly asking what is or is not Jewish about three modern texts: the Primal History Scene in Freud's *Totem and Taboo;* some moments in Kafka's uncanny fragment, *The Hunter Gracchus;* a few paragraphs in a celebrated essay by Scholem, "Tradition and New Creation in the Ritual of the Kabbalists" (reprinted in the collection, *On the Kabbalah and Its Symbolism*). Of these three passages or scatterings, I will venture to advance observations that the first two—by Freud and Kafka—appear to have no Jewish referentiality, and the third—by Scholem—implicitly appears to devalue the ritual of rabbinical Judaism. But Freud's brutal fantasia of "that memorable and criminal deed" of patricide and cannibalism is an early version of his even crazier fantasy in *Moses and Monotheism,* where the murder of Moses the Egyptian, by the Jews, becomes the founding event of Judiasm. Kafka's dead but undying hunter is no Wandering Jew, but his consciousness of isolation and election is a paradigm for the mouse people and Josephine, their prophetess and singer, in the last and, I think, most Jewish of all Kafka's stories. Scholem's exaltation of Lurianic ritual and its Gnostic creativity hints at a new sense of what we may not be aware of in rabbinical ritual. What Kafka, Freud, and Scholem share is a kind of prolepsis of a still hidden form of Judaism, one that necessarily is still unapparent to us. (Somewhere Scholem remarked that of all the Jewish writers who write in German, only Freud, Kafka, Walter Benjamin, and Scholem himself truly were Jewish rather than German writers.) The remark was extreme, but I think suggestive, and part of the suggestion is what I intend to explore now.

Some years back Cynthia Ozick printed a lively essay, called "Judaism and Harold Bloom," the very title of which placed me under the ban. If I recall rightly, the essay insisted that: "In Jewish thought there *are* no latecomers." The work of Leo Strauss demonstrated that Maimonides, Jehudah Halevi in his *Kuzari,* and Spinoza all shared a sense of belatedness, of needing to write "between the lines," and in some clear sense Maimonides, the *Kuzari,* and even Spinoza *are* Jewish thought. It must seem disturbing to suggest that, centuries hence, *Beyond the Pleasure Principle,* Kafka's *Letter to his Father,* and Scholem's memoir of Benjamin may seem no less monuments of Jewish spirituality than the *Guide for the Perplexed* or the *Kuzari*. But nothing need be unexpected in the disturbing relation between Jewish memory and Jewish history, to employ the terms eloquently demonstrated by Yerushalmi to be in dialectical tension with one another. My reference is to his remarkable little book *Zakhor* (upon which I have written elsewhere). Yerushalmi emphasized how the Lurianic Kabbalah so flooded Jewish consciousness in the sixteenth century as to cancel what would have been the rebirth of Jewish historiography, dormant for the fifteen hundred years since Josephus. Yet who could have prophesied the extraordinary rapidity with which the palpable Gnosticism of Luria's Kabbalah captured nearly the whole of Jewry, only a generation or two after the Ari died in Safed of Galilee? (The stories of Kafka, the speculations of Freud, the revival of Jewish Gnosis in the scholarship of Scholem—will the generations ahead somehow so amalgamate and diffuse these as to formulate a new Jewish myth, rationalizing again a Dispersion that has lost its messianic rationalization?) The state of Israel exists and will go on existing, but three-quarters of surviving Jewry will continue to prefer to live elsewhere. Normative Judaism will hold its remnants and, as ever, much of Jewry will vanish away into the nations. But there will also be a secular Jewry, culturally identifiable, by self and by others. What will constitute Jewish memory for the elite of this Jewry? What indeed already constitutes the recent phase of Jewish cultural memory for contemporary Jewish intellectuals who are unable to see the normative religion of Akiba as anything other than an anachronism or a pious antiquarianism?

I begin some tentative answers by turning to Freud's overt Jewish stance, immensely problematic as that was. What *is* most Jewish about Freud's work? I am not much impressed by the answers to this question that follow the pattern: from Oedipus to Moses, and thus center themselves upon Freud's own Oedipal relation to his father Jakob. Such answers only tell me that Freud had a Jewish father, and doubtless books and essays yet will be written hypothesizing Freud's relation to his indubitably Jewish mother. Nor am I persuaded by any attempts to relate Freud to esoteric Jewish traditions. As a speculator, Freud may be said to have founded a kind of Gnosis, but there are no Gnostic elements in the Freudian dualism. Nor am I convinced by any of the attempts to connect Freud's Dream Book to supposed Talmudic antecedents. And yet the center of Freud's work, his concept of repression, does seem to me profoundly Jewish, and in its patterns even normatively Jewish, Freudian memory and Freudian forgetting are a very Jewish memory and a very Jewish forgetting. It is their reliance upon a version of Jewish memory, a parody-version if you will, that makes Freud's writings profoundly and yet all too originally Jewish.

To be originally Jewish, and yet to be original, is a splendid paradox, as Freudian as it is Kafkan. Perhaps one has to be Freud or Kafka to embody such a paradox, and perhaps all that I am saying reduces to this and this alone: the mystery or problem of originality, peculiarly difficult in the context of the oldest, more or less continuous tradition in the West. But Freudian repression, like that uncanny quality or idea we cannot name except by calling it "Kafkan," is culturally not so primal as it may seem. *Verdrangung* is now poorly translated by "repression," if only because "represssion" has become a political and ideological term. Freud, as several Freudians have remarked, did not intend the trope of pushing down or under, but rather, the trope of flight, as befits the estrangement from representations, an estrangement resulting from an inner drive. (To fly from or be estranged from memories, images, desires that are prohibited, and to be forced into flight by an inner drive, is to presuppose a universe in which all memories, images and desires are overwhelmingly meaningful unless and until the estrangement is enacted.) What kind of a world is that, in which there is sense in everything? For there to be sense in everything already must be in the past, and there can be nothing new. I am echoing the critique of Freud's theory of repression first made by the great Dutch phenomenological psychiatrist, J. H. Van den Berg, but I echo also the Jewish historian Yerushalmi, when in *Zakhor* he vividly describes the dialectic of Jewish memory and Jewish history that dominates the vision of the normative rabbis of the second century, C.E. They were master theoreticians of repression eighteen centuries before their descendent, Solomon (or Sigmund) Freud.

Rabbinical memory founded itself upon the insistence that all meanings, and indeed all permissible representations, whether images, memories, or desires, were already present in the Hebrew Bible and in its normative commentaries, or else in the oral law as embodied by the contemporary interpreters who stood fast in the chain of tradition. Conversely, everything in the Scripture, and in its written and spoken commentaries, was and had to be totally meaningful. There was sense and overwhelming sense in every *yod,* indeed in every space between the letters. If you combine this conviction of total sense, with a rejection of all idolatry, of every mythology, and so of every irrationality, then you have arrived already at something very near to the authentic Freudian stance.

I think that Freud consciously was aware of all this, and affirmed the inner Jewishness of his science upon just such a basis. Primal repression, which ensues before there is anything to be repressed, is Freud's version of the Second Commandment.

Yet even this, I suspect, was not the innermost center of Freudian Jewishness. Kafka was not the innermost center of Freudian Jewishness. Kafka once, in effect, called Freud the Rashi of contemporary Jewish anxieties, and though there is a sardonic element in the remark, Kafka generally was not merely sardonic, particularly where the Jews or his own Jewishness was concerned. Freud obsessively collected classical artifacts, and yet toward the Greeks and the Romans, as toward the Christians, Freud spiritually was not even ambivalent. As a speculator, Freud had come to replace all gentile anteriority whatsoever. But towards Jewish anteriority, Freud indeed was ambivalent. Yahweh, in Freudian terms, had to represent the universal longing for the father but Freud's own internalization of Yahweh issued at last in the most Jewish of his psychic agencies, the superego. To argue against an old vulgarism with a new one, the ego may be the gentile but the id is not the Yid. As the "above-I," the superego has no transcendental element or function. It is not a reality-instructor for the hapless ego, but something much darker. In his late book that we know as *Civilization and its Discontents,* Freud writes a kind of tragicomedy or even apocalyptic farce, in which the superego compels the ego to abandon its aggressivities, but then goes on punishing the ego for supposedly manifesting precisely those aggressivities.

This sadomasochistic scenario is a parody of the role of the prophets and of their precursor, Moses, in regard to the ancient Israelites. But it is also an allegory, not so parodistic, of Freud's vision of his own function, as exemplar Jew, in regard to gentile culture, of which he belatedly regarded Jung as too true a representative. We are almost in the grotesque plot of Freud's "novel," *The Man Moses,* which we know as *Moses and Monotheism.* There, in a kind of absurdist revision of Freud's Primal History Scene from *Totem and Taboo,* the Jews murder Moses the Egyptian, who thenceforth becomes in effect, their superego. Freud's account of St. Paul then internalizes this superego further through the concept of original sin, thus setting up Christianity as the religion of the son against Judaism as the religion of the father. In one of the most striking of Freudian leaps, Christian anti-Semitism, with its accusation of deicide, is exposed as a polytheistic rebellion against the triumph of the Mosaic and so Jewish superego:

under the thin veneer of Christianity they have remained what their
ancestors were, barbarically polytheistic. They have not yet overcome their
grudge against the new religion which was forced on them, and they
have projected it onto the source from which Christianity came to them.
The fact that the Gospels tell a story which is enacted among Jews, and
in truth treats only of Jews has facilitated such a projection. The hatred
for Judaism is at bottom hatred for Christianity. . . .

Whether this is convincing is a matter quite apart from its ethos, which
is positively Judaistic. After all, why should monotheism be considered
an advance upon polytheism, in strictly Freudian terms? Is one really more
rational, let alone scientistic, than the other? Manifestly, Freud thought
so. But is "thought" really the right word in that sentence? Freud's obsession with Moses was complex, and the element of identification in it
is therefore very difficult to interpret. Still, as I have written elsewhere,
Freud's hidden model for the analytical transference was his own mytho-
poeic account of the taboo, and his even more hidden model for the an-
alyst was his rather frightening vision of the totem-father. I venture now
that the most surprising invention in the book *Totem and Taboo* is Freud's
singular transference of the Hebraic trope of the fatherhood of Yahweh
to the slain and so deified father of the Primal Horde. In biblical terms,
Baal or Moloch are anything but a father, and Freud's curious emphasis
has the effect of somehow Judaizing animism, almost as though the Yahwist
were composing *The Origin of Species*. What turns out to be most Jewish
in Freud is the Yahweh in whom Freud overtly did not care to believe.

Kafka's original mode of Jewishness if far more elusive and even eva-
sive, as we would expect. Adorno, in his "Notes on Kafka," says that
Kafka's "literalness," meaning the "fidelity to the letter" required of Kafka's reader, probably echoes Jewish exegesis of Torah. Adorno advises the
reader to "dwell on the incommensurable, opaque details, the blind spots,"
which I would say is equally essential advice for the reader of the Yahwist. But Adorno went strangely astray when he interpreted "The Hunter
Gracchus," which he saw as the transposition, into archetypes, of the end
of the bourgeois.

Adorno perhaps forgot his own admonition, as to the authority of
Kafka's uncanny literalism. The force of Adorno's allegory is undeniable,
but what (even in death, or undeath) is bourgeois about the Hunter
Gracchus, whom Adorno later rightly compares to the biblical hunter
Nimrod? After all, the bourgeois world is well-represented in Kafka's tale
by the fussy seaport mayor, whose final dialogue with Gracchus juxta-

poses bureaucratic inanity with Kafka's truly weird Sublime. Do you mean
to linger with us in our beautiful town of Riva is the mundane query,
and the more-than-courteous response of Gracchus is that he thinks not,
since his ship has no rudder, and is driven by winds that come from the
icy regions of death. This weird sublimity is no more Jewish than Kafka's
subjectivity considered itself to be a Jewish instance of culture. But then,
several critics have cited another moment in the Hunter's dialogue with
the mayor as a fearful prolepsis of the fate of European Jewry. How are
we to read this moment? The mayor asks: "whose is the guilt?," and here
is the astonishing reply:

> "The boatman's," said the Hunter, "Nobody will read what I say here,
> no one will come to help me; even if all the people were commanded
> to help me, every door and window would remain shut, everybody would
> take to bed and draw the bedclothes over his head, the whole earth would
> become an inn for the night. And there is sense in that, for nobody knows
> of me, and if anyone knew he would not know how to deal with me,
> he would not know how to help me. The thought of helping me is an
> illness that has to be cured by taking to one's bed."

"Turn it and turn it, for everything is in it," says the sage Ben Bag
Bag. By "it," he meant Torah, but we may say the same of Freud and of
Kafka, or rather of Freud *and* Kafka, taken together. "There is sense in
that," says the Hunter Gracchus, and he is more than justified, because
of the terrifying Jewish principle, Freudian and Kafkan, that *there is sense
in everything*, which indeed does mean that everything is past already and
that there can never be anything new again. That is precisely how
Yerushalmi interprets what he calls "Jewish memory." The Hunter Gracchus is no Wandering Jew, but the Hunter too is a theoretician of what
has become, more than ever, Jewish memory.

Kafka's final story and testament, "Josephine the Singer and the Mouse
Folk," is now another monument of Jewish memory, though all we could
say of it accurately is that their Mouse Folk are not *and* are the Jewish
people, and that their singer Josephine is not *and* is their writer, Franz
Kafka. But toward what principle of disavowal *and* affirmation does Kafka
thus drive us? Well, perhaps toward *his* version of what Freud called
"Verneinung" (in a profound, very brief paper of 1925). Freudian *Verneinung* is anything but an Hegelian dialectical negation. Rather, it is
properly dualistic, as befits a High Freudian concept, and mingles simultaneously and so ambivalently a cognitive return of the repressed and an

affective continuation of repression, or of flight away from prohibited and yet desired images, memories, desires. (Call Hegelian negation the most profound of gentile idealizations, and then say of the Freudian and Kafkan mode of negation that always it was fated to reenact endless repetitions of the Second Commandment.)

I turn to Gershom Scholem as my coda, and this is a reverent turn, since that great loss to Jewish culture is so agonizingly fresh and recent. Scholem wrote so many remarkable books and essays that a choice among them cannot be other than arbitrary, but I myself always have been obsessed with, and most influenced by, his essay "Tradition and New Creation in the Ritual of the Kabbalists." This essay opposes the ritual of Rabbinical Judaism in *Galut* to the ritual of Isaac Luria. Whereas the ritual of *Galut* before Luria replaces the natural year by Jewish memory, the ritual of Lurianic Kabbalah is a theurgy, a mode of "representation and excitation," as Scholem says. This theurgy, Scholem adds, is expected to accomplish a fourfold change: harmony between supernal judgment and mercy, sacred marriage of masculine and feminine, redemption of the *Shekhina* (Divine Presence) from dark powers of "the other side," and general defense against, or mastery over, the powers of "the other side." Such a ritual desires triumph, rather than mere negation, and compels awe and shock in us, as normative Jews. For it could not be more antithetical to the ritual of Rabbinical Judaism which, as Scholem memorably remarks, "makes nothing happen and transforms nothing." A ritual that makes nothing happen and transforms nothing, call it the ritual of the great Akiba, nevertheless has a quiet persistence and an ongoing force that, as Scholem recognized, quite eclipses the Lurianic extravagences. I recall, as all of us do, almost the most memorable of all the grandly memorable apothegms in *Pirke Aboth,* the Rabbi Tarphon's magnificent admonition: "It is not required of you that you complete the work, but neither are you free to desist from it." The work makes nothing happen and indeed transforms nothing, yet perhaps the whole greatness of the Jewish normative tradition is in such a conception of "the work." If Yahweh's work *is* the work, then it is hardly for us to go against the *Yahweh-dabar* that comes to us, and which does not bid us to alter the balance between his judgment and his mercy, or to will those other Gnostic intentions of Lurianic ritual.

And yet, Scholem activates our imaginations now, and Tarphon does not. Scholem's versions of revisions of Kabbalah move us in ways that the normative tradition does not, and certainly Scholem seems closer to

Kafka than either seems close to any part of the normative rabbinical heritage. Scholem's Gnosticism, masking as historical scholarship, is somehow more available as an emergent Jewish theology than is *The Star of Redemption,* or Buber's curious softenings and idealizations of Hasidism. In a phantasmagoria that I believe to be already existent, many of us shape a still inchoate and perhaps heretical new Torah out of the writings of Freud, Kafka, and Scholem. I say "perhaps" because who can say, or ever could say, what is heretical in regard to our traditions? We call Elisa ben Abuya *Acher,* but was he truly "the other" for us, simply because like the Gnostics he believed in two Powers, rather than one?

Yerushalmi ends his *Zakhor* by observing that all of us must understand the degree to which we now are the products of rupture. And he adds, once we are aware of this rupture, we not only are bound to accept it, but we are free to use it. I think that we are using it already, not always with full awareness that we are doing so. We study the nostalgias, and wish we could persuade ourselves that we are in continuity with Hillel, Akiba, and Tarphon, or at least with Maimonides, Jehudah Halevi, and Spinoza (hardly even now an exemplar of the normative!). But, on some level, we are aware that our continuity must be with Freud, Kafka, Scholem. They are the Jewish culture that is now available to us, when we do not deceive ourselves, and in remembering and studying them we also join ourselves again to an ongoing version of Jewish memory.

THREE
SCIENCE

[8]

On the Very Idea of a Conceptual Scheme

DONALD DAVIDSON

PHILOSOPHERS of many persuasions are prone to talk of conceptual schemes. Conceptual schemes, we are told, are ways of organizing experience; they are systems of categories that give form to the data of sensation; they are points of view from which individuals, cultures, or periods survey the passing scene. There may be no translating from one scheme to another, in which case the beliefs, desires, hopes, and bits of knowledge that characterize one person have no true counterparts for the subscriber to another scheme. Reality itself is relative to a scheme: what counts as real in one system may not in another.

Even those thinkers who are certain there is only one conceptual scheme are in the sway of the scheme concept; even monotheists have religion. And when someone sets out to describe "our conceptual scheme," his homey task assumes, if we take him literally, that there might be rival systems.

Conceptual relativism is a heady and exotic doctrine, or would be if we could make good sense of it. The trouble is, as so often in philosophy, it is hard to improve intelligibility while retaining the excitement. At any rate that is what I shall argue.

We are encouraged to imagine we understand massive conceptual change or profound contrasts by legitimate examples of a familiar sort. Sometimes an idea, like that of simultaneity as defined in relativity theory, is

Presidential Address delivered before the Seventieth Annual Eastern Meeting of the American Philosophical Association in Atlanta, December 28, 1973.

so important that with its addition a whole department of science takes on a new look. Sometimes revisions in the list of sentences held true in a discipline are so central that we may feel that the terms involved have changed their meanings. Languages that have evolved in distant times or places may differ extensively in their resources for dealing with one or another range of phenomena. What comes easily in one language may come hard in another, and this difference may echo significant dissimilarities in style and value.

But examples like these, impressive as they occasionally are, are not so extreme but that the changes and the contrasts can be explained and described using the equipment of a single language. Whorf, wanting to demonstrate that Hopi incorporates a metaphysics so alien to ours that Hopi and English cannot, as he puts it, "be calibrated," uses English to convey the contents of sample Hopi sentences. Kuhn is brilliant at saying what things were like before the revolution using what else? our postrevolutionary idiom. Quine gives us a feel for the "pre-individuative phase in the evolution of our conceptual scheme," while Bergson tells us where we can go to get a view of a mountain undistorted by one or another provincial perspective.

The dominant metaphor of conceptual relativism, that of differing points of view, seems to betray an underlying paradox. Different points of view make sense, but only if there is a common coordinate system on which to plot them; yet the existence of a common system belies the claim of dramatic incomparability. What we need, it seems to me, is some idea of the considerations that set the limits to conceptual contrast. There are extreme suppositions that founder on paradox or contradiction; there are modest examples we have no trouble understanding. What determines where we cross from the merely strange or novel to the absurd?

We may accept the doctrine that associates having a language with having a conceptual scheme. The relation may be supposed to be this: if conceptual schemes differ, so do languages. But speakers of different languages may share a conceptual scheme provided there is a way of translating one language into the other. Studying the criteria of translation is therefore a way of focusing on criteria of identity for conceptual schemes. If conceptual schemes aren't associated with languages in this way, the original problem is needlessly doubled, for then we would have to imagine the mind, with its ordinary categories, operating with a language with *its* organizing structure. Under the circumstances we would certainly want to ask who is to be master.

Alternatively, there is the idea that *any* language distorts reality, which implies that it is only wordlessly, if at all, that the mind comes to grips with things as they really are. This is to conceive language as an inert (though necessarily distorting) medium independent of the human agencies that employ this view of language that surely cannot be maintained. Yet if the mind can grapple without distortion with the real, the mind itself must be without categories and concepts. This featureless self is familiar from theories in quite different parts of the philosophical landscape. There are, for example, theories that make freedom consist in decisions taken apart from all desires, habits, and dispositions of the agent; and theories of knowledge that suggest that the mind can observe the totality of its own perceptions and ideas. In each case, the mind is divorced from the traits that constitute it; a familiar enough conclusion to certain lines of reasoning, as I said, but one that should always persuade us to reject the premises.

We may identify conceptual schemes with languages, then, or better, allowing for the possibility that more than one language may express the same scheme, sets of intertranslatable languages. Languages we will think of as separate from souls; speaking a language is not a trait a man can lose while retaining the power of thought. So there is no chance that someone can take up a vantage point for comparing conceptual schemes by temporarily shedding his own. Can we say that two people have different conceptual schemes if they speak languages that fail of intertranslatability?

In what follows I consider two kinds of case that might be expected to arise: complete, and partial, failures of translatability. There would be complete failure if no significant range of sentence in one language could be translated into the other; there would be partial failure if some range could be translated and some range could not (I shall neglect possible asymmetrics). My strategy will be to argue that we cannot make sense of total failure, and then to examine more briefly cases of partial failure.

First, then, the purported cases of complete failure. It is tempting to take a very short line indeed: nothing, it may be said, could count as evidence that some form of activity could not be interpreted in our language that was not at the same time evidence that that form of activity was not speech behavior. If this were right, we probably ought to hold that a form of activity that cannot be interpreted as language in our language is not speech behavior. Putting matters this way is unsatisfactory, however, for it comes to little more than making translatability into a familiar tongue a criterion of languagehood. As fiat, the thesis lacks the appeal of self-evidence; if it is a truth, as I think it is, it should emerge as the conclusion of an argument.

The credibility of the position is improved by reflection on the close relations between language and the attribution of attitudes such as belief, desire, and intention. On the one hand, it is clear that speech requires a multitude of finely discriminated intentions and beliefs. A person who asserts that perseverance keeps honor bright must, for example, represent himself as believing that perseverance keeps honor bright, and he must intend to represent himself as believing it. On the other hand, it seems unlikely that we can intelligibly attribute attitudes as complex as these to a speaker unless we can translate his words into ours. There can be no doubt that the relation between being able to translate someone's language and being able to describe his attitudes is very close. Still, until we can say more about *what* this relation is, the case against untranslatable languages remains obscure.

It is sometimes thought that translatability into a familiar language, say English, cannot be a criterion of languagehood on the grounds that the relation of translatability is not transitive. The idea is that some language, says Saturnian, may be translatable into English, and some further language, like Plutonian, may be translatable into Saturnian, while Plutonian is not translatable into English. Enough translatable differences may add up to an untranslatable one. By imagining a sequence of languages, each close enough to the one before to be acceptably translated into it, we can imagine a language so different from English as to resist totally translation into it. Corresponding to this distant language would be a system of concepts altogether alien to us.

This exercise does not, I think, introduce any new element into the discussion. For we should have to ask how we recognized that what the Saturnian was doing was *translating* Plutonian (or anything else). The Saturnian speaker might tell us that that was what he was doing or rather, we might for a moment assume that that was what he was telling us. But then it would occur to us to wonder whether our translations of Saturnian were correct.

According to Kuhn, scientists operating in different scientific traditions (within different "paradigms") "live in different worlds." Strawson's *The Bounds of Sense* begins with the remark that "It is possible to imagine kinds of worlds very different from the world as we know it."[1] Since there is at most one world, these pluralities are metaphorical or merely imagined. The metaphors are, however, not at all the same. Strawson invites us to imagine possible nonactual worlds, worlds that might be described, using our present language, by redistributing truth values over sentences in various systematic ways. The clarity of the contrasts between worlds in this case depends on supposing our scheme of concepts, our descriptive resources, to remain fixed. Kuhn, on the other hand, wants us to think of different observers of the same world who come to it with incommensurable systems of concepts. Strawson's many imagined worlds are seen (or heard)—anyway described—from the same points of view; Kuhn's one world is seen from different points of view. It is the second metaphor we want to work on.

The first metaphor requires a distinction within language of concept and content: using a fixed system of concepts (words with fixed meanings) we describe alternative universes. Some sentences will be true simply because of the concepts or meanings involved, others because of the way of the world. In describing possible worlds, we play with sentences of the second kind only.

The second metaphor suggests instead a dualism of quite a different sort, a dualism of total scheme (or language) and uninterpreted content. Adherence to the second dualism, while not inconsistent with adherence to the first, may be encouraged by attacks on the first. Here is how it may work.

To give up the analytic-synthetic distinction as basic to the understanding of language is to give up the idea that we can clearly distinguish between theory and language. Meaning, as we might loosely use the world, is contaminated by theory, by what is held to be true. Feyerabend puts it this way:

> Our argument against meaning invariance is simple and clear. It proceeds from the fact that usually some of the principles involved in the determinations of the meanings of older theories or points of view are inconsistent with the new . . . theories. It points out that it is natural to resolve this contradiction by eliminating the troublesome . . . older principles, and to replace them by principles, or theorems, of a new . . . theory. And it concludes by showing that such a procedure will also lead to the elimination of the old meanings.[2]

We may now seem to have a formula for generating distinct conceptual schemes. We get a new out of an old scheme when the speakers of a language come to accept as true an important range of sentences they previously took to be false (and, of course, vice versa). We must not describe this change simply as a matter of their coming to view old falsehoods as truths, for a truth is a proposition, and what they come to accept, in accepting a sentence as true, is not the same thing that they rejected when formerly they held the sentence to be false. A change has come over the meaning of the sentence because it now belongs to a new language.

This picture of how new (perhaps better) schemes result from new and better science is very much the picture philosophers of science, like Putnam and Feyerabend, and historians of science, like Kuhn, have painted for us. A related idea emerges in the suggestion of some other philosophers, that we could improve our conceptual lot if we were to tune our language to an improved science. Thus both Quine and Smart, in somewhat different ways, regretfully admit that our present ways of talking make a serious science of behavior impossible. (Wittgenstein and Ryle have said similar things without regret.) The cure, Quine and Smart think, is to change how we talk. Smart advocates (and predicts) the change in order to put us on the scientifically straight path of materialism. Quine is more concerned to clear the way for a purely extensional language. (Perhaps I should add that I think our *present* scheme and language are best understood as extensional and materialist.)

If we were to follow this advice, I do not myself think science or understanding would be advanced, though possibly morals would. But the present question is only whether, if such changes were to take place, we should be justified in calling them alterations in the basic conceptual apparatus. The difficulty in so calling them is easy to appreciate. Suppose that in my office of Minister of Scientific Language I want the new man to stop using words that refer, say, to emotions, feelings, thoughts, and intentions, and to talk instead of the physiological states and happenings that are assumed to be more or less identical with the mental riff and raff. How do I tell whether my advice has been heeded if the new person speaks a new language? For all I know, the shiny new phrases, though stolen from the old language in which they refer to physiological stirrings may in his mouth play the role of the messy old mental concepts.

The key phrase is: "for all I know." What is clear is that retention of some or all of the old vocabulary in itself provides no basis for judging the new scheme to be the same as, or different from, the old. So what sounded at first like a thrilling discovery—that truth is relative to a conceptual scheme—has not so far been shown to be anything more than the pedestrian and familiar face that the truth of a sentence is relative to (among other things) the language to which it belongs. Instead of living in different worlds, Kuhn's scientists may, like those who need Webster's dictionary, be only words apart.

Giving up the analytic-synthetic distinction has not proven a help in making sense of conceptual relativism. The analytic-synthetic distinction is however explained in terms of something that may serve to buttress conceptual relativism, namely the idea of empirical content. The dualism of the synthetic and the analytic is a dualism of sentences some of which are true (or false) both because of what they mean and because of their empirical content, while others are true (or false) by virtue of meaning alone, having no empirical content. If we give up the dualism, we abandon the conception of meaning that goes with it, but we do not have to abandon the idea of empirical content: we can hold, if we want, that *all* sentences have empirical content. Empirical content is in turn explained by reference to the facts, the world, experience, sensation, the totality of sensory stimuli, or something similar. Meanings gave us a way to talk about categories, the organizing structure of language, and so on, but it is possible, as we have seen, to give up meanings and analyticity while retaining the idea of language as embodying a conceptual scheme. Thus in place of the dualism of the analytic-synthetic we get the dualism of conceptual scheme and empirical content. The new dualism is the foundation of an empiricism shorn of the untenable dogmas of the analytic-synthetic distinction and reductionism—shorn, that is, of the unworkable idea that we can uniquely allocate empirical content sentence by sentence.

I want to urge that this second dualism of scheme and content, of organizing system and something waiting to be organized, cannot be made intelligible and defensible. It is itself a dogma of empiricism, the third dogma. The third, and perhaps the last, for if we give it up it is not clear that there is anything distinctive left to call empiricism.

The scheme-content dualism has been formulated in many ways. Here are some examples. The first comes from Whorf, elaborating on a theme of Sapir's. Whorf says that:

> language produces an organization of experience. We are inclined to think of language simply as a technique of expression, and not to realize that language first of all is a classification and arrangement of the stream of sensory experience which results in a certain world-order. . . . In other words, language does in a cruder but also in a broader and more versatile way the same thing that science does. . . . We are thus introduced to a new principle of relativity, which holds that all observers are not led by the same physical evidence to the same picture of the universe, unless their linguistic backgrounds are similar, or can in some way be calibrated.[3]

Here we have all the required elements: language as the organizing force, not to be distinguished clearly from science: what is organized, referred to variously as "experience," "the stream of sensory experience," and "physical evidence"; and finally, the failure of intertranslatability is a necessary condition for difference of conceptual schemes; the common relation to experience or the evidence is what is supposed to help us make sense of the claim that it is languages or schemes that are under consideration when translation fails. It is essential to this idea that there be something neutral and common that lies outside all schemes. This common something cannot, of course, be the *subject matter* of contrasting languages, or translation would be possible. Thus Kuhn has recently written:

> Philosophers have now abandoned hope of finding a pure sense-datum language . . . but many of them continue to assume that theories can be compared by recourse to a basic vocabulary consisting entirely of words which are attached to nature in ways that are unproblematic and, to the extent necessary, independent of theory. . . . Feyerabend and I have argued at length that no such vocabulary is available. In the transition from one theory to the next words change their meanings or conditions of applicability in subtle ways. Though most of the same signs are used before and after a revolution . . . e.g. force, mass, element, compound, cell . . . the ways in which some of them attach to nature has somehow changed. Successive theories are thus, we say, incommensurable.[4]

"Incommensurable" is, of course, Kuhn and Feyerabend's word for "not intertranslatable." The neutral content waiting to be organized is supplied by nature.

Feyerabend himself suggests that we may compare contrasting schemes by "choosing a point of view outside the system or the language." He hopes we can do this because "there is still human experience as an actually existing process"[5] independent of all schemes.

The same, or similar, thoughts are expressed by Quine in many passages: "The totality of our so-called knowledge or beliefs . . . is a man-made fabric which impinges on experience only along the edges";[6] "total science is like a field of force whose boundary conditions are experience";[7] "as an empiricist I . . . think of the conceptual scheme of science as a tool . . . for predicting future experience in the light of past experience."[8] And again:

> We persist in breaking reality down somehow into a multiplicity of identifiable and discriminable objects. . . . We talk so inveterately of

objects that to say we do so seems almost to say nothing at all; for how else is there to talk? It is hard to say how else there is to talk, not because our objectifying pattern is an invariable trait of human nature, but because we are bound to adapt any alien pattern to our own in the very process of understanding or translating the alien sentences.[9]

The test of difference remains failure or difficulty of translation: "to speak of that remote medium as radically different from ours is to say no more than that the translations do not come smoothly."[10] Yet the roughness may be so great that the alien has an "as yet unimagined pattern beyond individuation."[11]

The idea is then that something is a language, and associated with a conceptual scheme, whether we can translate it or not, if it stands in a certain relation (predicting, organizing, facing, or fitting) to experience (nature, reality, sensory promptings). The problem is to say what the relation is, and to be clearer about the entities related.

The images and metaphors fall into two main groups: conceptual schemes (languages) either *organize* something, or they *fit* it (as in "he warps his scientific heritage to fit his . . . sensory promptings"[12]). The first group contains also *systematize, divide up* (the stream of experience); further examples of the second group are *predict, account for, face* (the tribunal of experience). As for the entities that get organized, or which the scheme must fit, I think again we may detect two main ideas; either it is reality (the universe, the world, nature), or it is experience (the passing show, surface irritations, sensory promptings, sense data, the given).

We cannot attach a clear meaning to the notion of organizing a single object (the world, nature, etc.) unless that object is understood to contain or consist in other objects. Someone who sets out to organize a closet arranges the things in it. If you are told not to organize the shoes and shirts, but the closet itself, you would be bewildered. How would you organize the Pacific Ocean? Straighten out its shores, perhaps, or relocate its islands, or destroy the fish.

A language may contain simple predicates whose extensions are matched by no simple predicates, or even by any predicates at all, in some other language. What enables us to make this point in particular cases is an ontology common to the two languages, with concepts that individuate the same objects. We can be clear about breakdowns in translation when they are local enough, for a background of generally successful translation provides what is needed to make the failures intelligible. But we were after larger game: we wanted to make sense of there being a language we

could not translate at all. Or, to put the point differently, we were looking for a criterion of languagehood that did not depend on, or entail,
translatability into a familiar idiom. I suggest that the image of organizing the closet of nature will not apply such a criterion.

How about the other kind of object, experience? Can we think of a
language organizing it? Much the same difficulties recur. The notion of
organization applies only to pluralities. But whatever plurality we take
experience to consist in—events like losing a button or stubbing a toe,
having a sensation of warmth or hearing an oboe—we will have to individuate according to familiar principles. A language that organizes *such*
entities must be a language very like our own.

Experience (and its classmates like surface irritations, sensations, and
sense data) also makes another and more obvious trouble for the organizing idea. For how could something count as a language that organized *only* experiences, sensations, surface irritations, or sense data? Surely
knives and forks, railroads and mountains, cabbages and kingdoms also
need organizing.

This last remark will no doubt sound inappropriate as a reason to the
claim that a conceptual scheme is a way of coping with sensory experience; and I agree that it is. But what was under consideration was the
idea of *organizing* experience, not the idea of *coping with* (or fitting or
facing) experience. The reply was apropos of the former, not the latter,
concept. So now let's see whether we can do better with the second idea.

When we turn from talk of organization to talk of fitting we turn our
attention from the referential apparatus of language—predicates, quanti-
fiers, variables, and singular terms—to whole sentences. It is sentences
that predict (or are used to predict), sentences that cope or deal with things,
that fit our sensory promptings, that can be compared or confronted with
the evidence. It is sentences also that face the tribunal of experience, though
of course they must face it together.

The proposal is not that experiences, sense data, surface irritations, or
sensory promptings are the sole subject matter of language. There is, it
is true, the theory that talk about brick houses on Elm Street is ultimately
to be construed as being about sense data or perceptions, but such re-
ductionistic views are only extreme, and implausible, versions of the general position we are considering. The general position is that sensory experience provides all the *evidence* for the acceptance of sentences (where
sentences may include whole theories). A sentence or theory fits our sen-

sory promptings, successfully faces the tribunal of experience, predicts future experience, or copes with the pattern of our surface irritations, provided it is borne out by the evidence.

In the common course of affairs, a theory may be borne out by the available evidence and yet be false. But what is in view here is not just actually available evidence; it is the totality of possible sensory evidence past, present, and future. We do not need to pause to contemplate what this might mean. The point is that for a theory to fit or face up to the totality of possible sensory evidence is for that theory to be true. If a theory quantifies over physical objects, numbers or sets, what it says about these entities is true provided the thory as a whole fits the sensory evidence. One can see how, from this point of view, such entities might be called posits. It is reasonable to call something a posit if it can be contrasted with something that is not. Here the something that is not is sensory experience, at least that is the idea.

The trouble is that the notion of fitting the totality of experience, like the notions of fitting the facts, or being true to the facts, adds nothing intelligible to the simple concept of being true. To speak of sensory experience rather than the evidence, or just the facts, expresses a view about the source or nature of evidence, but it does not add a new entity to the universe against which to test conceptual schemes. The totality of sensory evidence is what we want provided it is all the evidence there is; and all the evidence there is is just what it takes to make our sentences or theories true. Nothing, however, no *thing*, makes sentences and theories true; not experience, not surface irritations, not the world, can make a sentence true. That experience takes a certain course, that our skin is warmed or punctured, that the universe is finite, these facts, if we like to talk that way, make sentences and theories true. But this point is put better without mention of facts. The sentence "My skin is warm" is true if and only if my skin is warm. Here there is no reference to a fact, a world, an experience, or a piece of evidence.[13]

Our attempt to characterize languages or conceptual schemes in terms of the notion of fitting some entity has come down, then, to the simple thought that something is an acceptable conceptual scheme or theory if it is true. Perhaps we better say *largely* true in order to allow sharers of a scheme to differ on details. And the criterion of a conceptual scheme different from our own now becomes largely true but not translatable. The question whether this is a useful criterion is just the question how well we understand the notion of truth, as applied to language, independent of the notion of translation. The answer is, I think, that we do not understand it independently at all.

We recognize sentences like " 'Snow is white' is true if and only if snow is white" to be trivially true. Yet the totality of such English sentences uniquely determines the extension of the concept of truth for English. Tarski generalized this observation and made it a test of theories of truth: according to Tarski's Convention T, a satisfactory theory of truth for a language L must entail, for every sentence *s* of L, a theorem of the form "*s* is true if and only if *p*" where "*s*" is replaced by a description of *s* and "*p*" by *s* itself if L is English, and by a translation of *s* into English if L is not English.[14] This isn't, of course, a definition of truth, and it doesn't hint that there is a single definition or theory that applies to languages generally. Nevertheless, Convention T suggests, though it cannot state, an important feature common to all the specialized concepts of truth. It succeeds in doing this by making essential use of the notion of translation into a language we know. Since Convention T embodies our best intuition as to how the concept of truth is used, there does not seem to be much hope for a test that a conceptual scheme is radically different from ours if that test depends on the assumption that we can divorce the notion of truth from that of translation.

Neither a fixed stock of meanings, nor a theory-neutral reality, can provide, then, a ground for comparison of conceptual schemes. It would be a mistake to look further for such a ground if by that we mean something conceived as common to incommensurable schemes. In abandoning this search, we abandon the attempt to make sense of the metaphor of a single space within which each scheme has a position and provides a point of view.

I turn now to the more modes approach: the idea of partial rather than total failure of translation. This introduces the possibility of making changes and contrasts in conceptual schemes intelligible by reference to the common part. What we need is a theory of translation or interpretation that makes no assumptions about shared meanings, concepts, or beliefs.

The interdependence of belief and meaning springs from the interdependence of two aspects of the interpretation of speech behavior; the attribution of beliefs and the interpretation of sentences. I remarked before that we can afford to associate coceptual schemes with languages because of these dependencies. Now we can put the point in a somewhat sharper way. Allow that a man's speech cannot be interpreted without knowing a good deal about what he believes (and intends and wants), and that fine distinctions between beliefs are impossible without understood speech; how then are we to interpret speech or intelligibly to attribute beliefs and other attitudes? Clearly we must have a theory that simultaneously accounts for attitudes and interprets speech, a theory that rests on evidence which assumes neither.

I suggest, following Quine, that we may without circularity or unwarranted assumptions accept certain very general attitudes towards sentences as the basic evidence for a theory of radical interpretation. For the sake of the present discussion at least we may depend on the attitude of accepting as true, directed at sentences, as the crucial notion. (A more full-blooded theory would look to other attitudes toward sentences as well, such as wishing true, wondering whether true, intending to make true, and so on.) Attitudes are indeed involved here, but the fact that the main issue is not begged can be seen from this: if we merely know that someone holds a certain sentence to be true, we know neither what he means by the sentence nor what belief his holding it true represents. His holding the sentence true is thus the vector of two forces; the problem of interpretation is to abstract from the evidence a workable theory of meaning and an acceptable theory of belief.

The way this problem is solved is best appreciated from undramatic examples. If you see a ketch sailing by and your companion says, "Look at that handsome yawl," you may be faced with a problem of interpretation. One natural possibility is that your friend has mistaken a ketch for a yawl, and has formed a false belief. But if his vision is good and his line of sight favorable it is even more plausible that he does not use the word "yawl" quite as you do, and has made no mistake at all about the position of the jigger on the passing yacht. We do this sort of off-the-cuff interpretation all the time, deciding in favor of reinterpretation of words in order to preserve a reasonable theory of belief. As philosophers we are peculiarly tolerant of systematic malapropism, and practiced at interpreting the result. The process is that of constructing a viable theory of belief and meaning from sentences held true.

Such examples emphasize the interpretation of anomalous details against a background of common beliefs and a going method of translation. But the principles involved must be the same in less trivial cases. What matters is this: if all we know is what sentences a speaker holds true, and we cannot assume that his language is our own, then we cannot take even a first step toward interpretation without knowing or assuming a great deal about the speaker's beliefs. Since knowledge of beliefs comes only with the ability to interpret words, the only possibility at the start is to assume general agreement on beliefs. We get a first approximation to a finished theory by assigning to sentences of a speaker conditions of truth that actually obtain (in our own opinion) just when the speaker holds those sentences true. The guiding policy is to do this as far as possible—subject to considerations of simplicity, hunches about the effects of social conditioning, and of course our common sense, or scientific knowlege of explicable error.

The method is not designed to eliminate disagreement, nor can it; its purpose is to make meaningful disagreement possible, and this depends entirely on a foundation—*some* foundation—in agreement. The agreement may take the form of widespread sharing of sentences held true by speakers of "the same language," or agreement in the large mediated by a theory of truth contrived by an interpreter for speakers of another language.

Since charity is not an option, but a condition of having a workable theory, it is meaningless to suggest that we might fall into massive error by endorsing it. Until we have successfully established a systematic correlation of sentences held true with sentences held true, there are no mistakes to make. Charity is forced on us, whether we like it or not, if we want to understand others, we must count them right in most matters. If we can produce a theory that reconciles charity and the formal conditions for a theory, we have done all that could be done to ensure communication. Nothing more is possible, and nothing more is needed.

We make maximum sense of the words and thoughts of others when we interpret in a way that optimizes agreement (this includes room, as we said, for explicable error, i.e., differences of opinion). Where does this leave the case for conceptual relativism? The answer is, I think, that we must say much the same thing about differences in conceptual scheme as we say about differences in belief: we improve the clarity and bite of declarations of difference, whether of scheme or opinion, by enlarging the basis of shared (translatable) language or of shared opinion. Indeed, no clear line between the cases can be made out. If we choose to translate some alien sentence rejected by its speakers by a sentence to which we are strongly attached on a community basis, we may be tempted to call this a difference in schemes; if we decide to accommodate the evidence in other ways, it may be more natural to speak of a difference of opinion. But when others think differently from us, no general principle, or appeal to evidence, can force us to decide that the difference lies in our beliefs rather than in our concepts.

We must conclude, I think, that the attempt to give a solid meaning to the idea of conceptual relativism, and hence to the idea of a conceptual scheme, fares no better when based on partial failure of translation than when based on total failure. Given the underlying methodology of interpretation, we could not be in a position to judge that others had concepts or beliefs radically different from our own.

It would be wrong to summarize by saying I have shown how communication is possible between people who have different schemes, a way that works without need of what there cannot be, namely a neutral ground, or a common coordinate system. For we have found no intelligible basis on which it can be said that schemes are different. It would be equally wrong to announce the glorious news that all mankind, all speakers of language, at least, share a common scheme and ontology. For if we cannot intelligibly say that schemes are different, neither can we intelligibly say that they are one.

In giving up dependence on the concepts of an uninterpreted reality, something outside all schemes and science, we do not relinquish the notion of objective truth—quite the contrary. Given the dogma of a dualism of scheme and reality, we get conceptual relativity, and truth relative to a scheme. Without the dogma, this kind of relativity goes by the board. Of course truth of sentences remains relative to language, but that is as objective as can be. In giving up the dualism of scheme and world, we do not give up the world, but reestablish unmediated touch with the familiar objects whose antics make our sentences and opinions true or false.

NOTES

1. Peter Strawson, *The Bounds of Sense* (London, 1966), p. 15.

2. Paul Feyerabend, "Explanation, Reduction, and Empiricism," in H. Feigl and Grover Maxwell, eds., *Scientific Explanation, Space, and Time*. Minnesota Studies in the Philosophy of Science, vol. 3 (Minneapolis, University of Minnesota Press, 1962), p. 82.

3. Benjamin Lee Whorf, *Language, Thought, and Reality: Selected Writings of Benjamin Lee Whorf,* J. B. Carroll, ed. (Cambridge, Mass.: MIT Press, 1956), p. 55.

4. Thomas Kuhn, "Reflection on my Critics," in I. Lakatos and A. Musgrave, eds., *Criticism and the Growth of Knowledge* (Cambridge: Cambridge University Press, 1970), pp. 266, 267.

5. Paul Feyerabend, "Problems of Empiricism," in R. G. Colodny, ed., *Beyond the Edge of Certainty,* Englewood Cliffs, N.J.: Prentice-Hall, 1965), p. 214.

6. W. V. O. Quine, "Two Dogmas of Empiricism," reprinted in *From a Logical Point of View,* 2d ed. (Cambridge: Harvard University Press, 1961), p. 42.

7. *Ibid.*

8. *Ibid.,* p. 44.

9. W. V. O. Quine, "Speaking of Objects," reprinted in *Ontological Relativity and Other Essays* (New York: Columbia University Press, 1969), p. 1.

10. *Ibid.,* p. 25.

11. *Ibid.,* p. 24.

12. Quine, "Two Dogmas of Empiricism," p. 46.

13. These remarks are defended in my "True to the Facts," *The Journal of Philosophy* (1969) 66:748–764.

14. Alfred Tarski, "The Concept of Truth in Formalized Languages," in *Logics, Semantics, Metamathematics* (Oxford: Oxford University Press, 1956).

[9]
Styles of Scientific Reasoning

IAN HACKING

I WISH TO pose a relativist question from within the heartland of rationality. It is not about the confrontation between science and alien cultures, for it comes out of our own scientific tradition. It does not rehearse the Kuhnian stories of revolution, replacement, and incommensurability, but speaks chiefly of evolution and accumulation. Its sources are not hermeneutics but the canonical writings of positivism. Far from invoking "the dogma of the dualism of scheme and reality" from which, according to Donald Davidson, "we get conceptual relativity," it may well learn a trick from Davidson himself.

I start from the fact that there have been different styles of scientific reasoning. The wisest of the Greeks admired Euclidean thought. The best minds of the seventeenth century held that the experimental method put knowledge on a new footing. At least part of every modern social science deploys some statistics. Such examples bring to mind different styles of reasoning with different domains. Each has surfaced and attained maturity in its own time, in its own way.

An inane subjectivism may say that whether p is a reason for q depends on whether people have got around to reasoning that way or not. I have the subtler worry that whether or not a proposition is, as it were, up for grabs as a candidate fro being true-or-false, depends on whether we have ways to reason about it. The style of thinking that befits the sentence helps

This essay is a condensed and revised version of two earlier papers, "Language, Truth, and Reason," in M. Hollis and S. Lukes, eds., *Rationality and Relativism* (Oxford: Blackwell; Cambridge: M.I.T., 1982), pp. 48–66; and "The Accumulation of Styles of Scientific Reasoning," in D. Henrich, ed., *Kant oder Hegel* (Stuttgart: Klett-Cotta, 1983), pp. 453–465.

fix its sense and determines the way in which it has a positive reaction pointing to the truth or to falsehood. If we continue in this vein, we may come to fear that the rationality of a style of reasoning is all too built-in. The propositions on which the reasoning bears mean what they do just because that way of reasoning can assign them a truth value. Is reason, in short, all too self-authenticating?

My worry is about truth-or-falsehood. Consider Hamlet's maxim, that nothing's either good or bad, but thinking makes it so. If we transfer this to truth and falsehood, this is ambiguous between: *(a)* Nothing, which is true, is true, and nothing, which is false, is false, but thinking makes it so; *(b)* Nothing's either true-or-false but thinking makes it so. It is *(b)* that preoccupies me. My relativist worry is, to repeat, that the sense of a proposition *p,* the way in which it points to truth or falsehood, hinges on the style of reasoning appropriate to *p.* Hence we cannot criticize that style of reasoning, as a way of getting to *p,* or to not-*p,* because *p* simply is that proposition whose truth value is determined in this way.

The distinction between *(a)* and *(b)* furnishes a distinction between subjectivity and relativity. Let *(a)* be subjectivism: by thinking we might make something true, or make it false. Let *(b)* be the kind of relativity that I address in this essay: by thinking, new candidates for truth and falsehood may be brought into being. Many of the recent but already classical philosophical discussions of such topics as incommensurability, indeterminacy of translation, and conceptual schemes seem to me to discuss truth, where they ought to be considering truth-or-falsehood. Hence bystanders, hoping to learn from philosophers, have tended to discuss subjectivity rather than relativity. For may part, I have no doubt that our discoveries are "objective," simply because the styles of reasoning that we employ determine what counts as objectivity. My worry is that the very candidates for truth or falsehood have no existence independent of the styles of reasoning that settle what it is to be true or false in their domain.

Styles of Reasoning

It is not the case that *nothing* is either true or false but thinking makes it so. Plenty of things that we say need no reasons. That is the core of the discredited philosophical doctrine of observation sentences, the boring utterances that crop up in almost any language, and which make radical translation relatively easy. Translation is hard when one gets to whole new ranges of possibility that make no sense for the favoured styles of reasoning of another culutre. It is there that ethnographers begin to have problems. Every people has generated its own peculiar styles. We are no different from others, except that we can see, more clearly from our own written record, the historical emergence of new styles of reasoning.

I take the word "style" from the title of a forthcoming book by A. C. Crombie: *Styles of Scientific Thinking in the European Tradition.* He concludes an anticipatory paper with the words:

> The active promotion and diversification of the scientific methods of late medieval and early modern Europe reflected the general growth of a research mentality in European society, a mentality conditioned and increasingly committed by its circumstances to expect and to look actively for problems to formulate and solve, rather than for an accepted concensus without argument. The varieties of scientific methods so brought in to play may be distinguished as,
> a the simple postulation established in the mathematical sciences,
> b the experimental exploration and measurement of more complex observable relations,
> c the hypothetical construction of analogical models,
> d the ordering of variety by comparison and taxonomy,
> e the statistical analysis of regularities of populations and the calculus of probabilities, and
> f the historical derivation of genetic development.
> The first three of these methods concern essentially the science of individual regularities, and the second three the science of the regularities of populations ordered in space and time.[1]

Coincidentally, at the same conference to which Crombie read these words, Winifred Wisan announced another forthcoming work, *Mathematics and the Study of Motion: Emergence of a New Scientific Style in the Seventeenth Century.*[2] Both Crombie and Wisan's papers were about Galileo, who has long been a favorite candidate for advancing a new style of thought. Sometimes words more dramatic than "style" are used, as when Althusser writes of Thales opening up a new continent, that of methematics, Galileo opening up the continent of dynamics, and Marx that of history.[3] But often the word "style" is chosen. It is to be found in Collingwood. Stephen Weinberg, the theoretical physicist, recalls Husserl speaking of a Galilean style for "making abstract models of the universe to which at least the physicists give a higher degree of reality than they accord the ordinary world of sensation."[4] Weinberg finds it remarkable that this style should work, "for the universe does not seem to have been prepared with human beings in mind." The linguist Noam Chomsky picks up this remark in a recent book, urging that "we have no present alternative to pursuing the 'Galilean style' in the natural sciences at least.[5]

Paradigms

There is a temptation, in the philosophy of science, to fix on one fashionable word and imagine that it has a clearer meaning than it deserves. Kuhn's word 'paradigm' is a good example. I have been asked how styles of reasoning differ from paradigms. The difference is total. To begin with it is a matter of scale. A paradigm may cover a very small bit of a special science. Some people read Kuhn on scientific revolutions as if he were discussing big revolutions only, the Copernican revolution, or 'the scientific revolution' of the seventeenth century. On the contrary he is quite explicitly discussing little revolts too. The discovery of X-rays provides a scientific revolution. Indeed in those papers where he discusses large-scale changes at the level of the so-called scientific revolution, he never speaks of paradigms at all. His papers on mathematical and experimental traditions, and on measurement, are in my opinion among the most valuable and original of Kunn's many fundamental insights. They are far closer to the idea of a style of reasoning than his discussions in *The structure of Scientific Revolutions*. It is at any rate clear that any generalization of Crombie's list will involve styles of reasoning that persist and which involve a large number of thinkers. Indeed, styles of reasoning teach a lesson directly opposite to one of Kuhn's inferences from the idea of a paradigm. He wrote that paradigm shifts show that scientific knowledge is not cumulative. I can agree with that. *Knowledge* is less cumulative than we thought. But other things accumulate. In addition to technology and experimental technique, we can add one style of reasoning to another, as is illustrated by Crombie's list, and if a style dies out, the death is slow and often passes by unnoticed. In the present volume Kuhn describes the late merging of the mathematical and experimental traditions. I could use that as an example of the complex, and sometimes tortured, interweaving of two different styles. That event took so long, that it made it look as if, in Herbert Butterfield's phrase, part of the scientific revolution of the seventeenth century was "delayed." Kuhn provides a different analysis, that has nothing to do with paradigms.

Kuhn has said that he had two chief uses for the word 'paradigm'. One is the paradigm as achievement, a body of work evolved at a moment of scientific crisis, and which sets a standard for addressing certain classes of problems. It is the textbook model of how to carry on the ensuing normal science. In the other sense, a paradigm is a disciplinary matrix, a relatively small group of workers who decide what to teach, who will be taught, what counts as success, what problems to work on.

A style of reasoning is very different. It tends to be slower in evolution, and vastly more widespread. Within that style of reasoning I call statistical inference, there are many different paradigms associated with names such as Neyman, Fisher, or Bayes. A style of reasoning need not be committed to any positive items of knowledge. A paradigm surely assumes certain propositions as taken for granted: they are part of the achievement that sets the model for future work. They are stated in the paradigmatic textbooks. A style of reasoning makes it possible to reason towards certain kinds of propositions, but does not of itself determine their truth value. Even the Euclidean geometrical style does not fix which propositions are going to come out as theorems.

If one runs down Crombie's list of scientific styles, it goes almost without saying that they are not the private property of this or that "disciplinary matrix" numbering one hundred or so active workers. That may be so for a time: perhaps, to repeat a myth, Thales did singlehandedly open up the continent of mathematics. The typical case, however, is a large number of people approaching the same subject matter with related styles of argumentation. This must necessarily be the case. For a style of reason opens up a new field of discourse, with new positive propositions to assert or deny. Such a new field is a relatively large-scale social phenomenon. A body of discourse needs quite a lot of speakers.

Discourse

Comparing "styles of scientific reasoning" to other catchphrases in circulation, I find it natural to lean less to Kuhn's paradigms and more to Michel Foucault's terms like 'episteme' and 'discourse.' Foucault quite deliberately abandons nearly all his neologisms as soon as he has put them into currency in a book. Despite my debts to Foucault, I shall not attempt exegesis here. In my own verions of what Foucault is up to, I emphasize that any discourse has its own categories of possibility, its own range of propositions that are either-true-or-false. Each discourse has what Foucault calls its own field of positivity; I gloss this as its own field of candidates for a positive knowledge that is determined by a style of argumentation not only fitting that discourse but helping to define it. I follow Foucault in emphasizing that the discourse is not defined by the actual content of knowledge, by the expressed beliefs of this or that school of thought. It is defined by what it is possible to believe. What it is possible to believe, in the domain that we call scientific, has the convention of arguments and reasons. I do not naively hold that scientists believe what they do because of the arguments that they offer or mention. I maintain only that those arguments are what define the sense of what they believe.

I do not say that "style of reasoning" means Foucaultian *'episteme'* or whatever. On the contrary, if one could adequately define an *episteme,* one would surely have to include, as one of its elements, the styles of reason that bear on the positive propositions of that field of knowledge. I am inclined to suppose that this concept, of a style of reason, when added to the "concepts, strategies", and so forth that preoccupy Foucault in *The Archaeology of Knowledge,* would do much of the work demanded by Foucault's completely opaque notion of the *'archive.'*

Arch-Rationalism

The existence of styles of reasoning does not immediately suggest relativism. Before elaborating the relativist worry sketched at the beginning of this paper, I shall first state a rationlist position informed by a proper respect both for history and for the idiosyncracies of ourselves and others. I shall call it arch-rationalism. (I, too, am an arch-rationalist most of the time.)

The arch-rationalist believes what right-thinking people have known all along. There are good and bad reasons. It has taken millennia to evolve systems of reasoning. By and large our Western tradition has contributed more to this progress than any other. We have often been narrow, blinkered, and insensitive to foreign insights. We have repressed our own deviant and original thinkers, condemning many to irretrievable oblivion. Some of our own once-favored styles of reasoning have turned out to be dead ends and others are probably on the way. However, new styles of reasoning will continue to evolve. So we shall not only find out more about nature, but we shall also learn new ways to reason about it. Maybe Paul Feyerabend's advocacy of anarchy is right. To compel people to reason in approved ways is to limit us and our potentialities for novelty. Arch-rationalism is convinced that there are good and bad reasons, but since it does not commit us to any specific regimentation like that of formal logic or of Karl Popper, it is fairly receptive to Feyerband's imitation anarchy.

My arch-rationalist thinks that there is a fairly sharp distinction between reasons and the propositions they support. Reasons merely help us find out what is the case. The arch-rationalist wants to know how the world is. There are good and bad reasons for propositions about nature. They are not relative to anything. They do not depend on context. The arch-rationalist is not an imperialist about reason. Maybe there could be people who never reason nor deliberate at all. They tell jokes, make and break promises, feign insults, and so forth, but they never reason. Just as statistical reasons had no force for the Greeks, so one imagines a people for whom none of our reasons for belief have force. On the other hand the arch-rationalist is an optimist about human nature. We who value truth and reason do imagine that a truthless and unreasoning people would, if left alone, evolve truth and reason for themselves. They would in their own way acquire a taste for speculation about the diagonal of a square, for motion on the inclined plane, for the tracks of the planets, for the inner constitution of matter, the evolution of the species, the Oedipus complex and amino acids.

The arch-rationalist not only grants that our kinds of truth and reason may not play as great a role in the life of other peoples as in our own culture; he may also be a romantic, hankering after a simpler, less reason-impregnated life. He will grant that our values are not inevitable, nor perhaps the noblest to which our species can aspire. But he cannot escape his own past. His admission of the historicity of our own styles of reasoning in no way makes them less objective. Styles of reasoning have histories and some emerged sooner than others. Humankind has got better at reasoning. What ground for relativism could there be in all that?

Instead of challenging the assumptions of the arch-rationalist, I shall extract a hint of incoherence from his heartland, which is, in the end, positivism.

Positivism

Positivism is commonly taken to be a hardheaded antagonism to all forms of relativism. I shall create a question for the arch-rationalist from three aspects of positivism itself. I draw them from Auguste Comte, the original positivist of the 1840s, Moritz Schlick, the leader of the Vienna Circle in 1930, and Michael Dummett, the most gifted present exponent of one among that family of doctrines.

Comte. Comte was an historicist. His epistemology is a massive and almost unreadable account of human knowledge, a narrative of the human mind in which each intellectual innovation finds its own niche. One of his ideas is that a branch of knowledge acquires a "positivity" by the development of a new, positive, style of reasoning associated with it. He is none too clear what he means by "positive"; he sometimes says he chose the word chiefly because it had overtones of moral uplift in all European languages. A positive proposition can be investigated by a means befitting the branch of knowledge to which it belongs. We may pun on his word: a positive proposition is one that has a direction, a truth value. It is no distortion to say that for Comte a class of positive propositions is a class of propositions that are up for grabs as true-or-false.

There are many aspects of Comte's thought from which one hastily withdraws—I refer both to questions of ideology and to issues of interest to analytic philosophers of science (e.g., his analysis of causation). I draw attention only to the idea of an historical evolution of different syles of reasoning, each bringing in train its own body of positive knowledge. Each finds its place in the great tabular displays of the sciences that serve as pull-outs from his gigantic epistemological text, the *Cours de philosophie positive*. Comte did not think that the evolution of styles and of positive knowledges had come to an end. His life goal was the creation of a new postive science, sociology. This would require a new style of reasoning. He ill foresaw what this style would be, but his metaconception of what he was doing was sound.

Schlick. One of the more memorable statements of logical positivism is Moritz Schlick's, "the meaning of a sentence is its method of verification."[6] Those words could not stand unmodified, because the Vienna Circle had succumbed to Gottlob Frege's dictum that meanings are definite, objective, and fixed. Schlick's maxim would imply that a change or advance in a method of verification would change the meanings of a sentence. Rather than give up the idea of meanings handed down from generation to generation, tranquil and unmodified, logical positivists revised Schlick's maxim again and again, although with no satisfactory outcome.[7] But for Comte, or any other of those fortunate writers of 1840 not yet infected by Fregean theories of meaning, Schlick's statement would be just fine. It is precisely, for Comte, the methods of verification—the ways in which the positive truth values are to be established—that determine the content of a body of knowledge.

Dummett. In logic, a proposition that has a definite truth value, true or false, is called *bivalent.* Dummett's work has made philosophers think closely about bivalence.[8] He was first inspired by a philosophical reconstruction of some of the thoughts behind intuitionist mathematics. In what is called a nonconstructive proof, one cannot exhibit the mathematical objects that are proved to exist. (So one might have a step in which one asserts that there is a prime number with a certain property, but be unable to say which prime number it is.) Nonconstructive proofs may also assume of a proposition that it is either true or false, without being able to show which truth value it has. Some philosophical mathematicians, including Dummett, have doubted whether such nonconstructive proofs are admissible.

Dummett is attracted to the following basis of his doubt. Whether or not a proposition is bivalent must depend upon its meaning. He wonders how we can confer meanings on statements in nonconstructive mathematics—meanings in virtue of which the statements are bivalent, although there is no known way to settle the truth values. It is we who through our linguistic practices are the sole source of the meanings of what we say. How then can we confer a meaning on a statement, such that it is bivalent, when nothing we know how to do bears on the truth or the falsehood of the statement? Maybe statements of nonconstructive mathematics acquire bivalence only as we perfect means of determining their truth values or exhibiting the mathematical objects of which they speak?

Although this subtle question arose in sharp form in the intuitionist critique of classical mathematics, Dummett extends it to other forms of discourse. Many statements about the past cannot now be settled by any practicable means. Are they bivalent? Might bivalence recede into the past as historical data become irrevocably erased? Dummett does not claim that his worries are conclusive, nor does he expect parallel answers for every kind of discourse. One might, on reflection, come out for bivalence in the case of history, but reject it for nonconstructive mathematics.

Positivity and bivalence. I have spoken of being true-or-false, and have used Comte's word "positive." Is this the same idea as bivalence? Not as I shall use the words. Being positive is a less strong characteristic than bivalence. Outside of mathematics I suspect that whether a statement is bivalent or not is an abstraction imposed by logicians to facilitate their analysis of deductive arguments forms. It is a noble abstraction, but it is a consequence of art, not nature. In the speculative sciences that concern me here, the interesting sentences are the ones that are up for grabs as true or false—ones for which we believe we have methods that will determine the truth values. The applications of these methods may require as yet unimagined technological innovation. Moreover as we find out more about the world, we find out that many of our questions no longer make sense. Bivalence is not the right concept for science. Allow me a couple of examples to point to the distinction required.

At the time of Laplace it was very sensible to think that there are particles of caloric, the substance of heat, that have repulsive forces that decay rapidly with distance. On such an hypothesis Laplace solved many of the outstanding problems about sound. Propositions about the rate of extinction of the repulsive force of caloric were up for grabs as true or false and one knew how to obtain information bearing on the question. Laplace had an excellent estimate of the rate of extinction of the repulsive force, yet it turns out that the whole idea is wrongheaded. I would say that Laplace's sentences once were "positive." They were never bivalent. Conversely, Maxwell once said that some propositions about the relative velocity of light were intrinsically incapable of determination, yet a few years after he said that, Michelson had invented the technology to give precise answers to Maxwell's questions. I would say that the sentences of interest to Maxwell had positivity when he uttered them, but were bivalent only after a transformation in technology—a transformation whose success depends on delicate experimental details about how the world works.

In short, Comte's "positive" is drawing attention to a less demanding concept than Dummett's "bivalent." Yet the two are connected and so are the thoughts of both writers. Dummett says: not bivalent unless we have a proof of the truth value, or a known surefire method for generating the proof. Comte says: not positive, not in the running for being true-or-false, until there is some style of reasoning that will bear on the question.

The whiff of circularity from the heartland of positivism

Comte, Schlick, and Dummett are no more relativist than Crombie or Chomsky. Yet a positivist train of thought, combined with an emphasis

on styles of reasoning, has the germ of relativism. If positivity is consequent upon a style of reasoning, then a range of possibilities depends upon
that style. They would not be possibilities, candidates for truth or falsehood, unless that style were in existence. The existence of the style arises
from historical events. Hence although whichever propositions are true
may depend on the data, the fact that they are candidates for being true,
is a consequence of a historical event. Conversely the rationality of a style
of reasoning as a way of bearing on the truth of a class of propositions
does not seem open for independent criticism, because the very sense of
what can be established by that style depends upon the style itself.

Is that a nasty circle?

I shall proceed as follows. First, I observe that by reasoning I don't
mean logic. I mean the very opposite, for logic is the preservation of truth,
while a style of reasoning is what brings in the possibility of truth or
falsehood. Then I separate my idea of style of reasoning from the incommensurability of Kuhn and Feyerabend, and from the indeterminacy of
translation urged by Quine. Then I examine Davidson's fundamental objection to the supposition that there are alternative ways of thinking. He
may refute subjectivity, as I understand it, but not relativity. The key distinction throughout the following discussion is the difference between
truth-and-falsehood as opposed to truth. A second important idea is the
looseness of fit between those propositions that have a sense for almost
all human beings regardless of reasoning, and those that get a sense only
within a style of reasoning.

Induction, Deduction

Neither deductive logic nor induction occur on Crombie's list. How
strange, for are they not said to be the basis of science? It is instructive
that no list like Crombie's would include them. The absence reminds us
that styles of reasoning create the possibility for truth and falsehood. Deduction and induction merely preserve it.

We now understand deduction as that mode of inference that preserves
truth. It cannot pass from true premises to a false conclusion. The nature
of induction is more controversial. The word has been used in many ways.
There is an important tradition represented alike by the philosopher C.
S. Peirce and the statistician Jerzy Neyman: induction is that mode of
argument that preserves truth most of the time.

Deduction and induction were important human discoveries. But they play little role in the scientific method, no more than the once revered syllogism. They are devices for jumping from truth to truth. Not only will they give us no original truth from which to jump, but also they take for granted the class of sentences that assert possibilities of truth or falsehood. That is why they do not occur in Crombie's list. In deduction and induction alike, truth plays the purely formal role of a counter on an abacus. It matters not what truth is, when we employ the mechanics of the model theory of modern logicians. Their machine works well so long as we suppose that the class of sentences that have truth values is already given. (Or, in the case of intuitionist logic, one supposes the class of sentences that may, through proof, acquire truth values is already given.) Induction equally assumes that the class of possible truths is predetermined. Styles of reasoning of the sort described by Crombie do something different. When they come into being they generate new classes of possibilities.

Indeterminacy/incommensurability

Philosophers have recently given us two doctrines that pull in opposite directions. Both seem to use the idea of a conceptual scheme, a notion that goes back at least to Kant but whose modern nominalist version is due to Quine. He says that a conceptual scheme is a set of sentences held to be true. He uses the metaphor of core and periphery. Sentences at the core have a kind of permanence and are seldom relinquished, while those on the periphery are more empirical and more readily given up in the light of "recalcitrant experience."

My talk of styles of reasoning does not mesh well with Quine's idea of a conceptual scheme. In his opinion two schemes differ when some substantial number of core sentences of one scheme are not held to be true in another scheme. A style of reasoning, in contrast, is concerned with truth-or-falsehood. Two parties, agreeing to the same styles of reasoning, may well totally disagree on the upshot, one party holding for true what the other party rejects. Styles of reasoning may determine possible truth values but, unlike Quine's schemes, are not characterized by assignments of truth values. It is to be expected, then, that Quine's application of the idea of a conceptual scheme will not coincide with my idea of styles of reasoning.

Donald Davidson, in his paper in this volume, follows Quine in thinking of a conceptual scheme as a set of sentences held for true, and argues that the idea of alternative schemes is incoherent. Thus he tries to slay the specter of incommensurability. I too hold, for different reasons, that incommensurability is no problem.[9] I also hold that as a matter of fact, indeterminacy of translation is also an empty idea. But there is one odd way in which my notion of styles of reasoning meshes more with Quine than with Davidson. This is because Quine holds that there is a wide range of low-grade rather boring sentences, which are mere responses to familiar sensory stimuli, and which pose no problem for translation. It is only in the higher reaches of thought that a problem arises. Now Davidson rejects this structure because he doubts the Quinean notion of "stimulus meaning." More important, although both Quine and Davidson assert their holism, Davidson, student of Quine, is holier than he. All of language is one of a piece for Davidson—one of a piece with a total theory of interaction with another person. I am with Quine. I think that there is a great looseness of fit between our boring utterances and our interesting ones, and I think that the interesting things that we say occur in more or less unrelated contexts, and fit together loosely. We might even get some value out of Wittgenstein's obscure and overworked idea of "language game" here. There are many language games only loosely related. My reflections on styles of reasoning make me an iconoclast about that grand old dream, the unity of science. I firmly believe in the disunity of science.

On looseness of fit

I used Hamlet's exaggeration only to make a distinction between subjectivity and relativity. It is not the case that *nothing* is either-true-or-false but thinking makes it so. Lots of propositions are perfectly intelligible without knowing how to reason for them. This is part of the truth in the timeworn doctrine of 'observation sentences', that we just see to be true by looking or feeling. It was a pernicious doctrine for the philosophy of science, for in science observation is a skill and even noticing has to be learned often on the basis of theory. Now I have strongly criticized Quine's own account of observation,[10] which I take to be radically at odds with the role of observation in science, yet I agree with him at least in this, that there are boring intertranslatable sentences and interesting ones that are unproblematic. But the issue is hardly one of translation. It is one of how we think, how we understand, how we reason. In the philosophy of language we can make a rough distinction along a continuum between those propositions for which we reason and those for which we do not.

Members of the former class are what make translation so relatively easy between different civilizations. Members of the latter class are what make it so hard. There are two strands that affect the philosophical anthropology of translation. One is well called Whorfian: alien ways of thought are not expressible without working your way into the other culture. The opposite, which is having something of a renaissance among ethnographers, holds that different ways of organizing the world are pretty invariant across cultures: Indians on the top of the high sierras in Mexico classify plants pretty much the way Linnaeus did.[11] I think there is truth in both these views. Many things to say arise from biological universals about humans, facts about how the eye or the stomach works. Sentences expressing such thoughts occur, rather boringly, in any language. They are what make translation easy. They are also rather boring things to translate, except for the sheer thrill of establishing communication across the barrier of strange sounds. On the other hand, the things that interest us may be so embedded in local cultural practices as to make it truly necessary to move into the other culture to understand anything of what's being said. There is a great looseness of fit between these two aspects of language. You can master "the pen of my aunt (or the shrunken skull of my uncle) is on the table." But it may take you some time to understand what pens or skulls are for. In the case of one of our own subcultures, scientific reasoning, one has to know how to reason before one can understand what is being reasoned about. The very sense of the propositions for which we reason is determined by the styles of reasoning we use.

Conceptual Schemes

In his famous paper, "On the Very Idea of a Conceptual Scheme," Donald Davidson argues more against incommensurability than indeterminacy, but he is chiefly against the idea of a conceptual scheme that gives sense to either. He provides "an underlying methodology of interpretation" such that "we could not be in a position" to judge "that others had concepts or beliefs different from our own." He makes plain that he does not reach this result by postulating "a neutral ground, or a common co-ordinate system" between schemes. It is the notion of a scheme itself to which he is opposed. He rejects a "dogma of dualism between scheme and reality" from which we derive the bogey of "conceptual relativity, and of truth relative to a scheme."

Davidson distinguishes two claims. Total translatabiltity between schemes may be impossible, or there may be only partial untranslatability. Even if we do not follow the intricacies of his argument, nor even accept its premises, we can, like Davidson, dismiss the idea of total untranslatabil-ity. As a matter of brute fact all human languages are fairly easily partially translatable. That fact is closely connected with what I said earlier, that there is a common human core of verbal performances connected with what people tend to notice around them. But I said that there is a loose-ness of fit between that broad base of shared humanity and the interest-ing things that people like to talk about. That looseness leaves some space for incommensurability. It is not only the topics of discussion that may vary from group to group, but what counts as a point of saying some-thing.[12] Yet Davidson counters there too, and mounts a magnificent at-tack against even the notion of partial untranslatability between groups of people. Since in fact the solution of the problem of even partial un-translatability is chiefly a matter of coming to share the interests of an-other, and since lots of travelers are pretty sympathetic people, interests do get shared, so we should welcome an argument against partial un-translatability too. Yet since Davidson's argument may seem founded up-on a lack of concern for alternative interests, we may fear his premises while we accept his conclusions.

My diagnosis has two parts. First of all, Davidson, like Quine, assumes that a conceptual scheme is defined in terms of what counts as true, rather than of what counts as true-or-false. Secondly, unlike Quine, Davidson is a superholist. He cannot grant that we could agree about everything boring, and yet be unable even to understand the interesting thoughts of others. The inability is not a difficulty about seeing what the other counts as true, but of grasping what possibilities are in question. We learn about that only through coming to share a style of reasoning, or many styles. Such reflections do not lead to indeterminacy of translation. They lead from a state of no traslation of some parts of language, to a shared un-derstanding of what before was incomprehensible. Nor do such reflec-tions lead to incommensurability. They lead only to the fact that the thoughts of another may have to be made commensurate with ours, by our coming to share a style of reasoning. But since styles of reasoning fit so loosely together we are well able to add the alien to our own, without giving up a thought. I may of course choose homeopathic medicine over surgery, or vice versa. Here I give up one treatment for another, but I well understand where each path leads, what truths ensue. I then decide what to do.

Truth versus truth-or-falsehood

Davidson concludes his argument against relativity with the words, "Of course the truth of sentences remains relative to a language, but that is as objective as can be." Earlier he rightly states what is wrong with the idea of making a sentence true:

> No *thing* makes sentences and theories true; not experience, not surface irritations [he there alluded to Quine], not the world . . . *That* experience takes a certain course, that our skin is warmed or punctured . . . these facts, if we like to talk that way, make sentences and theories true. But this point is better made without mention of facts. The sentence "my skin is warm" is true if and only if my skin is warm. Here there is no reference to a fact, a world, an experience, or a piece of evidence (p. 139).

Davidson's example, "my skin is warm," serves me well. I urge a distinction between statements that may be made in any language, and which require no style of reasoning, and statements whose sense depends upon a style of reasoning. Davidson writes as if all sentences were of the former class. I agree that "my skin is warm" is of that class. When I once looked for the best example of a sense-datum sentence to be actually published in the annals of real science, I hit upon precisely this sentence, or rather, "my skin is warmed." It begins William Herschel's investigations of 1800 which are said to commence the theory of radiant heat. (He noticed that using filters of some colors, his skin was warmed, while using other colors he had much light but little heat.)

Herschel went on to pose a theory of invisible rays of heat, a theory that we now call correct, although his own experiments made him give it up. In the course of this reasoning he abandoned the following sentence, "The heat which has the refrangibility of the red rays is occasioned by the light of those rays." We can certainly write out a truth condition of the form "*s* is true if and only if *p*" for this sentence. But there arises a problem for the sufficiently foreign translator. It is not that words like "ray" and "refrangible" are mildly theoretical and the translator may have no such notions in his vocabulary. If another culture has acquired the styles of reasoning enumerated by Crombie it can perfectly well learn Herschel's physics from the ground up—that is just what I do in making sense of Herschel's text. The problem is that the sufficiently foreign person will not have Herschel's kind of sentence as the sort of thing that can be true-or-false, because the ways of reasoning that bear on it are unknown. To exaggerate the case, say the translator is Archimedes. I do not choose him at random, for he wrote a great tract on burning mirrors and was a greater scientist than Herschel. Yet I say he would not be able to effect a translation until he had caught up on some scientific method.

I should repeat my opposition to usual versions of incommensurability. It is not that Herschel's science had some Newtonian principles about rays and refrangibility that determine the meaning of sentences in which those words occur, and so those sentences could not have the same meaning in another theory. On the contrary, Herschel's sentences were fairly immune to change in theory. They were up for grabs as true or false in 1800; Herschel thought first that a crucial sentence is true and later held it to be false; many years later the world agreed on the truth of the sentence. Herschel, then, first grabbed the right end of the stick and then grabbed the wrong one. My claim about a translator less well placed than Archimedes is that until he learns how to reason more like Herschel, there are no ends of a stick to grab.

Schemes without Dogma

"Truth of sentences," writes Davidson, "remains relative to a language, but that is as objective as can be." I claim that for part of our language, and perhaps as part of any language, being true-or-false is a property of sentences only because we reason about those sentences in certain ways. Subjectivists put their worries in the form of saying that with different customs we could "rightly" take some propositions for true while at present we take them for false. Davidson has dealt sharply with all such formulations. But he has left a space for a relativist fear. The relativist ought to say that there might be whole other categories of truth-or-falsehood than ours.

Perhaps I am proposing a version of the conceptual scheme idea. Quine's conceptual schemes are sets of sentences held for true. Mine would be sets of sentences that are candidates for truth or falsehood. Does such a notion fall into the "dogma of scheme and reality" that Davidson resents? I do not think so. The idea of a style of reasoning is as internal to what we think and say as the Davidsonian form, "*s* is true if and only if *p*" is internal to a language. *A style is not a scheme that confronts reality.* I did speak earlier of styles of reasoning being applied to data and to the formation of data. But data are uttered and are subject to Davidsonian treatment. There is much to be said about the neglected field of study, experimental science, but it has nothing much to do with scheme/reality. Experiment has a life of its own unrelated to theories or schemes.

Anarcho-Rationalism

This paper makes two assertions and draws some inferences from them. Each assertion and every inference is in need of clarification. To list them is to show how much more must be done.

1. There are different styles of reasoning. Many of these are discernible in our own history. They emerge at definite points and have distinct trajectories of maturation. Some die out, others are still going strong.

2. Propositions of the sort that necessarily require reasoning to be substantiated have a positivity, a being true-or-false, only in consequence of the styles of reasoning in which they occur.

3. Hence many categories of possibility, of what may be true or false, are contingent upon historical events, namely the development of certain styles of reasoning.

4. It may then be inferred that there are other categories of possibility than have emerged in our tradition.

5. We cannot reason as to whether alternative systems of reasoning are better or worse than ours, because the propositions to which we reason get their sense only from the method of reasoning employed. The propositions have no existence independent of the ways of reasoning toward them.

This chain of reflections does not lead to subjectivity. It does not imply that some proposition, with a content independent of reasoning, could be held to be true, or to be false, according to the mode of reasoning we adopt. Yet this defeat of subjectivity seems hollow because the propositions that are objectively found to be true are determined as true by styles of reasoning for which in principle there can be no external justification. A justification would be an independent way of showing that the style gets at the truth, but there is no characterization of the truth over and above what is reached by the styles of reason itself.

W. Newton-Smith has protested that my own doctrine of looseness of fit vitiates this conclusion. There are lots of low-grade propositions with truth values independent of styles of reasoning. Do not these lead us back to the comfortable picture of theories being tested against theory-neutral observation sentences? I do not reply that observation sentences are theory loaded. On the contrary, I hold that styles of scientific reasoning virtually never lead to observation sentences. That is a straightforward empirical claim. Try to find an observation sentence in the reports of the experimenter, the geometer or even the statistician. Go to the laboratory or the bureau of standards, go the survey samplers employed by the Pepsi-Cola company or to aviation engineers, and try to weasle out a single observation sentence, a single sentence which has a truth value independent of a style of reasoning. You will find a few. My reply lies not in the absence of such sentences but in the labor required to find them. One of the nice things about technology and the experimental sciences is that the practitioners seldom utter those boring "observation-sentences."

Can there not be a meta-reason justifying a style of reason? Can one not, for example, appeal to success? It need not be success in generating technology, although that does matter. Nor is it to be success in getting at the truth, for that would be circular. There can, however, be noncircular successes in truth-related matters. For example, following Imre Lakatos, one might revamp Popper's method of conjecture and refutation, urging that a methodology of research programs constantly opens up new things to think about. I have quoted Chomsky giving a similar meta-reason. On his analysis of the Galilean style, it has not only worked remarkably well, but also, in the natural sciences, at least, we have no alternative but to go on using that style, although, of course, in the future it may not work. Although Chomsky does not make the distinction, his meta-reason is less that Galileo's style continues to find out the truth about the universe, than that it poses new kinds of probing and answering. It has produced an open-ended dialogue. That might terminate in the face of a Nature that ceased to participate in ways that the Galilean can make sense of. We know she might cease to cater to our interests, but at present (says Chomsky) we have no alternative to a Galilean style.

Chomsky is saying that if we want to engage in certain pursuits (call them the natural sciences or even the pursuit of truth in our tradition), we must reason with our reasons. Other styles of reasoning may occur; some are current. Other people may have other interests. We ought at least to be cautious, in the social sciences, when it is proposed that some non-Galilean, non-"hypothetico-deductive" approach is to be desired. The arch-rationalist may even be a stick-in-the-mud, claiming that the Galilean style is the only show in town, for both natural and social science. But that is not the only possible opinion.

Some arch-rationalists may even find themselves agreeing that an anarcho-rationalism I have learned from Feyerabend is appealing. Our overall interests in truth and reason may well be served by letting other styles of reason evolve in their own ways, unfettered by a more imperial kind of rationalism. But that does not mean to say that I, as anarcho-rationalist, will take up something so recently killed off in our own tradition as homeopathic medicine and its appeal to similitudes. That is for others (though if they look healthier than I, I might join up). Anarcho-rationalism is tolerance for other people combined with the discipline of one's own standards of truth and reason. The anarcho-rationalist is at home with the sentiment expressed by Sartre in his last interview:

> C'est ça ma tradition, je n'en ai pas d'autre.
> Ni la tradition orientale, ni la tradition juive.
> Elles me manquent par mon historicité.[13]

NOTES

1. A. C. Crombie, "Philosophical Presuppositions and Shifting Interpretations of Galileo," in J. Hintikka, D. Gruender, and E. Agazzi, eds., *Theory Change, Ancient Axiomatics and Galileo's Methodology, Proceedings of the 1978 Pisa Conference on the History and Philosophy of Science* for ease of reference I have inserted letters (a) to (f). (Dordrecht: Reidel, 1981), 1:284.

2. W. L. Wisan, "Galileo and the Emergence of a New Scientific Style," *ibid.,* pp. 311–339.

3. Louis Althusser, *Politics and History,* (London: New Left Books, 1972), p. 185.

4. Stephen Weinberg, "The Forces of Nature," *Bulletin of the American Academy of Arts and Sciences* (1976), 29:28.

5. Noam Chomsky, *Rules and Representations,* (New York: Columbia University Press, 1980), p. 9.

6. Moritz Schlick, "Meaning and Verification," *The Philosophical Review* (1936), 46:261.

7. For an account of repeated failures, see Ian Hacking, *Why Does Language Matter to Philsophy?* (Cambridge: Cambridge University Press, 1975), ch. 9.

8. Michael Dummett, *Truth and Other Enigmas* (London: Duckworth, 1976).

9. Ian Hacking, *Representing and Intervening* (Cambridge: Cambridge University Press, 1983), ch. 5.

10. *Ibid.,* pp. 81–83.

11. Eugene S. Hung, *Zeltal Folk Zoology: The Classification of Discontinuities in Nature* (New York: Academic Press, 1977).

12. Michelle Z. Rosaldo, "The Things We Do With Words: Ilongot Speech Acts and Speech Act Theory in Philosophy," Language and Society 11 (203–237).

13. *Le Nouvel observateur,* March 10, 1980, p. 93.

[10]
Mathematical Versus Experimental Traditions in the Development of Physical Science

THOMAS S. KUHN

ANY ONE WHO STUDIES the history of scientific development repeatedly encounters a question, one version of which would be, "Are the sciences one or many?" Ordinarily that question is evoked by concrete problems of narrative organization, and these become especially acute when the historian of science is asked to survey his subject in lectures or in a book of significant scope. Should he or she take up the sciences one by one, beginning, for example, with mathematics, proceeding to astronomy, then to physics, to chemistry, to anatomy, physiology, botany, and so on? Or should he reject the notion that his object is a composite account of individual fields and take it instead to be knowledge of nature *tout court*?

Reprinted by permission from *The Journal of Interdisciplinary History* (1976), 7:1–31. © 1976 Massachusetts Institute of Technology and the editors of the *Journal of Interdisciplinary History*.
This essay is the revised and extended version of a George Sarton Memorial Lecture, delivered in Washington, D.C., in 1972, at a joint session of the American Association for the Advancement of Scinece and the History of Science Society. A preliminary version had been read at Cornell University during the preceding month. In the years that have elapsed since, I have benefited from the comments of colleagues too numerous to mention. Some special debts will be acknowledged in footnotes which follow. Here I record only my thanks for the encouragement and aid to clarification provided, during the course of revision, by two historians whose concerns overlap my own: Theodore Rabb and Quentin Skinner. The version that resulted was published in French translation in *Annales* (1975), 30:975–998. A number of additional changes, mostly minor, have been introduced into the English version.

In that case, he is bound insofar as possible, to consider all scientific subject matters together, to examine what men knew about nature at each period of time, and to trace the manner in which changes in method, in philosophical climate, or in society at large have affected the body of scientific knowledge conceived as one.

Given a more nuanced description, both approaches can be recognized as long-traditional and generally noncommunicating historiographic modes.[1] The first, which treats science as, at most, a loose-linked congeries of separate sciences, is also characterized by its practitioners' insistence on examining closely the technical content, both experimental and theoretical, of past versions of the particular specialty being considered. That is a considerable merit, for the sciences are technical, and a history which neglects their content often deals with another enterprise entirely, sometimes fabricating it for the purpose. On the other hand, historians who have aimed to write the history of a technical specialty have ordinarily taken the bounds of their topic to be those prescribed by recent textbooks in the corresponding field. If, for example, their subject is electricity, then their definition of an electrical effect often closely resembles the one provided by modern physics. With it in hand, they may search ancient, medieval, and early modern sources for appropriate references, and an impressive record of gradually accumulating knowledge of nature sometimes results. But that record is drawn from scattered books and manuscripts ordinarily described as works of philosophy, literature, history, scripture, or mythology. Narratives in this genre thus characteristically obscure the fact that most items they group as "electrical"—for example, lightning, the amber effect, and the torpedo (electric eel)—were not, during the period from which their descriptions are drawn, ordinarily taken to be related. One may read them carefully without discovering that the phenomena now called "electrical" did not constitute a subject matter before the seventeenth century and without finding even scattered hints about what then brought the field into existence. If a historian must deal with enterprises that did exist in the periods that concern him, then traditional accounts of the development of individual sciences are often profoundly unhistorical.

No similar criticism may be directed at the other main historiographic tradition, the one that treats science as a single enterprise. Even if attention is restricted to a selected century or nation, the subject matter of that putative enterprise proves too vast, too dependent on technical detail, and, collectively, too diffuse to be illuminated by historical analysis. Despite ceremonial bows to classics like Newton's *Principia* or Darwin's *Origin*, historians who view science as one have therefore paid little attention to its evolving content, concentrating instead on the changing intellectual, ideological, and institutional matrix within which it developed. The technical content of modern textbooks is thus irrelevant to their subject, and the works they produce have, especially in recent decades, been fully historical and sometimes intensely illuminating. The development of scientific institutions, values, methods, and worldviews is clearly in itself a worthy subject for historical research. Experience suggests, however, that it is by no means so nearly coextensive with the study of scientific development as its practitioners have ordinarily supposed. The relationship between the metascientific environment, on the one hand, and the development of particular scientific theories and experiments, on the other, has proved to be indirect, obscure, and controversial.

To an understanding of that relationship, the tradition which takes science to be one can in principle contribute nothing, for it bars *by presupposition* access to phenomena upon which the development of such understanding must depend. Social and philosophical commitments that fostered the development of a particular field at one period of time have sometimes hampered it at another; if the period of concern is specified, then conditions that promoted advance in one science often seem to have been inimical to others.[2] Under these circumstances, historians who wish to illuminate actual scientific development will need to occupy a difficult middle ground between the two traditional alternatives. They may not, that is, assume science to be one, for it clearly is not. But neither may they take for granted the subdivisions of subject matter embodied in contemporary science texts and in the organization of contemporary university departments.

Textbooks and institutional organization are useful indices of the natural divisions the historian must seek, but they should be those of the period he studies. Together with the other materials, they can then provide at least a preliminary roster of the various fields of scientific practice at a given time. Assembling such a roster is, however, only the beginning of the historian's task, for he needs also to know something about the relations between the areas of activity it names, asking, for example, about the extent of interaction between them and the ease with which practitioners could pass from one to the next. Inquiries of that sort can gradually provide a map of the complex structure of the scientific enterprise of a selected period, and some such map is prerequisite to an examination of the complex effects of metascientific factors, whether intellectual or social, on the development of the sciences. But a structural map alone is not sufficient. To the extent that the effects to be examined vary from field to field, the historian who aims to understand them will also have to examine at least representative parts of the sometimes recondite technical activities within the field or fields that concern him. Whether in the history or the sociology of science, the list of topics that can usefully be studied without attention to the content of the relevant sciences is extremely short.

Historical research of the sort just demanded has barely begun. My conviction that its pursuit will be fruitful derives not from new work, my own or someone else's, but from repeated attempts as a teacher to synthesize the apparently incompatible products of the two noncommunicating traditions just described.[3] Inevitably, all results of that synthesis are tentative and partial, regularly straining and sometimes overstepping the limits of existing scholarship. Nevertheless, schematic presentation of one set of those results may serve both to illustrate what I have had in mind when speaking of the changing natural divisions between the sciences and also to suggest the gains which might be achieved by closer attention to them. One consequence of a more developed version of the position to be examined below could be a fundamental reformulation of an already overlong debate about the origins of modern science. Another would be the isolation of an important novelty which, during the nineteenth century, helped to produce the discipline of modern physics.

The Classical Physical Sciences

My main theme may be introduced by a question. Among the large number of topics now included in the physical sciences, which ones were already in antiquity foci for the continuing activity of specialists? The list is extremely short. Astronomy is its oldest and most developed component; during the Hellenistic period, as research in that field advanced to a previously unprecedented level, it was joined by an additional pair, geometrical optics and statics, including hydrostatics. These three subjects—astronomy, statics, and optics—are the only parts of physical science which, during antiquity, became the objects of research traditions characterized by vocabularies and techniques inaccessible to laymen and thus by bodies of literature directed exclusively to practitioners. Even today Archimedes' *Floating Bodies* and Ptolemy's *Almagest* can be read only by those with developed technical expertise. Other subjects, which, like heat and electricity, later came to be included in the physical sciences, remained throughout antiquity simply interesting classes of phenomena, subjects for passing mention or for philosophic speculation and debate. (Electrical effects, in particular, were parceled out among several such classes.) Being restricted to initiates does not, of course, guarantee scientific advance, but the three fields just mentioned did advance in ways that required the esoteric knowledge and technique responsible for their isolation. If, furthermore, the accumulation of concrete and apparently permanent problem solutions is a measure of scientific progress, these fields are the only parts of what were to become the physical sciences in which unequivocal progress was made during antiquity.

At that time, however, the three were not practiced alone but were instead intimately associated with two others—mathematics and harmonics[4]—no longer ordinarily regarded as physical sciences. Of this pair, mathematics was even older and more developed than astronomy. Dominated, from the fifth century B.C., by geometry, it was conceived as the science of real physical quantities, especially spatial, and it did much to determine the character of the four others clustered around it. Astronomy and harmonics dealt with positions and ratios, respectively, and they were thus literally mathematical. Statics and geometric optics drew concepts, diagrams, and technical vocabulary from geometry, and they shared with it also a generally logical deductive structure common to both presentation and research. Not surprisingly, under these circumstances, men like Euclid, Archimedes, and Ptolemy, who contributed to one of these subjects, almost always made significant contributions to others as well. More than developmental level thus made the five a natural cluster, setting them apart from other highly evolved ancient specialties such as anatomy and physiology. Practiced by a single group and participating in a shared mathematical tradition, astronomy, harmonics, mathematics, optics, and statics are therefore grouped together here as the classical physical sciences or, more simply, as the classical sciences.[5] Indeed, even listing them as distinct topics is to some extent anachronistic. Evidence to be encountered below will suggest that, from some significant points of view, they might better be described as a single field, mathematics.

To the unity of the classical sciences one other shared characteristic was also prerequisite, and it will play an especially important role in the balance of this paper. Though all five fields, including ancient mathematics, were empirical rather than a priori, their considerable ancient development required little refined observation and even less experiment. For a person schooled to find geometry in nature, a few relatively accessible and mostly qualitative observations of shadows, mirrors, levers, and the motions of stars and planets provided an empirical basis sufficient for the elaboration of other powerful theories. Apparent exceptions to this broad generalization (systematic astronomical observation in antiquity as well as experiments and observations on refraction and prismatic colors then and in the Middle Ages) will only reinforce its central point when examined in the next section. Although the classical sciences (including, in important respects, mathematics) were empirical, the data their development required were of a sort which everyday observation, sometimes modestly refined and systematized, could provide.[6] That is among the reasons why this cluster of fields could advance so rapidly under circumstances that did not significantly promote the evolution of a second natural group, the one to which my title refers as the products of an experimental tradition.

Before examining that second cluster, consider briefly the way in which the first developed after its origin in antiquity. All five of the classical sciences were actively pursued in Islam from the ninth century, often at a level of technical proficiency comparable with that of antiquity. Optics advanced notably, and the focus of mathematics was in some places shifted by the intrusion of algebraic techniques and concerns not ordinarily valued within the dominantly geometric Hellenistic tradition. In the Latin West, from the thirteenth century, further technical elaboration of these generally mathematical fields was subordinated to a dominantly philosophical-theological tradition, important novelty being restricted primarily to optics and statics. Significant portions of the corpus of ancient and Islamic mathematics and astronomy were, however, preserved and occasionally studied for their own sake until they became the objects of continuing erudite European research during the Renaissance.[7] The cluster of mathematical sciences then reconstituted closely resembled its Hellenistic progenitor. As these fields were practiced during the sixteenth century, however, research on a sixth topic was increasingly associated with them. Partly as a result of fourteenth-century scholastic analysis, the subject of local motion was separated from the traditional philosophic problem of general qualitative change, becoming a subject of study in its own right. Already highly developed within the ancient and medieval philosophical tradition, the problem of motion was a product of everyday observation, formulated in generally mathematical terms. It therefore fitted naturally into the cluster of mathematical sciences with which its development was thereafter firmly associated.

Thus enlarged, the classical sciences continued from the Renaissance onward to constitute a closely knit set. Copernicus specified the audience competent to judge his astronomical classic with the words, "Mathematics is written for mathematicians." Galileo, Kepler, Descartes, and Newton are only a few of the many seventeenth-century figures who moved easily and often consequentially from mathematics to astronomy, to harmonics, to statics, to optics, and to the study of motion. With the partial exception of harmonics, furthermore, the close ties between these relatively mathematical fields endured with little change into the early nineteenth century, long after the classical sciences had ceased to be the only parts of physical science subject to continuing intense scrutiny. The scientific subjects to which an Euler, Laplace, or Gauss principally contributed are almost identical with those illuminated earlier by Newton and Kepler. Very nearly the same list would encompass the work of Euclid, Archimedes, and Ptolemy as well. Like their ancient predecessors, furthermore, the men who practiced these classical sciences in the seventeenth and eighteenth centuries had, with a few notable exceptions, little of consequence to do with experimentation and refined observation even though, after about 1650, such methods were for the first time intensively employed to study another set of topics later firmly associated with parts of the classical cluster.

One last remark about the classical sciences will prepare the way for consideration of the movement that promoted new experimental methods. All but harmonics[8] were radically reconstructed during the sixteenth and seventeenth centuries, and in physical science such transformations occurred nowhere else.[9] Mathematics made the transition from geometry and "the art of the coss" to algebra, analytic geometry, and calculus; astronomy acquired noncircular orbits based on the newly central sun; the study of motion was transformed by new, fully quantitative laws; and optics gained a new theory of vision, the first acceptable solution to the classical problem of refraction, and a drastically altered theory of colors. Statics, conceived as the theory of machines, is an apparent exception. But as hydrostatics, the theory of fluids, it was extended during the seventeenth century to pneumatics, the "sea of air," and it can therefore be included in the list of reconstructed fields. These conceptual transformations of the classical sciences are the events through which the physical sciences participated in a more general revolution of Western thought. If, therefore, one thinks of the Scientific Revolution as a revolution of ideas, it is the changes in these traditional, quasi-mathematical fields which one must seek to understand. Although other vitally important things also happened to the sciences during the sixteenth and seventeenth centuries (the Scientific

Revolution was not merely a revolution in thought), they prove to be of a different, and to some extent independent, sort.

The Emergence of Baconian Sciences

Turning now to the emergence of another cluster of research fields, I again begin with a question, this time with one about which there is much confusion and disagreement in the standard historical literature. What, if anything, was new about the experimental movement of the seventeenth century? Some historians have maintained that the very idea of basing science upon information acquired through the senses was novel. Aristotle, according to this view, believed that scientific conclusions could be deduced from axiomatic first principles; not until the end of the Renaissance did men escape his authority sufficiently to study nature rather than books. These residues of seventeenth-century rhetoric are, however, absurd. Aristotle's methodological writings contain many passages which are just as insistent upon the need for close observation as the writings of Francis Bacon. Randall and Crombie have isolated and studied an important medieval methodological tradition which, from the thirteenth century into the early seventeenth, elaborated rules for drawing sound conclusions from observation and experiment.[10] Descartes' *Regulae* and Bacon's *New Organon* owe much to that tradition. An empirical *philosophy* of science was no novelty at the time of the Scientific Revolution.

Other historians point out that, whatever people may have believed about the need for observations and experiments, they made them far more frequently in the seventeenth century than they had before. That generalization is doubtless correct, but it misses the essential qualitative differences between the older forms of experiment and the new. The participants in the new experimental movement, often called Baconian after its principal publicist, did not simply expand and elaborate the empirical elements present in the tradition of classical physical science. Instead they created a different sort of empirical science, one that for a time existed side by side with, rather than supplanting, its predecessor. A brief characterization of the occasional role played in the classical sciences by experiment and systematic observation will help to isolate the qualitative differences that distinguish the older form of empirical practice from its seventeenth-century rival.

Within the ancient and medieval tradition, many experiments prove on

examination to have been "thought experiments," the construction in mind
of potential experimental situations the outcome of which could safely be
foretold from previous everyday experience. Others were performed, especially in optics, but it is often extremely difficult for the historian to
decide whether a particular experiment discovered in the literature was
mental or real. Sometimes the results reported are not what they would
be now; on other occasions the apparatus required could not have been
produced with existing materials and techniques. Real problems of historical decision result, and they also haunt students of Galileo. Surely he
did experiments, but he is even more noteworthy as the man who brought
the medieval thought-experimental tradition to its highest form. Unfortunately, it is not always clear in which guise he appears.[11]

Finally, those experiments that clearly were performed seem invariably
to have had one of two objects. Some were intended to demonstrate a
conclusion known in advance by other means. Roger Bacon writes that,
though one can in principle deduce the ability of flame to burn flesh, it
is more conclusive, given the mind's propensity for error, to place one's
hand in the fire. Other actual experiments, some of them consequential,
were intended to provide concrete answers to questions posed by existing theory. Ptolemy's experiment on the refraction of light at the boundary between air and water is an important example. Others are the medieval optical experiments that generated colors by passing sunlight through
globes filled with water. When Descartes and Newton investigated prismatic colors, they were extending this ancient and, more especially, medieval tradition. Astronomical observation displays a closely related characteristic. Before Tycho Brahe, astronomers did not systematically search
the heavens or track the planets in their motions. Instead they recorded
first risings, oppositions, and other standard planetary configurations of
which the times and positions were needed to prepare ephemerides or to
compute parameters called for by existing theory.

Contrast this empirical mode with the one for which Bacon became
the most effective proponent. When its practitioners, men like Gilbert,
Boyle, and Hooke, performed experiments, they seldom aimed to demonstrate what was already known or to determine a detail required for
the extension of existing theory. Rather they wished to see how nature
would behave under previously unobserved, often previously nonexistent, circumstances. Their typical products were the vast natural or
experimental histories in which were amassed the miscellaneous data that
many of them thought prerequisite to the construction of scientific the-

ory. Closely examined, these histories often prove less random in choice and arrangement of experiments than their authors supposed. From 1650 at the latest, the men who produced them were usually guided by one or another form of the atomic or corpuscular philosophy. Their preference was thus for experiments likely to reveal the shape, arrangement, and motion of corpuscles; the analogies which underlie their juxtaposition of particular research reports often reveal the same set of metaphysical commitments.[12] But the gap between metaphysical theory on the one hand and particular experiments on the other was initially vast. The corpuscularism which underlies much seventeenth-century experimentation seldom demanded the performance or suggested the detailed outcome of any individual experiment. Under these circumstances, experiment was highly valued and theory often decried. The interaction that did occur between them was usually unconscious.

That attitude toward the role and status of experiment is only the first of the novelties which distinguish the new experimental movement from the old. A second is the major emphasis given to experiments which Bacon himself described as "twisting the lion's tail." These were the experiments that constrained nature, exhibiting it under conditions it could never have attained with the forceful intervention of man. The men who placed grain, fish, mice, and various chemicals seriatim in the artificial vacuum of a barometer or an air pump exhibit just this aspect of the new tradition.

Reference to the barometer and air pump highlights a third novelty of the Baconian movement, perhaps the most striking of all. Before 1590 the instrumental armory of the physical sciences consisted solely of devices for astronomical observation. The next hundred years witnessed the rapid introduction and exploitation of telescopes, microscopes, thermometers, barometers, air pumps, electric charge detectors, and numerous other new experimental devices. The same period was characterized by the rapid adoption by students of nature of an arsenal of chemical apparatus previously to be found only in the workshops of practical craftsmen and the retreats of alchemical adepts. In less than a century physical science became instrumental.

These marked changes were accompanied by several others, one of which merits special mention. The Baconian experimentalists scorned thought experiments and insisted upon both accurate and circumstantial reporting. Among the results of their insistence were sometimes amusing confrontations with the older experimental tradition. Robert Boyle, for example, pilloried Pascal for a book on hydrostatics in which, though the principles were found to be unexceptionable, the copious experimental illustrations had clearly been mentally manufactured to fit. Monsieur Pascal does not tell us, Boyle complained, how a man is to sit at the bottom of a twenty-foot tub of water with a cupping glass held to his leg. Nor does he say where one is to find the superhuman craftsman able to construct the refined instruments upon which some of his other experiments depended.[13] Reading the literature of the tradition within which Boyle stands, the historian has no difficulty telling which experiments were performed. Boyle himself often names witnesses, sometimes supplying their patents of nobility.

Granting the qualitative novelty of the Baconian movement, how did its existence affect the development of science? To the conceptual transformations of the classical sciences, the contributions of Baconianism were very small. Some experiments did play a role, but they all have deep roots in the older tradition. The prism Newton purchased to examine "the celebrated phenomena of colors" descends from medieval experiments with water-filled globes. The inclined plane is borrowed from the classical study of simply machines. The pendulum, though literally a novelty, is first and foremost a new physical embodiment of a problem the medieval impetus theorists had considered in connection with the oscillatory motion of a vibrating string or of a body falling through the center of the earth and then back toward it. The barometer was first conceived and analyzed as a hydrostatic device, a water-filled pumpshaft without leaks designed to realize the thought experiment with which Galileo had "demonstrated" the limits to nature's abhorrence of a vacuum.[14] Only after an extended vacuum had been produced and the variation of column height with weather and altitude had been demonstrated did the barometer and its child the air pump join the cabinet of Baconian instruments.

Equally to the point, although the experiments just mentioned were of consequence, there are few like them, and all owe their special effectiveness to the closeness with which they could confront the evolving theories of classical science, which had called them forth. The outcome of Torricelli's barometer experiment and of Galileo's with the inclined plane had been largely foreseen. Newton's prism experiment would have been no more effective than its traditional predecessors in transforming the theory of colors if Newton had not had access to the newly discovered law of refraction, a law sought within the classical tradition from Ptolemy to Kepler. For the same reason, the consequences of that experiment contrast markedly with those of the nontraditional experiments that during the seventeenth century revealed qualitatively novel optical effects like interference, diffraction, and polarization. The latter, because they were not products of classical science and could not be closely juxtaposed with its theories, had little bearing on the development of optics until the early nineteenth century. After all due qualification, some of it badly needed, Alexandre Koyré and Herbert Butterfield will prove to have been right. The transformation of the classical sciences during the Scientific Revolution is more accurately ascribed to new ways of looking at old phenomena than to a series of unanticipated experimental discoveries.[15]

Under those circumstances, numerous historians, Koryé included, have described the Baconian movement as a fraud, of no consequence to the development of science. That evaluation is, however, like the one it sometimes stridently opposed, a product of seeing the sciences as one. If Baconianism contributed little to the development of the classical sciences, it did give rise to a large number of new scientific fields, often with their roots in prior crafts. The study of magnetism, which derived its early data from prior experience with the mariner's compass, is a case in point. Electricity was spawned by efforts to find the relation of the magnet's attraction for iron to that of rubbed amber for chaff. Both these fields, furthermore, were dependent for their subsequent development upon the elaboration of new, more powerful, and more refined instruments. They are typical new Baconian sciences. Very nearly the same generalization applies to the study of heat. Long a topic for speculation within the philosophical and medical traditions, it was transformed into a subject for systematic investigation by the invention of the thermometer. Chemistry presents a case of a different and far more complex sort. Many of its main instruments, reagents, and techniques had been developed long before the Scientific Revolution. But until the late sixteenth century they were primarily the property of craftsmen, pharmacists, and alchemists. Only after a reevaluation of the crafts and of manipulative techniques were they regularly deployed in the experimental search for natural knowledge.

Since these fields and others like them were new foci for scientific activity in the seventeenth century, it is not surprising that their pursuit at first produced few transformations more striking than the repeated discovery of previously unknown experimental effects. If the possession of a body of consistent theory capable of producing refined predictions is the mark of a developed scientific field, the Baconian sciences remained underdeveloped throughout the seventeenth and much of the eighteenth centuries. Both their research literature and their patterns of growth were less like those of the contemporary classical sciences than like those discoverable in a number of the social sciences today. By the middle of the eighteenth century, however, experiment in these fields had become more systematic, increasingly clustering about selected sets of phenomena thought to be especially revealing. In chemistry, the study of displacement reactions and of saturation were among the newly prominent topics; in electricity, the study of conduction and of the Leyden jar; in thermometry and heat, the study of the temperature of mixtures. Simultaneously, corpuscular and other concepts were increasingly adapted to these particular areas of experimental research, the notions of chemical affinity or of electric fluids and their atmospheres providing particularly well-known examples.

The theories in which concepts like these functioned remained for some time predominantly qualitative and often correspondingly vague, but they could nonetheless be confronted by individual experiments with a precision unknown in the Baconian sciences when the eighteenth century began. Furthermore, as the refinements that permitted such confrontations continued into the last third of the century and became increasingly the center of the corresponding fields, the Baconian sciences rapidly achieved a state very like that of the classical sciences in antiquity. Electricity and magnetism became developed sciences with the work of Aepinus, Cavendish, and Coulomb; heat with that of Black, Wilcke, and Lavoisier; chemistry more gradually and equivocally, but not later than the time of Lavoisier's chemical revolution. At the beginning of the following century the qualitatively novel optical discoveries of the seventeenth century were for the first time assimilated to the older science of optics. With the occurrence of events like these, Baconian science had at last come of age, vindicating the faith, though not always the methodology, of its seventeenth-century founders.

How, during the almost two centiries of maturation, did the cluster of Baconian sciences relate to the cluster here called "classical"? The question has been far too little studied, but the answer, I think, will prove to be: not a great deal and then often with considerable difficulty—intellectual, institutional, and sometimes political. Into the nineteenth century the two clusters, classical and Baconian, remained distinct. Crudely put, the classical sciences were grouped together as "mathematics"; the Baconian were generally viewed as "experimental philosophy" or, in France, as *"physique expérimentale"*; chemistry, with its continuing ties to pharmacy, medicine, and the various crafts, was in part a member of the latter group, and in part a congeries of more practical specialties.[16]

This separation between the classical and Baconian sciences can be traced from the origin of the latter. Bacon himself was distrustful, not only of mathematics, but of the entire quasi-deductive structure of classical science. Those critics who ridicule him for failing to recognize the best science of his day have missed the point. He did not reject Copernicanism because he preferred the Ptolemaic system. Rather, he rejected both because he thought that no system so complex, abstract, and mathematical could contribute to either the understanding or the control of nature. His followers in the experimental tradition, though they accepted Copernican cosmology, seldom even attempted to acquire the mathematical skill and sophistication required to understand or pursue the classical sciences. This situation endured through the eighteenth century: Franklin, Black, and Nollet display it as clearly as Boyle and Hooke.

Its converse is far more equivocal. Whatever the causes of the Baconian movement, they impinged also on the previously established classical sciences. New instruments entered those fields, too, especially astronomy. Standards for reporting and evaluating data changed as well. By the last decade of the seventeenth century confrontations like that between Boyle and Pascal are no longer imaginable. But, as previously indicated, the effect of these developments was a gradual refinement rather than a substantial change in the nature of the classical sciences. Astronomy had been instrumental and optics experimental before; the relative merits of quantitative telescopic and naked-eye observation were in doubt throughout the seventeenth century; excepting the pendulum, the instruments of mechanics were predominantly tools for pedagogic demonstration rather than for research. Under these circumstances, though the ideological gap between the Baconian and classical sciences narrowed, it by no means disappeared. Through the eighteenth century, the main practitioners of the established mathematical sciences performed few experiments and made fewer substantive contributions to the development of the new experimental fields.

Galileo and Newton are apparent exceptions. But only the latter is a real one, and both illuminate the nature of the classical-Baconian split. A proud member of the Lincei, Galileo was also a developer of the telescope, the pendulum escapement, an early form of thermometer, and other new instruments besides. Clearly he participated significantly in aspects of the movement here called Baconian. But, as Leonardo's career also indicates, instrumental and engineering concerns do not make a man an experimentalist, and Galileo's dominant attitude toward that aspect of science remained within the classical mode. On some occasions he proclaimed that the power of his mind made it unnecessary for him to perform the experiments he described. On others, for example when considering the limitations of water pumps, he resorted without comment to apparatus that transcended the capacity of existing technology. Boyle's critique of Pascal applies to Galileo without change. It isolates a figure who could and did make epochal contributions to the classical sciences but not, except through instrumental design, to the Baconian.

Educated during the years when British Baconianism was at its height, Newton did participate unequivocally in both traditions. But, as I. B. Cohen emphasized two decades ago, what results are two distinct lines of Newtonian influence, one traceable to Newton's *Principia,* the other to his *Opticks.*[17] That insight gains special significance if one notes that, though the *Principia* lies squarely within the tradition of the classical sciences, the *Opticks* is by no means unequivocally in the Baconian. Because his subject was optics, a previously well-developed field, Newton was able constantly to juxtapose selected experiments with theory, and it is from those juxtapositions that his achievements result. Boyle, whose *Experimental History of Colours* includes several of the experiments on which Newton founded his theory, made no such attempt, contenting himself with the remark that his results suggested speculations that might be worth pursuing.[18] Hooke, who discovered "Newton's rings," the first subject of the *Opticks,* book 2, accumulated data in much the same way. Newton, instead, selected and utilized them to elaborate theory, very much as his predecessors in the classical tradition had used the less recondite information usually provided by everyday experience. Even when he turned, as in the "Queries" to his *Opticks,* to such new Baconian topics as chemistry, electricity, and heat, Newton chose from the growing experimental literature those particular observations and experiments that could illuminate theoretical issues. Though no achievements so profound as those in optics could have been forthcoming in these still emerging fields, concepts like chemical affinity, scattered through the "Queries," proved a rich source for the more systematic and selective Baconian practitioners of the eighteenth century, and they therefore returned to them again and again. What they found in the *Opticks* and its "Queries" was a non-Baconian use of Baconian experiment, a product of Newton's deep and simultaneous immersion in the classical scientific tradition.

With the partial exception, however, of his continental contemporaries, Huyghens and Mariotte, Newton's example is unique. During the eighteenth century, by the beginning of which his scientific work was complete, no one else participated significantly in both traditions, a situation reflected also by the development of scientific institutions and career lines, at least into the nineteenth century. Although much additional research in this area is needed, the following remarks will suggest the gross pattern which research is likely to refine. At least at the elementary level, the classical sciences had established themselves in the standard curriculum of the medieval university. During the seventeenth and eighteenth centuries the number of chairs devoted to them increased. The men who held them, together with those appointed to positions in the newly founded national scientific academies of France, Prussia, and Russia, were the principal contributors to the developing classical sciences. None of them is properly described as an amateur, though the term has often been applied indiscriminately to the practitioners of seventeenth- and eighteenth-century science as a whole. Practitioners of Baconian science were, however, usually amateurs, excepting only chemists, who found careers in pharmacy, industry, and some medical schools during the eighteenth century. For other experimental sciences the universities had no place before the last half of the nineteenth. Although some of their practitioners did receive positions in the various national scientific academies, they were there often second-class citizens. Only in England, where the classical sciences had begun to decline markedly before Newton's death, were they well represented, a contrast to be further developed below.

The example of the French Academy of Sciences is instructive in this respect, and its examination will simultaneously provide background for a point to be discussed in the next section. Guillaume Amontons (1663–1705), well known for his contributions to both the design and theory of such Baconian instruments as the thermometer and hygrometer, never rose in the academy beyond the status of *élève*, in which capacity he was attached to the astronomer Jean Le Fèver. Pierre Polinière (1671–1734), often cited as the man who introduced *physique exérimentale* to France, was never formally associated with the academy at all. Although the two main French contributors to eighteenth-century electrical sciences were academicians, the first, C. F. de C. Dufay (1698–1739), was placed in the chemistry section, while the second, the Abbé Nollet (1700–1770), was a member of the somewhat motley section officially reserved for practitioners of *arts mécaniques*. There, but only after his election to the

Royal Society of London, Nollet rose through the ranks, succeeding among others, both the Comte de Buffon and Ferchauld de Réaumur. The famous instrument maker Abraham Bréguet, on the other hand, a man with the sorts of talents for which the mechanics section had been designed, found no place in the academy until, in 1816 at age sixty-nine, his name was inscribed on its rolls by royal ordinance.

What these isolated cases suggest is indicated also by the academy's formal organization. A section for *physique expérimentale* was not introduced until 1785, and it was then grouped in the mathematical division (with geometry, astronomy, and mechanics) rather than in the division for the more manipulative sciences physiques (anatomy, chemistry and metallurgy, botany and agriculture, and natural history and mineralogy). After 1815, when the new section's name was changed to *physique générale,* the experimentalists among its members were for some time very few. Looking at the eighteenth century as a whole, the contributions of academicians to the Baconian physical sciences were minor compared with those of doctors, pharmacists, industrialists, instrument makers, itinerant lecturers, and men of independent means. Again the exception is England, where the Royal Society was largely populated by such amateurs, rather than by men whose careers were first and foremost in the sciences.

The Origins of Modern Science

Return now briefly from the end of the eighteenth century to the middle of the seventeenth. The Baconian sciences were then in gestation, the classical being radically transformed. Together with concomitant changes in the life sciences, these two sets of events constitute what has come to be called the Scientific Revolution. Although no part of this essay purports to explain its extraordinarily complex causes, it is worth noting how different the question of causes becomes when the developments to be explained are subdivided.

That only the classical sciences were transformed during the Scientific Revolution is not surprising. Other fields of physical science scarcely existed until late in the period. To the extent that they did, furthermore, they lacked any significant body of unified technical doctrine to reconstruct. Conversely, one set of reasons for the transformation of the classical sciences lies within their own previous lines of development. Although historians differ greatly about the weight to be attached to them, few now doubt that some medieval reformulations of ancient doctrine, Islamic or Latin, were of major significance to figures like Copernicus, Galileo, and Kepler. No similar scholastic roots for the Baconian sciences are visible to me, despite the claims sometimes made for the methodological tradition that descends from Grosseteste.

Many of the other factors now frequently invoked to explain the Scientific Revolution did contribute to the evolution of both classical and Baconian sciences, but often in different ways and to different degrees. The effects of new intellectual ingredients—initially Hermetic and then corpuscular-mechanical—in the environment where early modern science was practiced provide a first example of such differences. Within the classical sciences, Hermetic movements sometimes promoted the status of mathematics, encouraged attempts to find mathematical regularities in nature, and occasionally licensed the simple mathematical forms thus discovered as formal causes, the terminus of the scientific causal chain.[19] Both Galileo and Kepler provide examples of this increasingly ontological role of mathematics, and the latter displays a second, more occult, Hermetic influence as well. From Kepler and Gilbert to Newton, though by then in an attenuated form, the natural sympathies and antipathies prominent in Hermetic thought helped to fill the void created by the collapse of the Aristotelian spheres that had previously kept the planets in their orbits.

After the first third of the seventeenth century, when Hermetic mysticism was increasingly rejected, its place, still in the classical sciences, was rapidly taken by one or another form of corpuscular philosophy derived from ancient atomism. Forces of attraction and repulsion between either gross or microscopic bodies were no longer favored, a source of much opposition to Newton. But within the infinite universe demanded by corpuscularism, there could be no preferred centers or directions. Natural enduring motions could only occur in straight lines and could only be disturbed by intercorpuscular collisions. From Descartes on, that new perspective leads directly to Newton's first law of motion and—through the study of collisions, a new problem—to his second law as well. One factor in the transformation of the classical sciences was clearly the new intellectual climate, first Hermetic and then corpuscular, within which they were practiced after 1500.

The same new intellectual milieus affected the Baconian sciences, but often for other reasons and in different ways. Doubtless, the Hermetic emphasis on occult sympathies helps to account for the growing interest in magnetism and electricity after 1550; similar influences promoted the status of chemistry from the time of Paracelsus to that of van Helmont. But current research increasingly suggests that the major contribution of Hermeticism to the Baconian sciences and perhaps to the entire Scientific Revolution was the Faustian figure of the magus, concerned to manipulate and control nature, often with the aid of ingenious contrivances, instruments, and machines. Recognizing Francis Bacon as a transition figure between the magus Paracelsus and the experimental philosopher Robert Boyle has done more than anything else in recent years to transform historical understanding of the manner in which the new experimental sciences were born.[20]

For these Baconian fields, unlike their classical contemporaries, the effects of the transition to corpuscularism were equivocal, a first reason why Hermeticism endured longer in subjects like chemistry and magnetism than in, say, astronomy and mechanics. To declare that sugar is sweet because its round particles soothe the tongue is not obviously an advance on attributing to it a saccharine potency. Eighteenth-century experience was to demonstrate that the development of Baconian sciences often required guidance from concepts like affinity and phlogiston, not categorically unlike the natural sympathies and antipathies of the Hermetic movement. But corpuscularism did separate the experimental sciences from magic, thus promoting needed independence. Even more important, it provided a rationale for experiment, as no form of Aristotelianism or Platonism could have done. While the tradition governing scientific explanation demanded the specification of formal causes or essences, only data provided by the natural course of events could be relevant to it. To experiment or to constrain nature was to do it violence, thus hiding the role of the "natures" or forms which made things what they were. In a corpuscular universe, on the other hand, experimentation had an obvious relevance to the sciences. It could not change and might specially illuminate the mechanical conditions and laws from which natural phenomena followed. That was the lesson Bacon attached repeatedly to the fable of Cupid in chains.

A new intellectual milieu was not, of course, the sole cause of the Scientific Revolution, and the other factors most often invoked in its explanation also gain cogency when examined separately in classical and Baconian fields. During the Renaissance the medieval university's monopoly on learning was gradually broken. New sources of wealth, new ways of life, and new values combined to promote the status of a group formerly classified as artisans and craftsmen. The invention of printing and the recovery of additional ancient sources gave its members access to a scientific and technological heritage previously available, if at all, only within the clerical university setting. One result, epitomized in the careers of Brunelleschi and Leonardo, was the emergence from craft guilds during the fifteenth and sixteenth centuries of the artist-engineers whose expertise included painting, sculpture, architecture, fortification, water supply, and the design of engines of war and construction. Supported by an increasingly elaborate system of patronage, these men were at once employees and increasingly also ornaments of Renaissance courts and later sometimes of the city governments of northern Europe. Some of them were also informally associated with humanist circles, which introduced them to Hermetic and Neoplatonic sources. Those sources were not, however, what primarily legitimated their status as participants in a newly polite learning. Rather it was their ability to invoke and comment cogently upon such works as Vitruvius's *De architectura,* Euclid's *Geometry and Optics,* the pseudo-Aristotelian *Mechanical Problems,* and, after the mid-sixteenth century, both Archimedes' *Floating Bodies* and Hero's *Pneumatica.*[21]

The importance of this new group to the scientific revolution is indisputable. Galileo, in numerous respects, and Simon Stevin, in all, are among its products. What requires emphasis, however, is that the sources its members used and the fields they primarily influenced belong to the cluster here called classical. Whether as artists (perspective) or as engineers (construction and water supply), they mainly exploited works on mathematics, statics, and optics. Astronomy, too, occasionally entered their purview, though to a lesser extent. One of Vitruvius' concerns had been the design of precise sundials; the Renaissance artist-engineers sometimes extended it to the design of other astronomical instruments as well.

Although only here and there seminal, the concern of the artist-engineers with these classical fields was a significant factor in their reconstruction. It is probably the source of Brahe's new instruments and certainly of Galileo's concern with the strength of materials and the limited power of water pumps, the latter leading directly to Torricelli's barometer. Plausibly, but more controversially, engineering concerns, promoted especially by gunnery, helped to separate the problem of local motion from the larger philosophical problem of change, simultaneously making numbers rather than geometric proportions relevant to its further pursuit. These and related subjects are the ones that led to the inclusion of a section of arts mécaniques in the French academy and that caused that section to be grouped with the sections for geometry and astronomy. That it there-after provided no natural home for the Baconian sciences finds its coun-terpart in the concerns of the Renaissance artist-engineers, which did not include the nonmechanical, nonmathematical aspects of such crafts as dyeing, weaving, glass-making, and navigation. These were, however, precisely the crafts that played so large a role in the genesis of the new experimental sciences. Bacon's programmatic statements called for natu-ral histories of them all, and some of those histories of nonmechanical crafts were written.

Because the possible utility of even an analytic separation between the mechanical and nonmechanical crafts has not previously been suggested, what follows must be even more tentative than what precedes. As sub-jects for learned concern, however, the latter appear to have arrived later than the former. Presumably promoted at the start by Paracelsan atti-tudes, their establishment is demonstrated in such works as Biringuccio's *Pyrotechnia,* Agricola's *De re metallica,* Robert Norman's *Newe Attractive,* and Bernard Palissy's *Discours,* the earliest published in 1540. The status previously achieved by the mechanical arts doubtless helps to explain the appearance of books like these, but the movement which produced them is nevertheless distinct. Few practitioners of the nonmechanical crafts were supported by patronage or succeeded before the late seventeenth century in escaping the confines of craft guilds. None could appeal to a signifi-cant classical literary tradition, a fact that probably made the pseudoclas-sical Hermetic literature and the figure of the magus more important to them than to their contemporaries in the mathematical-mechanical fields.[22] Except in chemistry, among pharmacists and doctors, actual practice was seldom combined with learned discourse about it. Doctors do, however, figure in disproportionate numbers among those who wrote learned works not only on chemistry but also on the other nonmechanical crafts which provided data required for the development of the Baconian sciences. Agricola and Gilbert are only the earliest examples.

These differences between the two traditions rooted in prior crafts may help to explain still another. Although the Renaissance artist-engineers were socially useful, knew it, and sometimes based their claims upon it, the utilitarian elements in their writings are far less persistent and strident than those in the writings of men who drew upon the nonmechanical crafts. Remember how little Leonardo cared whether or not the mechan-ical contrivances he invented could actually be built; or compare the writ-ings of Galileo, Pascal, Descartes, and Newton with those of Bacon, Boyle, and Hooke. Present in both sets of writings, utilitarianism is central only to the second, a fact that may provide a clue to a last major difference between the classical and the Baconian sciences.

Excepting chemistry, which had found a variegated institutional base by the end of the seventeenth century, the Baconian and classical sciences flourished in different national settings from at least 1700. Practitioners of both can be found in most European countries, but the center for the Baconian sciences was clearly Britain, for the mathematical the Continent, especially France. Newton is the last British mathematician before the mid-nineteenth century who can compare with continental figures like the Bernoullis, Euler, Lagrange, Laplace, and Gauss. In the Baconian sciences, the contrast begins earlier and is less clear-cut, but continental experimentalists with reputations to rival those of Boyle, Hooke, Hauksbee, Gray, Hales, Black, and Priestley are difficult to find before the 1780s. Furthermore, those who first come to mind tend to cluster in Holland and Switzerland, especially the former. Boerhaave, Musschenbroek, and de Saussure, all provide examples.[23] That geographical pattern needs more systematic investigation, but, if account is taken of relative populations and, especially, of relative productivity in the Baconian and classical sciences, it is likely to prove striking. Such investigation may also show that the national differences just sketched emerged only after the mid-seventeenth century, becoming slowly more striking during the generations that followed. Are not the differences between the eighteenth-century activities of the French Academy of Sciences and the Royal Society greater than those between the activities of the Accademia del Cimento, the Montmor Academy, and the British "Invisible College"?

Among the numerous competing explanations of the Scientific Revolution, only one provides clue to this pattern of geographical divergences. It is the so-called Merton thesis, a redevelopment for the sciences of explanations for the emergence of capitalism provided earlier by Weber, Troeltsch, and Tawney.[24] After their initial evangelical proselytizing phases, it is claimed, settled Puritan or Protestant communities provided an "ethos" or "ethic" especially congenial to the development of science. Among its primary components were a strong utilitarian strain, a high valuation of work, including manual and manipulative work, and a distrust of system which encouraged each man to be his own interpreter first of Scripture and then of nature. Leaving aside, as others may not, the difficulties of identifying such an ethos and of determining whether it may be ascribed to all Protestant or only to certain Puritan sects, the main drawbacks of this viewpoint have always been that it attempts to explain too much. If Bacon, Boyle, and Hooke seem to fit the Merton thesis, Galileo, Descartes, and Huyghens do not. It is in any case far from clear that postevangelical Puritan or Protestant communities existed anywhere until the Scientific Revolution had been under way for some time. Not surprisingly the Merton thesis has been controversial.

Its appeal is, however, vastly larger if it is applied not to the Scientific Revolution as a whole, but rather to the movement which advanced the Baconian sciences. That movement's initial impetus toward power over nature through manipulative and instrumental techniques was doubtless supported by Hermeticism. But the corpuscular philosophies, which in the sciences increasingly replaced Hermeticism after the 1630s, carried no similar values, and Baconianism continued to flourish. That it did so especially in non-Catholic countries suggests that it may yet be worth discovering what, with respect to the sciences, a "Puritan" and an "ethos" are. Two isolated bits of biographical information may make that problem especially intriguing. Denis Papin, who built Boyle's second air pump and invented the pressure cooker, was a Huguenot driven from France by the mid-seventeenth-century persecutions. Abraham Bréguet, the instrument maker forced on the French Academy of Sciences in 1816, was an immigrant from Neuchâtel, to which his family had fled after the revocation of the Edict of Nantes.

The Genesis of Modern Physics

My final topic must be presented as an epilogue, a tentative sketch of a position to be developed and modified by further research. But, having traced the generally separate development of the classical and Baconian sciences into the late eighteenth century, I must at least ask what happened next. Anyone acquainted with the contemporary scientific scene will recognize that the physical sciences no longer fit the pattern sketched above, a fact that has made the pattern itself difficult to see. When and how did the change occur? What was its nature?

Part of the answer is that the physical sciences during the nineteenth century participated in the rapid growth and transformation experienced by all learned professions. Older fields like medicine and law gained new institutional forms, more rigid and with intellectual standards more exclusive than any they had known before. In the sciences, from the late eighteenth century, the number of journals and societies increased rapidly, and many of them, unlike the traditional national academies and their publications, were restricted to individual scientific fields. Long-standing disciplines like mathematics and astronomy became for the first time professions with their own institutional forms.[25] Similar phenomena occurred only slightly more slowly in the newer Baconian fields, and one result was a loosening of ties which had previously bound them together. Chemistry, in particular, had by midcentury at the latest became a separate intellectual profession, still with ties to industry and to other experimental fields but with an identity now distinct from either. Partly for those institutional reasons and partly because of the effect on chemical research, first, of Dalton's atomic theory and, then, of increased attention to organic compounds, chemical concepts rapidly diverged from those used elsewhere in the physical sciences. As this occurred, topics like heat and electricity were increasingly barred from chemistry and left to experimental philosophy or to a new field, physics, that was increasingly taking its place.

A second important source of change during the nineteenth century was a gradual shift in the perceived identity of mathematics. Until perhaps the middle of the century such topics as celestial mechanics, hydrodynamics, elasticity, and the vibrations of continuous and discontinuous media were at the center of professional mathematical research. Seventy-five years later, they had become "applied mathematics," a concern separate from and usually of lower status than the more abstract questions of "pure mathematics" which had become central to the discipline. Through courses in topics like celestial mechanics or even electromagnetic faculties, they had become service courses, their subjects no longer on the frontier of mathematical thought.[26] The resulting separation between research in mathematics and in the physical sciences urgently needs more study, both for itself and for its effect on the development of the latter. That is doubly the case because it occurred in different ways and at different rates in different countries, a factor in the development of the additional national differences to be discussed below.

A third variety of change, especially relevant to the topics considered in this essay, was the remarkably rapid and full mathematization of a number of Baconian fields during the first quarter of the nineteenth century. Among the topics that now constitute the subject matter of physics, only mechanics and hydrodynamics had demanded advanced mathematical skills before 1800. Elsewhere the elements of geometry, trigonometry, and algebra were entirely sufficient. Twenty years later, the work of Laplace, Fourier, and Sadi Carnot had made higher mathematics essential to the study of heat; Poisson and Ampère had done the same for electricity and magnetism; and Jean Fresnel, with his immediate followers, had had a similar effect on the field of optics. Only as their new mathematical theories were accepted as models did a profession with an identity like that of modern physics become one of the sciences. Its emergence demanded a lowering of the barriers, both conceptual and institutional, that had previously separated the classical and Baconian fields.

Why those barriers were lowered when and as they were is a problem demanding much additional research. But a major part of the answer will doubtless lie in the internal development of the relevant fields during the eighteenth century. The qualitative theories so rapidly mathematized after 1800 had come into existence only during and after the 1780s. Fourier's theory demanded the concept of specific heat and the consequent systematic separation of notions of heat and temperature. The contributions of Laplace and Carnot to thermal theory required in addition the recognition at the end of the century of adiabatic heating. Poisson's pioneering mathematization of static electrical and magnetic theory was made possible by the prior work of Coulomb, most of which appeared only in the 1790s.[27] Ampère's mathematization of the interaction between electric currents was supplied almost simultaneously with his discovery of the effects that his theory treated. Especially for the mathematization of electrical and thermal theory, recent developments in mathematical technique also played a role. Except perhaps in optics, the papers which between 1800 and 1825 made previously experimental fields fully mathematical could not have been written two decades before the burst of mathematization began.

Internal development, primarily of Baconian fields, will not, however, explain the manner in which mathematics was introduced after 1800. As the names of the authors of the new theories will already have suggested, the first mathematizers were uniformly French. Excepting in some initially little known papers by George Green and Gauss, nothing of the same sort occurred elsewhere before the 1840s, when the British and Germans began belatedly to adopt and adapt the example set by the French a generation before. Probably institutional and individual factors will prove primarily responsible for that early French leadership. Beginning very slowly in the 1760s, with the appointments of Nollet and then of Monge to teach *physique expérimentale* at the *Ecole de génie* at Mézières, Baconian subjects increasingly penetrated the education of French military engineers.[28] That movement culminated in the establishment during the 1790s of the *Ecole polytechnique,* a new sort of educational institution at which students were exposed not only to the classical subjects relevant to the *arts mécaniques* but also to chemistry, the study of heat, and other related subjects. It can be no accident that all of those who produced mathematical theories of previously experimental fields were either teachers or students at the *Ecole polytechnique.* Also of great importance to the direction taken by their work was the magistral leadership of Laplace in extending Newtonian mathematical physics to nonmathematical subjects.[29]

For reasons that are currently both obscure and controversial, the practice of the new mathematical physics declined rapidly in France after about 1830. In part it participated in a general decline in the vitality of French science, but an even more important role was probably played by a reassertion of the traditional primacy of mathematics, itself after midcentury moving further away from the concrete concerns of physics. As physics after 1850 became mathematical in all its parts, remaining nonetheless dependent on refined experiment, French contributions for a century declined to a level unmatched in such previously comparable fields as chemistry and mathematics.[30] Physics required, as other sciences did not, the establishment of a firm bridge across the classical-Baconian divide.

What had begun in France during the first quarter of the nineteenth century had, therefore, later to be re-created elsewhere, initially in Germany and Britain after the mid-1840s. In both countries, as might by now be expected, existing institutional forms at first inhibited the cultivation of a field dependent upon easy communication between practitioners skilled in experiment on the one hand and mathematics on the other. Part of Germany's quite special success—attested by the preponderant role of Germans in the twentieth-century conceptual transformations of physics—must be due to the rapid growth and consequent plasticity of German educational institutions during the years when men like Neumann, Weber, Helmholtz, and Kirchhoff were creating a new discipline in which both experimentalists and mathematical theorists would be associated as practitioners of physics.[31]

During the first decades of this century that German model increasingly spread to the rest of the world. As it did so, the long-standing division between the mathematical and the experimental physical sciences was more and more obscured and may even seem to have disappeared. But, from another viewpoint, it is perhaps more accurately described as having been displaced—from a position between separate fields to the interior of physics itself, a location from which it continues to provide a source of both individual and professional tensions. It is only, I suggest, because physical theory is now everywhere mathematical that theoretical and experimental physics appear as enterprises so different that almost no one can hope to achieve eminence in both. No such dichotomy between experiment and theory has characterized fields like chemistry or biology in which theory is less intrinsically mathematical. Perhaps, therefore, the cleavage between mathematical and experimental science still remains, rooted in the nature of the human mind.[32]

NOTES

1. For a somewhat more extended discussion of these two approaches, see Thomas S. Kuhn, "History of Science" in the *International Encyclopedia of the Social Sciences,* vol. 14 (New York: Macmillan, 1968), pp. 74–83. Note also the way in which distinguishing between them both deepens and obscures the now far better known distinction between internalist and externalist approaches to the history of science. Virtually all the authors now regarded as internalists fall amost invariably into the group that has treated the sciences as one. But the labels "internalist" and "externalist" then no longer quite fit. Those who have concentrated primarily on individual sciences, e.g., Alexandre Koyré, have not hesitated to attribute a significant role in scientific development to extrascientific *ideas*. What they have resisted primarily is attention to socioeconomic and institutional factors as treated by such writers as B. Hessen, G. N. Clark, and R. K. Merton. But these nonintellectual factors have not always been much valued by those who took the sciences to be one. The "internalist-externalist debate" is thus frequently about issues different from the ones its name suggests, and the resulting confusion is sometimes damaging.

2. On this point, in addition to the material below, see Thomas S. Kuhn, "Scientific Growth: Reflections on Ben-David's 'Scientific Role,' " *Minerva* (1972), 10:166–178.

3. Those problems of synthesis go back to the very beginning of my career, at which time they took two forms which initially seemed entirely distinct. The first, sketched in note 2, above, was how to make socioeconomic concerns relevant to narratives about the development of scientific ideas. The second, highlighted by the appearance of Herbert Butterfield's admirable and influential *Origins of Modern Science* (London: Macmillan 1949), concerned the role of experimental method in the Scientific Revolution of the seventeenth century. Butterfield's first four chapters plausibly explained the main conceptual transformations of early modern science as "brought about, not by new observations or additional evidence in the first instance, but by transpositions that were taking place inside the minds of the scientists themselves . . . [by their] putting on a different kind of thinking-cap" (p. 1). The next two chapters, "The Experimental Method in the Seventeenth Century" and "Bacon and Descartes," provided more traditional accounts of their subjects. Although they seemed obviously relevant to scientific development, the chapters which dealt with them contained little material actually put to work elsewhere in the book. One reason they did not, I belatedly recognized, was that Butterfield attempted, especially in his chapter "The Postponed Scientific Revolution in Chemistry," to assimilate the conceptual transformations in eighteenth-century science to the same model (not new observations but a new thinking-cap) which had succeeded so brilliantly for the seventeenth.

4. Henry Guerlac first urged on me the necessity of including music theory in the cluster of classical sciences. That I should initially have omitted a field no longer conceived as science indicates how easy it is to miss the force of the methodological precept offered in my opening pages. Harmonics was not, however, quite the field we would now call music theory. Instead, it was a mathematical science that attributed numerical proportions to the numerous intervals of various Greek scales or modes. Since there were seven of these, each available in three genera and in fifteen tonoi or keys, the discipline was complex, specification of some intervals requiring four- and five-digit numbers. Since only the simplest intervals were empirically accessible as the ratios of the lengths of vibrating strings, harmonics was also a highly abstract subject. Its relation to musical practice was at best indirect, and it remains obscure. Historically, harmonics dates from the fifth century B.C. and was highly developed by the time of Plato and Aristotle. Euclid is among the numerous figures who wrote treatises about it and whose work was largely superseded by Ptolemy's, a phenomenon familiar also in other fields. For these descriptive remarks and those in note 8, below, I am largely indebted to several illuminating conversations with Noel Swerdlow. Before they occurred, I had felt incapable of following Guerlac's advice.

5. The abbreviation "classical sciences" is a possible source of confusion, for anatomy and physiology were also highly developed sciences in classical antiquity, and they share a few, but by no means all, of the developmental characteristics here attributed to the classical physical sciences. These biomedical sciences were, however, parts of a second classical cluster, practiced by a distinct group of people, most of them closely associated with medicine and medical institutions. Because of these and other differences, the two clusters may not be treated together, and I restrict myself here to the physical science, partly on grounds of competence and partly to avoid excessive complexity. See, however, notes 6 and 9, below.

6. Elaborate or refined data generally become available only when their collection fulfills some perceived social function. That anatomy and physiology, which require such data, were highly developed in antiquity must be a consequence of their apparent relevance to medicine. That even that relevance was often hotly disputed (by the Empirics!) should help to account for the relative paucity, except in Aristotle and Theophrastus, of ancient data applicable to the more general taxonomic, comparative, and developmental concerns basic to the life sciences from the sixteenth century. Of the classical physical sciences, only astronomy required data of apparent social use (calendars and, from the second century B.C., horoscopy). If the others had depended upon the availability of refined data, they would probably have advanced no further than the study of topics such as heat.

7. This paragraph has considerably benefited from discussions with John Murdoch, who emphasizes the historiographic problems encountered if the classical sciences are conceived of as continuing research traditions in the Latin Middle Ages. On this topic see his "Philosophy and the Enterprise of Science in the Later Middle Ages," in Y. Elkana, ed., *The Interaction Between Science and Philosophy* (New York: Humanities Press, 1974), pp. 51–74.

8. Although harmonics was not transformed, its status declined greatly from

the late fifteenth to the early eighteenth century. More and more it was relegated to the first section of treatises directed primarily to more practical subjects: composition, temperament, and instrument construction. As these subjects became more and more central to even quite theoretical treatises, music was increasingly divorced from the classical sciences. But the separation came late and was never complete. Kepler, Mersenne, and Descartes, all wrote on harmonics; Galileo, Huyghens, and Newton displayed interest in it; Euler's *Tentamen novae theoriae musicae* is in a longstanding tradition. After its publication in 1739, harmonics ceased to figure for its own sake in the research of major scientists, but an initially related field had already taken its place: the study, both theoretical and experimental, of vibrating strings, oscillating air columns, and acoustics in general. The career of Joseph Sauveur (1653–1716) clearly illustrates the transition from harmonics as music to harmonics as acoustics.

9. They did, of course, occur in the classical life sciences, anatomy, and physiology. Also, these were the only parts of the biomedical sciences transformed during the Scientific Revolution. But the life sciences had always depended on refined observation and occasionally on experiment as well; they had drawn their authority from ancient sources (e.g., Galen) sometimes distinct from those important to the physical sciences; and their development was intimately involved with that of the medical profession and corresponding institutions. It follows that the factors to be discussed when accounting either for the conceptual transformation or for the newly enlarged range of the life sciences in the sixteenth and seventeenth centuries are by no means always the same as those most relevant to the corresponding changes in the physical sciences. Nevertheless, recurrent conversations with my colleague Gerald Geison reinforce my long-standing impression that they too can fruitfully be examined from a viewpoint like the one developed here. For that purpose the distinction between experimental and mathematical traditions would be of little use, but a division between the medical and nonmedical life sciences might be crucial.

10. A. C. Crombie, *Robert Grosseteste and the Origins of Experimental Science, 1100–1700* (Oxford: Oxford University Press, 1953); J. H. Randall, Jr., *The School of Padua and the Emergence of Modern Science* (Padua: 1961).

11. For a useful and easily accessible example of medieval experimentation, see canto 2 of Dante's *Paradiso*. Passages located through the index entry "experiment, role of in Galileo's work" in Ernan McMullin, ed., *Galileo: Man of Science* (New York: Basic Books, 1965), will indicate how complex and controversial Galileo's relation to the medieval tradition remains.

12. An extended example is provided by Thomas S. Kuhn, "Robert Boyle and Structural Chemistry in the Seventeenth Century," *Isis* (1952), 43:12–36.

13. "Hydrostatical Paradoxes, Made Out by New Experiments" in A. Millar, ed., *The Works of the Honourable Robert Boyle*, vol. 2 (London, 1744), 414–447, where the discussion of Pascal's books occurs on the first page.

14. For the medieval prelude to Galileo's approach to the pendulum, see Marshall Clagett, *The Science of Mechanics in the Middle Ages* (Madison: University of Wisconsin Press, 1959), pp. 537–538, 570–571). For the road to Torricelli's barometer, see the too little known monograph by C. de Waard, *L'expérience bar-*

ométrique, ses antécédents et ses explications (Thouars: Deux-Sèvres, 1936).

15. Alexandre Koyré, *Etudes Galiléennes* (Paris, 1939); Butterfield, *Origins of Modern Science*.

16. For an early stage in the development of chemistry as a subject of intellectual concern, see Marie Boas, *Robert Boyle and Seventeenth-Century Chemistry* (Cambridge: Cambridge University Press, 1958). For a vitally important later stage see Henry Guerlac, "Some French Antecedents of the Chemical Revolution," *Chymia* (1959), 5:73–112.

17. I. B. Cohen, *Franklin and Newton* (Philadelphia: American Philosophical Society, 1956).

18. Boyle, *Works,* 2:42–43.

19. The increased value ascribed to mathematics, as tool or as ontology, by many early-modern scientists has been recognized for almost half a century and was for many years described as a response to Renaissance Neoplatonism. Changing the label to "Hermeticism" does not improve the explanation of this aspect of scientific thought (though it has assisted in the recognition of other important novelties), and the change illustrates a decisive limitation of recent scholarship, one which I have not known how to avoid here. As currently used, "Hermeticism" refers to a variety of presumably related movements: Neoplatonism, Cabalism, Rosicrucianism, and what you will. They badly need to be distinguished: temporally, geographically, intellectually, and ideologically.

20. Frances A. Yates, "The Hermetic Tradition in Renaissance Science," in C. S. Singleton, ed., *Science and History in the Renaissance* (Baltimore: Johns Hopkins Univerity Press, 1968), pp. 255–274; Paolo Rossi, *Francis Bacon: From Magic to Science,* Sacha Rabinovitch, trans. (Chicago: University of Chicago Press, 1968).

21. P. Rossi, *Philosophy, Technology, and the Arts in the Early Modern Era,* Salvator Attanasio, trans. (New York: Harper, 1970). Rossi and earlier students of the subject do not, however, discuss the possible importance of distinguishing between the crafts practiced by the artist-engineers and those later introduced to the learned world by figures like Vanoccio Biringuccio and Agricola. For some aspects of that distinction, introduced below, I am much indebted to conversation with my colleague, Michael S. Mahoney.

22. Although neither deals quite directly with this point, two recent articles suggest the way in which, first, Hermeticism and, then, corpuscularism could figure in seventeenth-century battles for intellectual-social status: P. M. Rattansi, "The Helmontian-Galenist Controversy in Restoration England," *Ambix* (1964), 12:1–23; T. M. Brown, "The College of Physicians and the Acceptance of Iatromechanism in England, 1665–1695," *Bulletin of the History of Medicine,* (1970), 44:12–30.

23. Information relevant to this point is scattered throughout Pierre Brunet, *Les physiciens Hollandais et la méthode expérimentale en France au XVIIIe siècle* (Paris, 1926).

24. R. K. Merton, *Science, Technology, and Society in Seventeenth-Century England* (New York: Humanities Press, 1970). This new edition of a work first published in 1938 includes a "Selected Bibliography: 1970," which provides useful guidance to the controversy that has continued since its initial appearance.

25. Everett Mendelsohn, "The Emergence of Science as a Profession in Nine-

teenth-Century Europe," in Karl Hill, ed., *The Management of Scientists* (Boston: Beacon Press, 1964).

26. Relevant recollections about the relation of mathematics and mathematical physics in England, France, and the United States during the 1920s are contained in the interviews with Leon Brillouin, E. C. Kemble, and N. F. Mott on deposit in the various Archives for History of Quantum Physics. For information about these depositories, see T. S. Kuhn, J. L. Heilbron, P. F. Forman, and Lini Allen, *Sources for History of Quantum Physics: An Inventory and Report* (Philadelphia: American Philosophical Society, 1967).

27. Aspects of the problem of mathematizing physics are considered in Thomas S. Kuhn, "The Function of Measurement in Modern Physical Science," *Isis* (1961), 52:161–193, where the distinction between classical and Baconian sciences was first introduced in print. Others are to be found in Robert Fox, *The Caloric Theory of Gases from Lavoisier to Regnault* (Oxford: Oxford University Press, 1971).

28. Relevant information will be found in René Taton, "L'école royale du génie de Mézières," in R. Taton, ed., *Enseignement et diffusion des sciences en France au XVIIIe siècle* (Paris, 1964), pp. 559–615.

29. R. Fox, "The Rise and Fall of Lapalcian Physics," *Historical Studies in the Physical Sciences* (1976), 4:89–136; R. H. Silliman, "Fresnel and the Emergence of Physics as a Discipline," *ibid.*, pp. 137–162.

30. Relevant information as well as guidance to the still sparse literature on this topic will be found in R. Fox, "Scientific Enterprise and the Patronage of Research in France, 1800–70," *Minerva* (1973), 11:442–473; H. W. Paul, "La science Française de la second partie du XIXe siècle vue par les auteurs Anglais et Américains," *Revue d'histoire des sciences* (1974), 27:147–163. Note, however, that both are concerned primarily with the alleged decline in French science as a whole, an effect surely less pronounced and perhaps quite distinct from the decline of French physics. Conversations with Fox have reinforced my convictions and helped me to organize my remarks on these points.

31. Russel McCormmach, "Editor's Foreword," *Historical Studies in the Physical Sciences* vol. 3 (1971), ix–xxiv.

32. Other frequently remarked but still little investigated phenomena also hint at a psychological basis for this cleavage. Many mathematicians and theoretical physicists have been passionately interested in and involved with music, some having had great difficulty choosing between a scientific and a musical career. No comparably widespread involvement is visible in the experimental sciences including experimental physics (nor, I think, in other disciplines without an apparent relationship to music). But music, or part of it, was once a member of the cluster of mathematical sciences, never of the experimental. Also likely to be revealing is further study of a subtle distinction often remarked by physicists: that between a "mathematical" and a "theoretical" physicist. Both use much mathematics, often on the same problems. But the first tends to take the physics problem as conceptually fixed and to develop powerful mathematical techniques for application to it; the second thinks more physically, adapting the conception of his problem to the often more limited mathematical tools at his disposal. Lewis Pyenson, to whom I am indebted for helpful comments on my earliest draft, is developing interesting ideas on the evolution of the distinction.

FOUR
MORAL THEORY

[II]

A Kantian Conception
of Equality

JOHN RAWLS

M Y AIM in this paper is to give a brief account of the conception
of equality that underlies the view expressed in my book *A Theory
of Justice* and the principles considered there. I hope to state the fundamental intuitive idea simply and informally; and so I make no attempt to
sketch the argument from the original position. In fact, this construction
is not mentioned until the end and then only to indicate its role in giving
a Kantian interpretation to the conception of equality already presented.

I

When fully articulated, any conception of justice expresses a conception of the person, of the relations between persons, and of the general
structure and ends of social cooperation. To accept the principles that
represent a conception of justice is at the same time to accept an ideal of
the person; and in acting from these principles we realize such an ideal.
Let us begin, then, by trying to describe the kind of person we might
want to be and the form of society we might wish to live in and to shape
our interests and character. In this way we arrive at the notion of a well-
ordered society. I shall first describe this notion and then use it to explain
a Kantian conception of equality.

Reprinted with permission from *The Cambridge Review* (February 1975), pp. 94–99. The
original title was "A Kantian Conception of Equality." Sections 1, 3 and 4 of this discussion draw upon sections 1 and 3 of "Reply to Alexander and Musgrave," *Quarterly Journal
of Economics*, (November 1974). Sections 2, 5 and 6 of that paper take up some questions
about the argument from the original position.

First of all, a well-ordered society is effectively regulated by a public conception of justice. That is, it is a society all of whose members accept, and know that the others accept, the same principles (the same conception) of justice. It is also the case that basic social institutions and their arrangement into one scheme (the basic structure) actually satisfy, and are on good grounds believed by everyone to satisfy, these principles. Finally, publicity also implies that the public conception is founded on reasonable beliefs that have been established by generally accepted methods of inquiry; and the same is true of the application of its principles to basic social arrangements. This last aspect of publicity does not mean that everyone holds the same religious, moral, and theoretical beliefs; on the contrary, there are assumed to be sharp and indeed irreconcilable differences on such questions. But at the same time there is a shared understanding that the principles of justice, and their application to the basic structure of society, should be determined by considerations and evidence that are supported by rational procedures commonly recognized.

Second, I suppose that the members of a well-ordered society are, and view themselves as free and equal moral persons. They are moral persons in that, once they have reached the age of reason, each has, and views the others as having, a realized sense of justice; and this sentiment informs their conduct for the most part. That they are equal is expressed by the supposition that they each have, and view themselves as having a right to equal respect and consideration in determining the principles by which the basic arrangements of their society are to be regulated. Finally, we express their being free by stipulating that they each have, and view themselves as having, fundamental aims and higher-order interests (a conception of their good) in the name of which it is legitimate to make claims on one another in the design of their institutions. At the same time, as free persons they do not think of themselves as inevitably bound to, or as identical with, the pursuit of any particular array of fundamental interests that they may have at any given time; instead, they conceive of themselves as capable of revising and altering these final ends and they give priority to preserving their liberty in this regard.

In addition, I assume that a well-ordered society is stable relative to its conception of justice. This means that social institutions generate an effective supporting sense of justice. Regarding society as a going concern, its members acquire as they grow up an allegiance to the public conception and this allegiance usually overcomes the temptations and strains of social life.

Now we are here concerned with a conception of justice and the idea of equality that belongs to it. Thus, let us suppose that a well-ordered society exists under circumstances of justice. These necessitate some conception of justice and give point to its special role. First, moderate scarcity obtains. This means that although social cooperation is productive and mutually advantageous (one person's or group's gain need not be another's loss), natural resources and the state of technology are such that the fruits of joint efforts fall short of the claims that people make. And second, persons and associations have contrary conceptions of the good that lead them to make conflicting claims on one another; and they also hold opposing religious, philosophical, and moral convictions (on matters the public conception leaves open) as well as different ways of evaluating arguments and evidence in many important cases. Given these circumstances, the members of a well-ordered society are not indifferent as to how the benefits produced by their cooperation are distributed. A set of principles is required to judge between social arrangements that shape this division of advantages. Thus the role of the principles of justice is to assign rights and duties in the basic sturcture of society and to specify the manner in which institutions are to influence the overall distribution of the returns from social cooperation. The basic structure is the primary subject of justice and that to which the principles of justice in the first instance apply.

It is perhaps useful to observe that the notion of a well-ordered society is an extension of the idea of religious toleration. Consider a pluralistic society, divided along religious, ethnic, or cultural lines in which the various groups have reached a firm understanding on the scheme of principles to regulate their fundamental institutions. While they have deep differences about other things, there is public agreement on this framework of principles and citizens are attached to it. A well-ordered society had not attained social harmony in all things, if indeed that would be desirable; but it has achieved a large measure of justice and established a basis for civic friendship, which makes people's secure association together possible.

II

The notion of a well-ordered society assumes that the basic structure, the fundamental social institutions and their arrangement into one scheme, is the primary subject of justice. What is the reason for this assumption?

First of all, any discussion of social justice must take the nature of the basic structure into account. Suppose we begin with the initially attractive idea that the social process should be allowed to develop over time as free agreements fairly arrived at and fully honoured require. Straightaway we need an account of when agreements are free and the conditions under which they are reached are fair. In addition, while these conditions may be satisfied at an earlier time, the accumulated results of agreements in conjunction with social and historical contingencies are likely to change institutions and opportunities so that the conditions for free and fair agreements no longer hold. The basic structure specifies the background conditions against which the actions of individuals, groups, and associations take place. Unless this structure is regulated and corrected so as to be just over time, the social process with its procedures and outcomes is no longer just, however free and fair particular transactions may look to us when viewed by themselves. We recognize this principle when we say that the distribution resulting from voluntary market transactions will not in general be fair unless the antecedent distribution of income and wealth and the structure of the market is fair. Thus we seem forced to start with an account of a just basic structure. It's as if the most important agreement is that which establishes the principles must be acknowledged ahead of time, as it were. To agree to them now, when everyone knows their present situation, would enable some to take unfair advantage of social and natural contingencies, and of the results of historical accidents and accumulations.

Other considerations also support taking the basic structure as the primary subject of justice. It has always been recognized that the social system shapes the desires and aspirations of its members; it determines in large part the kind of persons they want to be as well as the kind of persons they are. Thus an economic system is not only an institutional device for satisfying existing wants and desires but a way of fashioning wants and desires in the future. By what principles are we to regulate a scheme of institutions that has such fundamental consequences for our view of ourselves and for our interests and aims? This question becomes all the more crucial when we consider that the basic structure contains social and economic inequalities. I assume that these are necessary, or highly advantageous, for various reasons: they are required to maintain and to run social arrangements, or to serve as incentives; or perhaps they are a way to put resources in the hands of those who can make the best social use of them, and so on. In any case, given these inequalities, individuals' life prospects are bound to be importantly affected by their family and class origins, by their natural endowments and the chance contingencies of their (particularly early) development, and by other accidents over the course of their lives. The social structure, therefore, limits people's ambitions and hopes in different ways, for they will with reason view themselves in part according to their place in it and take into account the means and opportunities they can realistically expect.

The justice of the basic structure is, then, of predominant importance. The first problem of justice is to determine the principles to regulate inequalities and to adjust the profound and long-lasting effects of social, natural, and historical contingencies, particularly since these contingencies combined with inequalities generate tendencies that, when left to themselves, are sharply at odds with the freedom and equality appropriate for a well-ordered society. In view of the special role of the basic structure, we cannot assume that the principles suitable to it are natural applications, or even extensions, of the familiar principles governing the actions of individuals and associations in everyday life which take place within its framework. Most likely we shall have to loosen ourselves from our ordinary perspective and take a more comprehensive viewpoint.

III

I shall now state and explain two principles of justice, and then discuss the appropriateness of these principles for a well-ordered society. They read as follows:

1. Each person has an equal right to the most extensive scheme of equal basic liberties compatible with a similar scheme of liberties for all.
2. Social and economic inequalities are to meet two conditions: they must be (a) to the greatest expected benefit of the least advantaged; and (b) attached to offices and positions open to all under conditions of fair opportunity.

The first of these principles is to take priority over the second; and the measure of benefit to the least advantaged is specified in terms of an index of social primary goods. These goods I define roughly as rights, liberties and opportunities, income and wealth, and the social bases of self-respect. Individuals are assumed to want these goods whatever else they want, or whatever their final ends. The least advantaged are defined very roughly, as they overlap between those who are least favored by each of the three main kinds of contingencies. Thus this group includes persons whose family and class origins are more disadvantaged than others, whose natural endowments have permitted them to fare less well, and whose fortune and luck have been relatively less favorable, all within the normal range (as noted below) and with the relevant measures based on social primary goods. Various refinements are no doubt necessary, but this definition of the least advantaged suitably expresses the link with the problem of contingency and should suffice for our purposes here.[1]

I also suppose that everyone has physical needs and psychological capacities within the normal range, so that the problems of special health care and of how to treat the mentally defective do not arise. Besides prematurely introducing difficult questions that may take us beyond the theory of justice, the consideration of these hard cases can distract our moral perception by leading us to think of people distant from us whose fate arouses pity and anxiety. Whereas the first problem of justice concerns the relations among those who in the normal course of things are full and active participants in society and directly or indirectly associated together over the whole course of their life.

Now the members of a well-ordered society are free and equal; so let us first consider the fittingness of the two principles to their freedom, and then to their equality. These principles reflect two aspects of their freedom, namely, liberty, and responsibility, which I take up in turn. In regard to liberty, recall that people in a well-ordered society view themselves as having fundamental aims and interests which they must protect, if this is possible. It is partly in the name of these interests that they have a right to equal consideration and respect in the design of their society. A familiar historical example is the religious interest; the interest in the integrity of the person, freedom from psychological oppression, and from physical assault and dismemberment is another. The notion of a well-ordered society leaves open what particular expression these interests take; only their general form is specified. But individuals do have interests of the requisite kind and the basic liberties necessary for their protection are guaranteed by the first principle.

It is essential to observe that these liberties are given by a list of liberties; important among these are freedom of thought and liberty of conscience, freedom of the person, and political liberty. These liberties have a central range of application within which they can be limited and compromised only when they conflict with other basic liberties. Since they may be limited when they clash with one another, none of these liberties is absolute; but however they are adjusted to form one system, this system is to be the same for all. It is difficult, perhaps impossible, to give a complete definition of these liberties independently from the particular circumstances, social, economic, and technological, of a given well-ordered society. Yet the hypothesis is that the general form of such a list could be devised with sufficient exactness to sustain this conception of justice. Of course, liberties not on the list, for example, the right to own certain kinds of property (e.g., means of production), and freedom of contract as understood by the doctrine of laissez–faire, are not basic: and so they are not protected by the priority of the first principle.

One reason, then, for holding the two principles suitable for a well-ordered society is that they assure the protection of the fundamental interests that members of such a society are presumed to have. Further reasons for this conclusion can be given by describing in more detail the notion of a free person. Thus we may suppose that such persons regard themselves as having a highest-order interest in how all their other interests, including even their fundamental ones, are shaped and regulated by social institutions. As I noted earlier, they do not think of themselves as unavoidably tied to any particular array of fundamental interests; instead they view themselves as capable of revising and changing these final ends. They wish, therefore, to give priority to their liberty to do this, and so their original allegiance and continued devotion to their ends are to be formed and affirmed under conditions that are free. Or, expressed another way, members of a well-ordered society are viewed as responsible for their fundamental interests and ends. While as members of particular associations some may decide in practice to yield much of this responsibility to others, the basic structure cannot be arranged so as to prevent people from developing their capacity to be responsible, or to obstruct their exercise of it once they attain it. Social arrangements must respect their autonomy and this points to the appropriateness of the two principles.

IV

These last remarks about responsibility may be elaborated further in connection with the role of social primary goods. As already stated, these are things that people in a well-ordered society may be presumed to want, whatever their final ends. And the two principles assess the basic structure in terms of certain of these goods: rights, liberties and opportunities, income and wealth, and the social bases of self-respect. The latter are features of the basic structure that may reasonably be expected to affect people's self-respect and self-esteem (these are not the same) in important ways.[2] Part (a) of the second principle (the difference principle, or as economists prefer to say, the maximin criterion) uses an index of these goods to determine the least advantaged. Now certainly there are difficulties in working out a satisfactory index, but I shall leave these aside. Two points are particularly relevant here: first, social primary goods are certain objective characteristics of social institutions and of people's situation with respect to them; and second, the same index of these goods is used to compare everyone's social circumstances. It is clear, then, that although the index provides a basis for interpersonal comparisons for the purposes of justice, it is not a measure of individuals' overall satisfaction or dissatisfaction. Of course, the precise weights adopted in such an index cannot be laid down ahead of time, for these should be adjusted, to some degree at least, in view of social conditions. What can be settled initially is certain constraints on these weights, as illustrated by the priority of the first principle.

Now, that the responsibility of free persons is implicit in the use of primary goods can be seen in the following way. We are assuming that people are able to control and to revise their wants and desires in the light of circumstances and that they are to have responsibility for doing so, provided that the principles of justice are fulfilled, as they are in a well-ordered society. Persons do not take their wants and desires as determined by happenings beyond their control. We are not, so to speak, assailed by them, as we are perhaps by disease and illness so that wants and desires fail to support claims to the means of satisfaction in the way that disease and illness support claims to medicine and treatment.

Of course, it is not suggested that people must modify their desires and ends whatever their circumstances. The doctrine of primary goods does not demand the stoic virtues. Society, for its part, bears the responsibility for upholding the principles of justice and secures for everyone a fair share of primary goods (as determined by the difference principle) within a framework of equal liberty and fair equality of opportunity. It is within the limits of this division of responsibility that individuals and associations are expected to form and moderate their aims and wants. Thus among the members of a well-ordered society there is an understanding that as citizens they will press claims for only certain kinds of things, as allowed for by the principles of justice. Passionate convictions and zealous aspirations do not, as such, give anyone a claim upon social resources or the design of social institutions. For the purposes of justice, the appropriate basis of interpersonal comparisons is the index of primary goods and not strength of feeling or intensity of desire. The theory of primary goods is an extension of the notion of needs, which are distinct from aspirations and desires. One might say, then, that as citizens the members of a well-ordered society collectively take responsibility for dealing justly with one another founded on a public and objective measure of (extended) needs, while as individuals and members of associations they take responsibility for their preferences and devotions.

V

I now take up the appropriateness of two principles in view of the equality of the members of a well-ordered society. The principles of equal liberty and fair opportunity (part (b) of the second principle) are a natural expression of this equality; and I assume, therefore, that such a society is one in which some form of democracy exists. Thus our question is by what principle can members of a democratic society permit the tendencies of the basic structure to be deeply affected by social chance, and natural and historical contingencies.

Now since we are regarding citizens as free and equal moral persons (the priority of the first principle of equal liberty gives institutional expression to this), the obvious starting point is to suppose that all other social primary goods, and in particular income and wealth, should be equal: everyone should have an equal share. But society must take organizational requirements and economic efficiency into account. So it is unreasonable to stop at equal division. The basic structure should allow inequalities so long as these improve everyone's situation, including that of the least advantaged, provided these inequalities are consistent with equal liberty and fair opportunity. Because we start from equal shares, those who benefit least have, so to speak, a veto; and thus we arrive at the difference principle. Taking equality as the basis of comparison, those who have gained more must do so on terms that are justifiable to those who have gained the least.

In explaining this principle, several matters should be kept in mind. First of all, it applies in the first instance to the main public principles and policies that regulate social and economic inequalities. It is used to adjust the system of entitlements and rewards, and the standards and precepts that this system employs. Thus the difference principle holds, for example, for income and property taxation, for fiscal and economic policy; it does not apply to particular transactions or distributions, nor, in general, to small-scale and local decisions, but rather to the background against which these take place. No observable pattern is required of actual distributions, nor even any measure of the degree of equality (such as the Gini coefficient) that might be computed from these.[3] What is enjoined is that the inequalities make a functional contribution to those least favoured. Finally, the aim is not to eliminate the various contingencies for some such contingencies seem inevitable. Thus, even if an equal distribution of natural assets seemed more in keeping with the equality of free persons, the question of redistributing these assets (were this conceivable) does not arise, since it is incompatible with the integrity of the person. Nor need we make any specific assumptions about how great these variations are; we only suppose that, as realized in later life, they are influenced by all three kinds of contingencies. The question, then, is by what criterion a democratic society is to organize cooperation and arrange the system of entitlements that encourages and rewards productive efforts. We have a right to our natural abilities and a right to whatever we become entitled to by taking part in a fair social process. The problem is to characterize this process.[4]

At first sight, it may appear that the difference principle is arbitrarily biased towards the least favored. But suppose, for simplicity, that there are only two groups, one significantly more fortunate than the other. Society could maximize the expectations of either group but not both, since we can maximize with respect to only one aim at a time. It seems plain that society should not do the best it can for those initially more advantaged; so if we reject the difference principle, we must prefer maximizing some weighted mean of the two expectations. But how should this weighted mean be specified? Should society proceed as if we had an equal chance of being in either group (in proportion to their size) and determine the mean that maximizes this purely hypothetical expectation? Now it is true that we sometimes agree to draw lots but normally only to things that cannot be appropriately divided or else cannot be enjoyed or suffered in common.[5] And we are willing to use the lottery principle even in matters of lasting importance if there is no other way out. (Consider the example of conscription.) But to appeal to it in regulating the basic structure itself would be extraordinary. There is no necessity for society as an enduring system to invoke the lottery principle in this case; nor is there any reason for free and equal persons to allow their relations over the whole course of their life to be significantly affected by contingencies to the greater advantage of those already favored by these accidents. No one had an antecedent claim to be benefited in this way; and so to maximize a weighted mean is, so to speak, to favour the more fortunate twice over. Society can, however, adopt the difference principle to arrange inequalities so that social and natural contingencies are efficiently used to the benefit of all, taking equal division as a benchmark. So while natural assets cannot be divided evenly, or directly enjoyed or suffered in common, the results of their productive efforts can be allocated in ways consistent with an initial equality. Those favored by social and natural contingencies regard themselves as already compensated, as it were, by advantages to which no one (including themselves) had a prior claim. Thus they think the difference principle appropriate for regulating the system of entitlements and inequalities.

VI

The conception of equality contained in the principles of justice I have described is Kantian. I shall conclude by mentioning very briefly the reasons for this description. Of course, I do not mean that this conception is literally Kant's conception, but rather that it is one of no doubt several conceptions sufficiently similar to essential parts of his doctrine to make the adjective appropriate. Much depends on what one counts as essential. Kant's view is marked by a number of dualisms, in particular, the dualisms between the necessary and the contingent, form and content, reason and desire, and noumena and phenomena. To abandon these dualisms as he meant them is, for many, to abandon what is distinctive in his theory. I believe otherwise. His moral conception has a characteristic structure that is more clearly discernible when these dualisms are not taken in the sense he gave them but reinterpreted and their moral force reformulated within the scope of an empirical theory. One of the aims of *A Theory of Justice* was to indicate how this might be done.

To suggest the main idea, think of the notion of a well-ordered society as an interpretation of the idea of a kingdom of ends thought of as a human society under circumstances of justice. Now the members of such a society are free and equal and so our problem is to find a rendering of freedom and equality that it is natural to describe as Kantian; and since Kant distinguished between positive and negative freedom, we must make room for this contrast. At this point I resorted to the idea of the original position: I supposed that the conception of justice suitable for a well-ordered society is the one that would be agreed to in a hypothetical situation that is fair between individuals conceived as free and equal moral persons, that is, as members of such a society. Fairness of the circumstances under which agreement is reached transfers to the fairness of the principles agreed to. The original position was designed so that the conception of justice that resulted would be appropriate.

Particularly important among the features of the original position for the interpretation of negative freedom are the limits on information, which I called the veil of ignorance. Now there is a stronger and a weaker form of these limits. The weaker supposes that we begin with full information, or else that which we possess in everyday life, and then proceed to eliminate only the information that would lead to partiality and bias. The stronger form has a Kantian explanation: we start from no information at all; for by negative freedom Kant means being able to act independently from the determination of alien causes; to act from natural necessity is to subject oneself to the heteronomy of nature. We interpret this as requiring that the conception of justice that regulates the basic structure, with its deep and long-lasting effects on our common life, should not be adopted on grounds that rest on a knowledge of the various contingencies. Thus when this conception is agreed to, knowledge of our social position, our peculiar desires and interests, or of the various outcomes and configurations of natural and historical accident is excluded. One allows only that information required for a rational agreement. This means that, so far as possible, only the general laws of nature are known together with such particular facts as are implied by the circumstances of justice.

Of course, we must endow the parties with some motivation, otherwise no acknowledgement would be forthcoming. Kant's discussion in the *Groundwork* of the second pair of examples indicates, I believe, that in applying the procedure of the categorical imperative he tacitly relied upon some account of primary goods. In any case, if the two principles would be adopted in the original position with its limits on information, the conception of equality they contain would be Kantian in the sense that by acting from this conception the members of a well-ordered society would express their negative freedom. They would have succeeded in regulating the basic structure and its profound consequences on their persons and mutual relationships by principles the grounds for which are suitably independent from chance and contingency.

In order to provide an interpretation of positive freedom, two things are necessary: first, that the parties are conceived as free and equal moral persons must play a decisive part in their adoption of the conception of justice; and second, the principles of this conception must have a content appropriate to express this determining view of persons and must apply to the controlling institutional subject. Now if correct, the argument from the original position seems to meet these conditions. The assumption that the parties are free and equal moral persons does have an essential role in this argument; and as regards content and application, these principles express, on their public face as it were, the conception of the person that is realized in a well-ordered society. They give priority to the basic liberties, regard individuals as free and responsible masters of their aims and desires, and all are to share equally in the means for the attainment of ends unless the situation of everyone can be improved, taking equal division as the starting point. A society that realized these principles would attain positive freedom, for these principles reflect the features of persons that determined their selection and so express a conception they give to themselves.

NOTES

1. This paragraph confirms H. L. A. Hart's interpretation. See his discussion of liberty and its priority, *Chicago Law Review* (April 1973), pp. 536–540.

2. I discuss certain problems in interpreting the account of primary goods in "Fairness to Goodness," *Philosophical Review* (October 1975), pp. 536–554.

3. For a discussion of such measures, see A. K. Sen, *On Economic Inequality* (Oxford: Oxford University Press, 1973), ch. 2.

4. The last part of this paragraph alludes to some objections raised by Robert Nozick in his *Anarchy, State, and Utopia* (New York: Basic Books, 1974), esp. pp. 213–229.

5. At this point I adapt some remarks of Hobbes. See *The Leviathan,* ch. 15, under the thirteenth and fourteenth laws of nature.

[12]

Contractualism and Utilitarianism

T. M. SCANLON

UTILITARIANISM occupies a central place in the moral philosophy of our time. It is not the view which most people hold; certainly there are very few who would claim to be act utilitarians. But for a much wider range of people it is the view toward which they find themselves pressed when they try to give a theoretical account of their moral beliefs. Within moral philosophy it represents a position one must struggle against if one wishes to avoid it. This is so in spite of the fact that the implications of act utilitarianism are wildly at variance with firmly held moral convictions, while rule utilitarianism, the most common alternative formulation, strikes most people as an unstable compromise.

The wide appeal of utilitarianism is due, I think, to philosophical considerations of a more or less sophisticated kind which pull us in a quite different direction than our first-order moral beliefs. In particular, utilitarianism derives much of its appeal from alleged difficulties about the foundations of rival views. What a successful alternative to utilitarianism must do, first and foremost, is to sap this source of strength by providing a clear account of the foundations of non-utilitarian moral reasoning. In what follows I will first describe the problem in more detail by setting out the questions which a philosophical account of the foundations of morality must answer. I will then put forward a version of contractualism

I am greatly indebted to Derek Parfit for patient criticism and enormously helpful discussion of earlier versions of this paper. Thanks are due also to audiences who have heard parts of those versions delivered as lectures and kindly responded with helpful comments. In particular, I am indebted to Marshall Cohen, Ronald Dworkin, Owen Fiss, and Thomas Nagel for valuable criticism. Reprinted by permission from *Utilitarianism and Beyond,* Amartya Sen and Bernard Williams, eds. (Cambridge: Cambridge University Press, 1981).

which, I will argue, offers a better set of responses to these questions than that supplied by straightforward versions of utilitarianism. Finally I will explain why contractualism, as I understand it, does not lead back to some utilitarian formula as its normative outcome.

Contractualism has been proposed as the alternative to utilitarianism before, notably by John Rawls in *A Theory of Justice* (Rawls 1971). Despite the wide discussion which this book has received, however, I think that the appeal of contractualism as a foundational view has been underrated. In particular, it has not been sufficiently appreciated that contractualism offers a particularly plausible account of moral motivation. The version of contractualism that I shall present differs from Rawls' in a number of respects. In particular, it makes no use, or only a different and more limited kind of use, of his notion of choice from behind a veil of ignorance. One result of this difference is to make the contrast between contractualism and utilitarianism stand out more clearly.

I

There is such a subject as moral philosophy for much the same reason that there is such a subject as the philosophy of mathematics. In moral judgments, as in mathematical ones, we have a set of putatively objective beliefs in which we are inclined to invest a certain degree of confidence and importance. Yet on reflection it is not at all obvious what, if anything, these judgments can be about, in virtue of which some can be said to be correct or defensible and others not. This question of subject matter, or the grounds of truth, is the first philosophical question about both morality and mathematics. Second, in both morality and mathematics it seems to be possible to discover the truth simply by thinking or reasoning about it. Experience and observation may be helpful, but observation in the normal sense is not the standard means of discovery in either subject. So given any positive answer to the first question—any specification of the subject matter or ground of truth in mathematics or morality—we need some compatible epistemology explaining how it is possible to discover the facts about this subject matter through something like the means we seem to use.

Given this similarity in the questions giving rise to moral philosophy and to the philosophy of mathematics, it is not surprising that the answers commonly given fall into similar general types. If we were to interview students in a freshman mathematics course many of them would,

I think, declare themselves for some kind of conventionalism. They would hold that mathematics proceeds from definitions and principles that are either arbitrary or instrumentally justified, and that mathematical reasoning consists in perceiving what follows from these definitions and principles. A few others, perhaps, would be realists or Platonists according to whom mathematical truths are a special kind of nonempirical fact that we can perceive through some form of intuition. Others might be naturalists who hold that mathematics, properly understood, is just the most abstract empirical science. Finally there are, though perhaps not in an average freshman course, those who hold that there are no mathematical facts in the world "outside of us," but that the truths of mathematics are objective truths about the mental constructions of which we are capable. Kant held that pure mathematics was a realm of objective mind-dependent truths, and Brouwer's mathematical Intuitionism is another theory of this type (with the important difference that it offers grounds for the warranted assertability of mathematical judgments rather than for their truth in the classical sense). All of these positions have natural correlates in moral philosophy. Intuitionism of the sort espoused by W. D. Ross is perhaps the closest analogue to mathematical Platonism, and Kant's theory is the most familiar version of the thesis that morality is a sphere of objective, mind-dependent truths.

All of the views I have mentioned (with some qualification in the case of conventionalism) give positive (i.e., non-sceptical) answers to the first philosophical question about mathematics. Each identifies some objective, or at least intersubjective, ground of truth for mathematical judgments. Outright scepticism and subjective versions of mind-dependence (analogues of emotivism or prescriptivism) are less appealing as philosophies of mathematics than as moral philosophies. This is so in part simply because of the greater degree of intersubjective agreement in mathematical judgment. But it is also due to the difference in the further questions that philosophical accounts of the two fields must answer.

Neither mathematics nor morality can be taken to describe a realm of facts existing in isolation from the rest of reality. Each is supposed to be connected with other things. Mathematical judgments give rise to predictions about those realms to which mathematics is applied. This connection is something that a philosophical account of mathematical truth must explain, but the fact that we can observe and learn from the correctness of such predictions also gives support to our belief in objective mathematical truth. In the case of morality the main connection is, or is generally supposed to be, with the will. Given any candidate for the role of subject matter of morality we must explain why anyone should care about it, and the need to answer this question of motivation has given strong support to subjectivist views.

But what must an adequate philosophical theory of morality say about moral motivation? It need not, I think, show that the moral truth gives anyone who knows it a reason to act which appeals to that person's present desires or to the advancement of his or her interests. I find it entirely intelligible that moral requirement might correctly apply to a person even though that person had no reason of either of these kinds for complying with it. Whether moral requriements give those to whom they apply reasons for compliance of some third kind is a disputed question which I shall set aside. But what an adequate moral philosophy must do, I think, is to make clearer to us the nature of the reasons that morality does provide, at least to those who are concerned with it. A philosophical theory of morality must offer an account of these reasons that is, on the one hand, compatible with its account of moral truth and moral reasoning and, on the other, supported by a plausible analysis of moral experience. A satisfactory moral philosophy will not leave concern with morality as a simple special preference, like a fetish or a special taste, which some people just happen to have. It must make understandable why moral reasons are ones that people can take seriously, and why they strike those who are moved by them as reasons of a special stringency and inescapability.

There is also a further question whether susceptibility to such reasons is compatible with a person's good or whether it is, as Nietzsche argued, a psychological disaster for the person who has it. If one is to defend morality one must show that it is not disastrous in this way, but I will not pursue this second motivational question here. I mention it only to distinguish it from the first question, which is my present concern.

The task of giving a philosophical explanation of the subject matter of morality differs both from the task of analyzing the meaning of moral terms and from that of finding the most coherent formulation of our first-order moral beliefs. A maximally coherent ordering of our first-order moral beliefs could provide us with a valuable kind of explanation: it would make clear how various, apparently disparate moral notions, precepts, and judgments are related to one another, thus indicating to what degree conflicts between them are fundamental and to what degree, on the other hand, they can be resolved or explained away. But philosophical inquiry into the subject matter of morality takes a more external view. It seeks to explain what kind of truths moral truths are by describing them in relation to other things in the world and in relation to our particular concerns. An explanation of how we can come to know the truth about morality must be based on such an external explanation of the kind of things moral truths are, rather than on a list of particular moral truths, even a maximally coherent list. This seems to be true as well about explanations of how moral beliefs can give one a reason to act.[1]

Coherence among our first-order moral beliefs—what Rawls has called narrow reflective equilibrium[2]—seems unsatisfying[3] as an account of moral truth or as an account of the basis of justification in ethics just because, taken by itself, a maximally coherent account of our moral beliefs need not provide us with what I have called a philosophical explanation of the subject matter of morality. However internally coherent our moral beliefs may be rendered, the nagging doubt may remain that there is nothing to them at all. They may be merely a set of socially inculcated reactions, mutually consistent perhaps but not judgments of a kind which can properly be said to be correct or incorrect. A philosophical theory of the nature of morality can contribute to our confidence in our first-order moral beliefs chiefly by allaying these natural doubts about the subject. Insofar as it includes an account of moral epistemology, such a theory may guide us toward new forms of moral argument, but it need not do this. Moral argument of more or less the kind we have been familiar with may remain as the only form of justification in ethics. But whether or not it leads to revision in our modes of justification, what a good philosophical theory should do is to give us a clearer understanding of what the best forms of moral argument amount to and what kind of truth it is that they can be a way of arriving at. (Much the same can be said, I believe, about the contribution which philosophy of mathematics makes to our confidence in particular mathematical judgments and particular forms of mathematical reasoning.)

Like any thesis about morality, a philosophical account of the subject matter of morality must have some connection with the meaning of moral terms: it must be plausible to claim that the subject matter described is in fact what these terms refer to, at least in much of their normal use. But the current meaning of moral terms is the product of many different moral beliefs held by past and present speakers of the language, and this meaning is surely compatible with a variety of moral views and with a variety of views about the nature of morality. After all, moral terms are used to express many different views of these kinds, and people who express these views are not using moral terms incorrectly, even though what some of them say must be mistaken. Like a first-order moral judgment, a philosophical characterization of the subject matter of morality is a substantive claim about morality, albeit a claim of a different kind.

While a philosophical characterization of morality makes a kind of claim that differs from a first-order moral judgment, this does not mean that a philosophical theory of morality will be neutral between competing normative doctrines. The adoption of a philosophical thesis about the nature of morality will almost always have some effect on the plausibility of particular moral claims, but philosophical theories of morality vary widely in the extent and directness of their normative implications. At one extreme is intuitionism, understood as the philosophical thesis that morality is concerned with certain non-natural properties. Rightness, for example, is held by Ross to be the property of "fittingness" or "moral suitability."[4] Intuitionism holds that we can identify occurrences of these properties, and that we can recognize as self-evident certain general truths about them, but that they cannot be further analyzed or explained in terms of other notions. So understood, intuitionism is in principle compatible with a wide variety of normative positions. One could, for example, be an intuitionistic utilitarian or an intuitionistic believer in moral rights, depending on the general truths about the property of moral rightness which one took to be self-evident.

The other extreme is represented by philosophical utilitarianism. The term "utilitarianism" is generally used to refer to a family of specific normative doctrines—doctrines which might be held on the basis of a number of different philosophical theses about the nature of morality. In this sense of the term one might, for example, be a utilitarian on intuitionist or on contractualist grounds. But what I will call "philosophical utilitarianism" is a particular philosophical thesis about the subject matter of morality, namely the thesis that the only fundamental moral facts are facts about individual well-being.[5] I believe that this thesis has a great deal of plausibility for many people, and that, while some people are utilitarians for other reasons, it is the attractiveness of philosophical utilitarianism which accounts for the widespread influence of utilitarian principles.

It seems evident to people that there is such a thing as individuals' being made better or worse off. Such facts have an obvious motivational force; it is quite understandable that people should be moved by them in much the way that they are supposed to be moved by moral considerations. Further, these facts are clearly relevant to morality as we now understand it. Claims about individual well-being are one class of valid starting points for moral argument. But many people find it much harder to see how there could be any other, independent starting points. Substantive moral requirements independent of individual well-being strike people as intuitionist in an objectionable sense. They would represent "moral facts" of a kind it would be difficult to explain. There is no problem about recognizing it as a fact that a certain act is, say, an instance of lying or of promise breaking. And a utilitarian can acknowledge that such facts as these often have (derivative) moral significance: they are morally significant because of their consequences for individual well-being. The problems, and the charge of "intuitionism," arise when it is claimed that such acts are wrong in a sense that is not reducible to the fact that they decrease individual well-being.

How could this independent property of moral wrongness be understood in a way that would give it the kind of importance and motivational force which moral considerations have been taken to have? If one accepts the idea that there are no moral properties having this kind of intrinsic significance, then philosophical utilitarianism may seem to be the only tenable account of morality. And once philosophical utilitarianism is accepted, some form of normative utilitarianism seems to be forced on us as the correct first-order moral theory. Utilitarianism thus has, for many people, something like the status which Hilbert's Formalism and Brouwer's Intuitionism have for their believers. It is a view which seems to be forced on us by the need to give a philosophically defensible account of the subject. But it leaves us with a hard choice: we can either abandon many of our previous first-order beliefs or try to salvage them by showing that they can be obtained as derived truths or explained away as useful and harmless fictions.

It may seem that the appeal of philosophical utilitarianism as I have described it is spurious, since this theory must amount either to a form of intuitionism (differing from others only in that it involves just one appeal to intuition) or else to definitional naturalism of a kind refuted by Moore and others long ago. But I do not think that the doctrine can be disposed of so easily. Philosophical utilitarianism is a philosophical thesis about the nature of morality. As such, it is on a par with intuitionism or with the form of contractualism which I will defend later in this paper. None of these theses need claim to be true as a matter of definition; if one of them is true it does not follow that a person who denies it is misusing the words "right," "wrong," and "ought." Nor are all these theses forms of intuitionism, if intuitionism is understood as the view that moral facts concern special non-natural properties, which we can apprehend by intuitive insight but which do not need or admit of any further analysis. Both contractualism and philosophical utilitarianism are specifically incompatible with this claim. Like other philosophical theses about the nature of morality (including, I would say, intuitionism itself), contractualism and philosophical utilitarianism are to be appraised on the basis of their success in giving an account of moral belief, moral argument, and moral motivation that is compatible with our general beliefs about the world: our beliefs about what kinds of things there are in the world, what kinds of observation and reasoning we are capable of, and what kinds of reasons we have for action. A judgment as to which account of the nature of morality (or of mathematics) is most plausible in this general sense is just that: a judgment of overall plausibility. It is not usefully described as an insight into concepts or as a special intuitive insight of some other kind.

If philosophical utilitarianism is accepted, then some form of utilitarianism appears to be forced upon us as a normative doctrine, but further argument is required to determine which form we should accept. If all that counts morally is the well-being of individuals, no one of whom is singled out as counting for more than the others, and if all that matters in the case of each individual is the degree to which his or her well-being is affected, then it would seem to follow that the basis of moral appraisal is the goal of maximizing the *sum* of individual well-being.[6] Whether this standard is to be applied to the criticism of individual actions, or to the selection of rules or policies, or to the inculcation of habits and dispositions to act, is a further question, as is the question of how "well-being" itself is to be understood. Thus the hypothesis that much of the appeal of utilitarianism as a normative doctrine derives from the attractiveness of philosophical utilitarianism explains how people can be convinced that some form of utilitariansim must be correct while yet being quite uncertain as to which form it is, whether it is "direct" or "act" utilitarianism or some form of indirect "rule" or "motive" utilitarianism. What these views have in common, despite their differing normative consequences, is the identification of the same class of fundamental moral facts.

II

If what I have said about the appeal of utilitarianism is correct, then what a rival theory must do is to provide an alternative to philosophical utilitarianism as a conception of the subject matter of morality. This is what the theory which I shall call contractualism seeks to do. Even if it succeeds in this, however, and is judged superior to philosophical utilitarianism as an account of the nature of morality, normative utilitarianism will not have been refuted. The possibility will remain that normative utilitarianism can be established on other grounds, for example as the normative outcome of contractualism itself. But one direct and, I think, influential argument for normative utilitarianism will have been set aside.

To give an example of what I mean by contractualism, a contractualist account of the nature of moral wrongness might be stated as follows.

An act is wrong if its performance under the circumstances would be disallowed by any system of rules for the general regulation of behavior which no one could reasonably reject as a basis for informed, unforced general agreement.

This is intended as a characterization of the kind of property which moral wrongness is. Like philosophical utilitarianism, it will have normative consequences, but it is not my present purpose to explore these in detail. As a contractualist account of one moral notion, what I have set out here is only an approximation, which may need to be modified considerably. Here I can offer a few remarks by way of clarification.

The idea of "informed agreement" is meant to exclude agreement based on superstition or false belief about the consequences of actions, even if these beliefs are ones which it would be reasonable for the person in question to have. The intended force of the qualification "reasonably," on the other hand, is to exclude rejections that would be unreasonable *given* the aim of finding principles which could be the basis of informed, unforced, general agreement. Given this aim, it would be unreasonable, for example, to reject a principle because it imposed a burden on you when every alternative principle would impose much greater burdens on others. I will have more to say about grounds for rejection later in the paper.

The requirement that the hypothetical agreement which is the subject of moral argument be unforced is meant not only to rule out coercion, but also to exclude being forced to accept an agreement by being in a weak bargaining position, for example because others are able to hold out longer and hence to insist on better terms. Moral argument abstracts from such considerations. The only relevant pressure for agreement comes from the desire to find and agree on principles which no one who had this desire could reasonably reject. According to contractualism, moral argument concerns the possiblity of agreement among persons who are all moved by this desire, and moved by it to the same degree. But this counterfactual assumption characterizes only the agreement with which morality is concerned, not the world to which moral principles are to apply. Those who are concerned with morality look for principles for application to their imperfect world which they could not reasonably reject, and which others in the world, who are not now moved by the desire for agreement, could not reasonably reject should they come to be so moved.[7]

The contractualist account of moral wrongness refers to principles "which no one could reasonably reject" rather than to principles "which everyone could reasonably accept" for the following reason.[8] Consider a principle under which some people will suffer severe hardships, and suppose that these hardships are avoidable. That is, there are alternative principles under which no one would have to bear comparable burdens. It might happen, however, that the people on whom these hardships fall are particularly self-sacrificing, and are willing to accept these burdens for the sake of what they see as the greater good of all. We would not say, I think, that it would be unreasonable of them to do this. On the other hand, it might not be unreasonable for them to refuse these burdens, and, hence, not unreasonable for someone to reject a principle requiring him to bear them. If this rejection would be reasonable, then the principle imposing these burdens is put in doubt, despite the fact that some particularly self-sacrificing people could (reasonably) accept it. Thus it is the reasonableness of rejecting a principle, rather than the reasonableness of accepting it, on which moral argument turns.

It seems likely that many non-equivalent sets of principles will pass the test of non-rejectability. This is suggested, for example, by the fact that there are many different ways of defining important duties, no one of which is more or less "rejectable" than the others. There are, for example, many different systems of agreement-making and many different ways of assigning responsibility to care for others. It does not follow, however, that any action allowed by at least one of these sets of principles cannot be morally wrong according to contractualism. If it is important for us to have *some* duty of a given kind (some duty of fidelity to agreements, or some duty of mutual aid) of which there are many morally acceptable forms, then one of these forms needs to be established by convention. In a setting in which one of these forms *is* conventionally established, acts disallowed by it will be wrong in the sense of the definition given. For, given the need for such conventions, one thing that could not be generally agreed to would be a set of principles allowing one to disregard conventionally established (and morally acceptable) definitions of important duties. This dependence on convention introduces a degree of cultural relativity into contractualist morality. In addition, what a person can reasonably reject will depend on the aims and conditions that are important in his life, and these will also depend on the society in which he lives. The definition given above allows for variation of both of these kinds by making the wrongness of an action depend on the circumstances in which it is performed.

The partial statement of contractualism which I have given has the abstract character appropriate in an account of the subject matter of morality. On its face, it involves no specific claim as to which principles could be agreed to or even whether there is a unique set of principles which could be the basis of agreement. One way, though not the only way, for a contractualist to arrive at substantive moral claims would be to give a technical definition of the relevant notion of agreement, e.g., by specifying the conditions under which agreement is to be reached, the parties to this agreement, and the criteria of reasonableness to be employed. Different contractualists have done this in different ways. What must be claimed for such a definition is that (under the circumstances in which it is to apply) what it describes is indeed the kind of unforced, reasonable agreement at which moral argument aims. But contractualism can also be understood as an informal description of the subject matter of morality on the basis of which ordinary forms of moral reasoning can be understood and appraised without proceeding via a technical notion of agreement.

Who is to be included in the general agreement to which contractualism refers? The scope of morality is a difficult question of substantive morality, but a philosophical theory of the nature of morality should provide some basis for answering it. What an adequate theory should do is to provide a framework within which what seem to be relevant arguments for and against particular interpretations of the moral boundary can be carried out. It is often thought that contractualism can provide no plausible basis for an answer to this question. Critics charge either that contractualism provides no answer at all, because it must begin with some set of contracting parties taken as given, or that contractualism suggests an answer which is obviously too restrictive, since a contract requires parties who are able to make and keep agreements and who are each able to offer the others some benefit in return for their cooperation. Neither of these objections applies to the version of contractualism that I am defending.

The general specification of the scope of morality which it implies seems to me to be this: morality applies to a being if the notion of justification to a being of that kind makes sense. What is required in order for this to be the case? Here I can only suggest some necessary conditions. The first is that the being have a good, that is, that there be a clear sense in which things can be said to go better or worse for that being. This gives partial sense to the idea of what it would be reasonable for a trustee to accept on the being's behalf. It would be reasonable for a trustee to accept at least those things that are good, or not bad, for the being in question. Using this idea of trusteeship we can extend the notion of acceptance to apply to beings that are incapable of literally agreeing to anything. But this minimal notion of trusteeship is too weak to provide a basis for morality, according to contractualism. Contractualist morality relies on notions of what it would be reasonable to accept, or reasonable to reject, which are essentially comparative. Whether it would be unreasonable for me to reject a certain principle, given the aim of finding principles which no one with this aim could reasonably reject, depends not only on how much actions allowed by that principle might hurt me in absolute terms but also on how that potential loss compares with other potential losses to others under this principle and alternatives to it. Thus, in order for a being to stand in moral relations with us it is not enough that it have a good, it is also necessary that its good be sufficiently similar to our own to provide a basis for some system of comparability. Only on the basis of such a system can we give the proper kind of sense to the notion of what a trustee could reasonably reject on a being's behalf.

But the range of possible trusteeship is broader than that of morality. One could act as a trustee for a tomato plant, a forest, or an ant colony, and such entities are not included in morality. Perhaps this can be explained by appeal to the requirement of comparability: while these entities have a good, it is not comparable to our own in a way that provides a basis for moral argument. Beyond this, however, there is in these cases insufficient foothold for the notion of justification *to* a being. One further minimum requirement for this notion is that the being constitute a point of view; that is, that there be such a thing as what it is like to be that being, such a thing as what the world seems like to it. Without this, we do not stand in a relation to the being that makes even hypothetical justification *to it* appropriate.

On the basis of what I have said so far, contractualism can explain why the capacity to feel pain should have seemed to many to count in favour of moral status: a being which has this capacity seems also to satisfy the three conditions I have just mentioned as necessary for the idea of justification to it to make sense. If a being can feel pain, then it constitutes a center of consciousness to which justification can be addressed. Feeling pain is a clear way in which the being can be worse off; having its pain alleviated is a way in which it can be benefited; and these are forms of weal and woe which seem directly comparable to our own.

It is not clear that the three conditions I have listed as necessary are also sufficient for the idea of justification to a being to make sense. Whether they are, and, if they are not, what more may be required, are difficult and disputed questions. Some would restrict the moral sphere to those to whom justifications could in principle be communicated, or to those who can actually agree to something, or to those who have the capacity to understand moral argument. Contractualism as I have stated it does not settle these issues at once. All I claim is that it provides a basis for argument about them which is at least as plausible as that offered by rival accounts of the nature of morality. These proposed restrictions on the scope of morality are naturally understood as debatable claims about the conditions under which the relevant notion of justification makes sense, and the arguments commonly offered for and against them can also be plausibly understood on this basis.

Some other possible restrictions on the scope of morality are more evidently rejectable. Morality might be restricted to those who have the capacity to observe its constraints, or to those who are able to confer some reciprocal benefit on other participants. But it is extremely implausible to suppose that the beings excluded by these requirements fall entirely outside the protection of morality. Contractualism as I have formulated it[9] can explain why this is so: the absence of these capacities alone does nothing to undermine the possibility of justification to a being. What it may do in some cases, however, is to alter the justifications which are relevant. I suggest that whatever importance the capacities for deliberative control and reciprocal benefit may have is as factors altering the duties which beings have and the duties others have towards them, not as conditions whose absence suspends the moral framework altogether.

III

I have so far said little about the normative content of contractualism. For all I have said, the act utilitarian formula might turn out to be a theorem of contractualism. I do not think that this is the case, but my main thesis is that whatever the normative implications of contractualism may be it still has distinctive content as a philosophical thesis about the nature of morality. This content—the difference, for example, between being a utilitarian because the utilitarian formula is the basis of general agreement and being a utilitarian on other grounds—is shown most clearly in the answer that a contractualist gives to the first motivational questions.

Philosophical utilitarianism is a plausible view partly because the facts which it identifies as fundamental to morality—facts about individual well-being—have obvious motivational force. Moral facts can motivate us, on this view, because of our sympathetic identification with the good of others. But as we move from philosophical utilitarianism to a specific utilitarian formula as the standard of right action, the form of motivation that utilitarianism appeals to becomes more abstract. If classical utilitarianism is the correct normative doctrine then the natural source of moral motivation will be a tendency to be moved by changes in aggregate well-being, however these may be composed. We must be moved in the same way by an aggregate gain of the same magnitude whether it is obtained by relieving the acute suffering of a few people or by bringing tiny benefits to a vast number, perhaps at the expense of moderate discomfort for a few. This is very different from sympathy of the familiar kind toward particular individuals, but a utilitarian may argue that this more abstract desire is what natural sympathy becomes when it is corrected by rational reflection. This desire has the same content as sympathy—it is a concern for the good of others—but it is not partial or selective in its choice of objects.

Leaving aside the psychological plausibility of this even-handed sympathy, how good a candidate is it for the role of moral motivation? Certainly sympathy of the usual kind is one of the many motives that can sometimes impel one to do the right thing. It may be the dominant motive, for example, when I run to the aid of a suffering child. But when I feel convinced by Peter Singer's 1972 article on famine, and find myself crushed by the recognition of what seems a clear moral requirement, there is something else at work. In addition to the thought of how much good I could do for people in drought-stricken lands, I am overwhelmed by the further, seemingly distinct thought that it would be wrong for me to fail to aid them when I could do so at so little cost to myself. A utilitarian may respond that his account of moral motivation cannot be faulted for not capturing this aspect of moral experience, since it is just a reflection of our non-utilitarian moral upbringing. Moreover, it must be groundless. For what kind of fact could this supposed further fact of moral wrongness be, and how could it give us a further, special reason for acting? The question for contractualism, then, is whether it can provide a satisfactory answer to this challenge.

According to contractualism, the source of motivation that is directly triggered by the belief that an action is wrong is the desire to be able to justify one's actions to others on grounds they could not reasonably reject.[10] I find this an extremely plausible account of moral motivation—a better account of at least my moral experience than the natural utilitarian alternative—and it seems to me to constitute a strong point for the contractualist view. We all might like to be in actual agreement with the people around us, but the desire which contractualism identifies as basic to morality does not lead us simply to conform to the standards accepted by others whatever these may be. The desire to be able to justify one's actions to others on grounds they could not reasonably reject will be satisfied when we know that there is adequate justification for our action even though others in fact refuse to accept it (perhaps because they have no interest in finding principles which we and others could not reasonably reject). Similarly, a person moved by this desire will not be satisfied by the fact that others accept a justification for his action if he regards this justification as spurious.

One rough test of whether you regard a justification as sufficient is whether you would accept that justification if you were in another person's position. This connection between the idea of "changing places" and the motivation which underlies morality explains the frequent occurrence of "Golden Rule" arguments within different systems of morality and in the teachings of various religions. But the thought experiment of changing places is only a rough guide; the fundamental question is what would it be unreasonable to reject as a basis for informed, unforced, general agreement. As Kant observed,[11] our different individual points of view, taken as they are, may in general be simply irreconcilable. "Judgmental harmony" requires the construction of a genuinely interpersonal form of justification which is nonetheless something that each individual could agree to. From this interpersonal standpoint, a certain amount of how things look from another person's point of view, like a certain amount of how they look from my own, will be counted as bias.

I am not claiming that the desire to be able to justify one's actions to others on grounds they could not reasonably reject is universal or "natural." "Moral education" seems to me plausibly understood as a process of cultivating this desire and shaping it, largely by learning what justifications others are in fact willing to accept, by finding which ones you yourself find acceptable as you confront them from a variety of perspectives, and by appraising your own and others' acceptance or rejection of these justifications in the light of greater experience.

In fact, it seems to me that the desire to be able to justify one's actions (and institutions) on grounds one takes to be acceptable is quite strong in most people. People are willing to go to considerable lengths, involving quite heavy sacrifices, in order to avoid admitting the unjustifiability of their actions and institutions. The notorious insufficiency of moral motivation as a way of getting people to do the right thing is not due to simple weakness of the underlying motive, but rather to the fact that it is easily deflected by self-interest and self-deception.

It could reasonably be objected here that the source of motivation I have described is not tied exclusively to the contractualist notion of moral truth. The account of moral motivation which I have offered refers to the idea of a justification which it would be unreasonable to reject, and this idea is potentially broader than the contractualist notion of agreement. For let M be some non-contractualist account of moral truth. According to M, we may suppose, the wrongness of an action is simply a moral characteristic of that action in virtue of which it ought not to be done. An act which has this characteristic, according to M, has it quite independently of any tendency of informed persons to come to agreement about it. However, since informed persons are presumably in a position to recognize the wrongness of a type of action, it would seem to follow that if an action is wrong then such persons would agree that it is not to be performed. Similarly, if an act is not morally wrong, and there is adequate moral justification to perform it, then there will presumably be a moral justification for it which an informed person would be unreasonable to reject. Thus, even if M, and not contractualism, is the correct account of moral truth, the desire to be able to justify my actions to others on grounds they could not reasonably reject could still serve as a basis for moral motivation.

What this shows is that the appeal of contractualism, like that of utilitarianism, rests in part on a qualified scepticism. A non-contractualist theory of morality can make use of the source of motivation to which contractualism appeals. But a moral argument will trigger this source of motivation only in virtue of being a good justification for acting in a certain way, a justification which others would be unreasonable not to accept. So a non-contractualist theory must claim that there are moral properties which have justificatory force quite independent of their recognition in any ideal agreement. These would represent what John Mackie has called instances of intrinsic "to-be-doneness" and "not-to-be-doneness."[12] Part of contractualism's appeal rests on the view that, as Mackie puts it, it is puzzling how there could be such properties "in the world."

By contrast, contractualism seeks to explain the justificatory status of moral properties, as well as their motivational force, in terms of the notion of reasonable agreement. In some cases the moral properties are themselves to be understood in terms of this notion. This is so, for example, in the case of the property of moral wrongness, considered above. But there are also right- and wrong-making properties which are themselves independent of the contractualist notion of agreement. I take the property of being an act of killing for the pleasure of doing so to be a wrong-making property of this kind. Such properties are wrong-making because it would be reasonable to reject any set of principles which permitted the acts they characterize. Thus, while there are morally relevant properties "in the world" which are independent of the contractualist notion of agreement, these do not constitute instances of intrinsic "to-be-doneness" and "not-to-be-doneness": their moral relevance—their force in justifications as well as their link with motivation—is to be explained on contractualist grounds.

In particular, contractualism can account for the apparent moral significance of facts about individual well-being, which utilitarianism takes to be fundamental. Individual well-being will be morally significant, according to contractualism, not because it is intrinsically valuable or because promoting it is self-evidently a right-making characteristic, but simply because an individual could reasonably reject a form of argument that gave his well-being no weight. This claim of moral significance is, however, only approximate, since it is a further difficult question exactly how "well-being" is to be understood and in what ways we are required to take account of the well-being of others in deciding what to do. It does not follow from this claim, for example, that a given desire will always and everywhere have the same weight in determining the rightness of an action that would promote its satisfaction, a weight proportional to its strength or "intensity." The right-making force of a person's desires is specified by what might be called a conception of morally legitimate interests. Such a conception is a product of moral argument; it is not given, as the notion of individual well-being may be, simply by the idea of what it is rational for an individual to desire. Not everything for which I have a rational desire will be something in which others need concede me to have a legitimate interest which they undertake to weigh in deciding what to do. The range of things which may be objects of my rational desires is very wide indeed, and the range of claims which others could not reasonably refuse to recognize will almost certainly be narrower than this. There will be a tendency for interests to conform to rational desire—for those conditions making it rational to desire something also to establish a legitimate interest in it—but the two will not always coincide.

One effect of contractualism, then, is to break down the sharp distinction, which arguments for utilitarianism appeal to, between the status of individual well-being and that of other moral notions. A framework of moral argument is required to define our legitimate interests and to account for their moral force. This same contractualist framework can also account for the force of other moral notions such as rights, individual responsibility, and procedural fairness.

IV

It seems unlikely that act utilitarianism will be a theorem of the version of contractualism which I have described. The positive moral significance of individual interests is a direct reflection of the contractualist requirement that actions be defensible to each person on grounds he could not reasonably reject. But it is a long step from here to the conclusion that each individual must agree to deliberate always from the point of view of maximum aggregate benefit and to accept justifications appealing to this consideration alone. It is quite possible that, according to contractualism, *some* moral questions may be properly settled by appeal to maximum aggregate well-being, even though this is not the sole or ultimate standard of justification.

What seems less improbable is that contractualism should turn out to coincide with some form of "two-level" utilitarianism. I cannot fully assess this possibility here. Contractualism does share with these theories the important features that the defense of individual actions must proceed via a defense of principles that would allow those acts. But contractualism differs from *some* forms of two-level utilitarianism in an important way. The role of principles in contractualism is fundamental; they do not enter merely as devices for the promotion of acts that are right according to some other standard. Since it does not establish two potentially conflicting forms of moral reasoning, contractualism avoids the instability which often plagues rule utilitarianism.

The fundamental question here, however, is whether the principles to which contractualism leads must be ones whose general adoption (either ideally or under some more realistic conditions) would promote maximum aggregate well-being. It has seemed to many that this must be the case. To indicate why I do not agree I will consider one of the best-known arguments for this conclusion and explain why I do not think it is successful. This will also provide an opportunity to examine the relation between the version of contractualism I have advocated here and the version set forth by Rawls.

The argument I will consider, which is familiar from the writings of Harsanyi and others, proceeds via an interpretation of the contractualist notion of acceptance and leads to the principle of maximum average utility. To think of a principle as a candidate for unanimous agreement I must think of it not merely as acceptable to *me* (perhaps in virtue of my particular position, my tastes, etc.) but as acceptable to others as well.[13] To be relevant, my judgment that the principle is acceptable must be impartial. What does this mean? To judge impartially that a principle is acceptable is, one might say, to judge that it is one which you would have reason to accept no matter who you were. That is, and here is the interpretation, to judge that it is a principle which it would be rational to accept if you did not know which person's position you occupied and believed that you had an equal chance of being in any of these positions. ("Being in a person's position" is here understood to mean being in his objective circumstances and evaluating these from the perspective of his tastes and preferences.) But, it is claimed, the principle which it would be rational to prefer under these circumstances—the one which would offer the chooser greatest expected utility—would be that principle under which the average utility of the affected parties would be highest.

This argument might be questioned at a number of points, but what concerns me at present is the interpretation of impartiality. The argument can be broken down into three stages. The first of these is the idea that moral principles must be impartially acceptable. The second is the idea of choosing principles in ignorance of one's position (including one's tastes, preferences, and so forth). The third is the idea of rational choice

under the assumption that one has an equal chance of occupying anyone's position. Let me leave aside for the moment the move from stage
two to stage three, and concentrate on the first step, from stage one to
stage two. There is a way of making something like this step which is, I
think, quite valid, but it does not yield the conclusion needed by the argument. If I believe that a certain principle, *P,* could not reasonably be
rejected as a basis for informed, unforced, general agreement, then I must
believe not only that it is something which it would be reasonable for me
to accept but something which it would be reasonable for others to accept as well, insofar as we are all seeking a ground for general agreement.
Accordingly, I must believe that I would have reason to accept *P* no matter which social position I were to occupy (though, for reasons mentioned above, I may not believe that I *would* agree to *P* if I were in some
of these positions).

Now it may be thought that no sense can be attached to the notion of
choosing or agreeing to a principle in ignorance of one's social position,
especially when this includes ignorance of one's tastes, preferences, etc.
But there is at least a minimal sense that might be attached to this notion. If it would be reasonable for everyone to choose or agree to *P,* then
my knowledge that I have reason to do so need not depend on my
knowledge of my particular position, tastes, preferences, etc. So, insofar
as it makes any sense at all to speak of choosing or agreeing to something
in the absence of this knowledge, it could be said that I have reason to
choose or agree to those things which everyone has reason to choose or
agree to (assuming, again, the aim of finding principles on which all could
agree). And indeed, this same reasoning can carry us through to a version of stage three. For if I judge *P* to be a principle which everyone has
reason to agree to, then it could be said that I would have reason to agree
to it if I thought that I had an equal chance of being anybody, or indeed,
if I assign any other set of probabilities to being one or another of the
people in question.

But it is clear that this is not the conclusion at which the original argument aimed. That conclusion concerned what it would be rational for
a self-interested person to choose or agree to under the assumption of
ignorance or equal probability of being anyone. The conclusion I have
reached appeals to a different notion: the idea of what it would be unreasonable for people to reject given that they are seeking a basis for general agreement. The direction of explanation in the two arguments is quite
different. The original argument sought to explain the notion of impar-

tial acceptability of an ethical principle by appealing to the notion of rational self-interested choice under special conditions, a notion which appears to be a clearer one. My revised argument explains how *a* sense might be attached to the idea of choice or agreement in ignorance of one's position, given some idea of what it would be unreasonable for someone to reject as a basis for general agreement. This indicates a problem for my version of contractualism: it may be charged with failure to explain the central notion on which it relies. Here I would reply that my version of contractualism does not seek to explain this notion. It only tries to describe it clearly and to show how other features of morality can be understood in terms of it. In particular, it does not try to explain this notion by reducing it to the idea of what would maximize a person's self-interested expectations if he were choosing from a position of ignorance or under the assumption of equal probability of being anyone.

The initial plausibility of the move from stage one to stage two of the original argument rests on a subtle transition from one of these notions to the other. To believe that a principle is morally correct one must believe that it is one which all could reasonably agree to and none could reasonably reject. But my belief that this is the case may often be distorted by a tendency to take its advantage to me more seriously than its possible costs to others. For this reason, the idea of "putting myself in another's place" is a useful corrective device. The same can be said for the thought experiment of asking what I could agree to in ignorance of my true position. But both of these thought experiments are devices for considering more accurately the question of what *everyone* could reasonably agree to or what no one could reasonably reject. That is, they involve the pattern of reasoning exhibited in my revised form of the three-stage argument, not that of the argument as originally given. The question, what would maximize the expectations of a single self-interested person choosing in ignorance of his true position, is a quite different question. This can be seen by considering the possibility that the distribution with the highest average utility, call it A, might involve extremely low utility levels for some people, levels much lower than the minimum anyone would enjoy under a more equal distribution.

Suppose that A is a principle which it would be rational for a self-interested chooser with an equal chance of being in anyone's position to select. Does it follow that no one could reasonably reject A? It seems evident that this does not follow.[14] Suppose that the situation of those who would fare worst under A, call them the Losers, is extremely bad, and that there is an alternative to *A,* call it *E,* under which no one's situation would be nearly as bad as this. Prima facie, the Losers would seem to have a reasonable ground for complaint against *A.* Their objection may be rebutted, by appeal to the sacrifices that would be imposed on some other individual by the selection of *E* rather than *A.* But the mere fact that *A* yields higher average utility, which might be due to the fact that many people do very slightly better under *A* than under *E* while a very few do much worse, does not settle the matter.

Under contractualism, when we consider a principle our attention is naturally directed first to those who would do worst under it. This is because if anyone has reasonable grounds for objecting to the principle it is *likely* to be them. It does not follow, however, that contractualism always requires us to select the principle under which the expectations of the worse off are highest. The reasonableness of the Losers' objection to *A* is not established simply by the fact that they are worse off under *A* and no one would be this badly off under *E.* The force of their complaint depends also on the fact that their position under *A* is, in absolute terms, very bad, and would be significantly better under *E.* This complaint must be weighed against those of individuals who would do worse under E. The question to be asked is, is it unreasonable for someone to refuse to put up with the Losers' situation under *A* in order that someone else should be able to enjoy the benefits which he would have to give up under *E?* As the supposed situation of the Loser under *A* becomes better, or his gain under *E* smaller in relation to the sacrifices required to produce it, his case is weakened.

One noteworthy feature of contractualist argument as I have presented it so far is that it is nonaggregative: what are compared are individual gains, losses, and levels of welfare. How aggregative considerations can enter into contractualist argument is a further question too large to be entered into here.

I have been criticizing an argument for Average Utilitarianism that is generally associated with Harsanyi, and my objections to this argument (leaving aside the last remarks about maximin) have an obvious similarity to objections raised by Rawls.[15] But the objections I have raised apply as well against some features of Rawls' own argument. Rawls accepts the first step of the argument I have described. That is, he believes that the correct principles of justice are those which "rational persons concerned to advance their interests" would accept under the conditions defined by his Original Position, where they would be ignorant of their own particular talents, their conception of the good, and the social position (or generation) into which they were born. It is the second step of the argument which Rawls rejects, i.e., the claim that it would be rational for persons so situated to choose those principles which would offer them greatest expected utility under the assumption that they have an equal chance of being anyone in the society in question. I believe, however, that a mistake has already been made once the first step is taken.

This can be brought out by considering an ambiguity in the idea of acceptance by persons "concerned to advance their interests." On one reading, this is an essential ingredient in contractual argument; on another it is avoidable and, I think, mistaken. On the first reading, the interests in question are simply those of the members of society to whom the principles of justice are to apply (and by whom those principles must ultimately be accepted). The fact that they have interests which may conflict, and which they are concerned to advance, is what gives substance to questions of justice. On the second reading, the concern "to advance their interests" that is in question is a concern of the parties to Rawls' Original Position, and it is this concern which determines, in the first instance,[16] what principles of justice they will adopt. Unanimous agreement among these parties, each motivated to do as well for himself as he can, is to be achieved by depriving them of any information that could give them reason to choose differently from one another. From behind the veil of ignorance, what offers the best prospects for one will offer the best prospects for all, since no one can tell what would benefit him in particular. Thus the choice of principles can be made, Rawls says, from the point of view of a single rational individual behind the veil of ignorance.

Whatever rules of rational choice this single individual, concerned to advance his own interests as best he can, is said to employ, this reduction of the problem to the case of a single person's self-interested choice should arouse our suspicion. As I indicated in criticizing Harsanyi, it is important to ask whether this single individual is held to accept a principle because he judges that it is one he could not reasonably reject whatever position he turns out to occupy, or whether, on the contrary, it is supposed to be acceptable to a person in any social position because it would be the rational choice for a single self-interested person behind the veil of ignorance. I have argued above that the argument for average utilitarianism involves a covert transition from the first pattern of reasoning to the second. Rawls' argument also appears to be of this second form; his defense of his two principles of justice relies, at least initially, on claims about what it would be rational for a person, concerned to advance his own interests, to choose behind a veil of ignorance. I would claim, however, that the plausibility of Rawls' arguments favoring his two principles over the principle of average utility is preserved, and in some cases enhanced, when they are interpreted as instances of the first form of contractualist argument.

Some of these arguments are of an informal moral character. I have already mentioned his remark about the unacceptability of imposing lower expectations on some for the sake of the higher expectations of others. More specifically, he says of the parties to the Original Position that they are concerned "to choose principles the consequences of which they are prepared to live with whatever generation they turn out to belong to"[17] or, presumably, whatever their social position turns out to be. This is a clear statement of the first form of contractualist argument. Somewhat later he remarks, in favor of the two principles, that they "are those a person would choose for the design of a society in which his enemy is to assign him a place."[18] Rawls goes on to dismiss this remark, saying that the parties "should not reason from false premises,"[19] but it is worth asking why it seemed a plausible thing to say in the first place. The reason, I take it, is this. In a contractualist argument of the first form, the object of which is to find principles acceptable to each person, assignment by a malevolent opponent is a thought experiment which has a heuristic role like that of a veil of ignorance: it is a way of testing whether one really does judge a principle to be acceptable from all points of view or whether, on the contrary, one is failing to take seriously its effect on people in social positions other than one's own.

But these are all informal remarks, and it is fair to suppose that Rawls' argument, like the argument for average utility, is intended to move from the informal contractualist idea of principles "acceptable to all" to the idea of rational choice behind a veil of ignorance, an idea which is, he hopes, more precise and more capable of yielding definite results. Let me turn then to his more formal arguments for the choice of the Difference Principle by the parties to the Original Position. Rawls cites three features of the decision faced by parties to the Original Position which, he claims, make it rational for them to use the maximin rule and, therefore, to select his Difference Principle as a principle of justice. These are (a) the absence of any objective basis for estimating probabilities, (b) the fact that some principles could have consequences for them which "they could hardly accept" while (c) it is possible for them (by following maximin) to ensure themselves of a minimum prospect, advances above which, in comparison, matter very little.[20] The first of these features is slightly puzzling, and I leave it aside. It seems clear, however, that the other considerations mentioned have at least as much force in an informal contractualist argument about what all could reasonably agree to as they do in determining the rational choice of a single person concerned to advance his interests. They express the strength of the objection that the "losers" might have to a scheme that maximized average utility at their expense, as compared with the counter-objections that others might have to a more egalitarian arrangement.

In addition to this argument about rational choice, Rawls invokes among "the main grounds for the two principles" other considerations which, as he says, use the concept of contract to a greater extent.[21] The parties to the Original Position, Rawls says, can agree to principles of justice only if they think that this agreement is one that they will actually be able to live up to. It is, he claims, more plausible to believe this of his two principles than of the principle of average utility, under which the sacrifices demanded ("the strains of commitment") could be much higher. A second, related claim is that the two principles of justice have greater psychological stability than the principle of average utility. It is more plausible to believe, Rawls claims, that in a society in which they were fulfilled people would continue to accept them and to be motivated to act in accordance with them. Continuing acceptance of the principle of average utility, on the other hand, would require an exceptional degree of identification with the good of the whole on the part of those from whom sacrifices were demanded.

These remarks can be understood as claims about the "stability" (in a quite practical sense) of a society founded on Rawls' two principles of justice. But they can also be seen as an attempt to show that a principle arrived at via the second form of contractualist reasoning will also satisfy the requirements of the first form, i.e., that it is something no one could reasonably reject. The question "is the acceptance of this principle an agreement you could actually live up to?" is, like the idea of assignment by one's worse enemy, a thought experiment through which we can use our own reactions to test our judgment that certain principles are ones that no one could reasonably reject. General principles of human psychology can also be invoked to this same end.

Rawls' final argument is that the adoption of his two principles gives public support to the self-respect of individual members of society, and gives "a stronger and more characteristic interpretation of Kant's idea"[22] that people must be treated as ends, not merely as means to the greater collective good. But, whatever difference there may be here between Rawls' two principles of justice and the principle of average utility, there is at least as sharp a contrast between the two patterns of contractualist reasoning distinguished above. The connection with self-respect, and with the Kantian formula, is preserved by the requirement that principles of justice be ones which no member of the society could reasonably reject. This connection is weakened when we shift to the idea of a choice which advances the interests of a single rational individual for whom the various individual lives in a society are just so many different possibilities. This is so whatever decision rule this rational chooser is said to employ. The argument from maximin seems to preserve this connection with self-respect because it reproduces as a claim about rational choice what is, in slightly different terms, an appealing moral argument.

The "choice situation" that is fundamental to contractualism as I have described it is obtained by beginning with "mutually disinterested" individuals with full knowledge of their situations and adding to this (not, as is sometimes suggested, benevolence but) a desire on each of their parts to find principles which none could reasonably reject insofar as they too have this desire. Rawls several times considers such an idea in passing.[23] He rejects it in favor of his own idea of mutually disinterested choice from behind a veil of ignorance on the ground that only the latter enables us to reach definite results: "if in choosing principles we required unanimity even where there is full information, only a few rather obvious cases could be decided."[24] I believe that this supposed advantage is questionable. Perhaps this is because my expectations for moral argument are more modest than Rawls'.

However, as I have argued, almost all of Rawls' own arguments have at least as much force when they are interpreted as arguments within the form of contractualism which I have been proposing.

One possible exception is the argument from maximin. If the Difference Principle were taken to be generally applicable to decisions of public policy, then the second form of contractualist reasoning through which it is derived would have more far-reaching implications than the looser form of argument by comparison of losses, which I have employed. But these wider applications of the principle are not always plausible, and I do not think that Rawls intends it to be applied so widely. His intention is that the Difference Principle should be applied only to major inequalities generated by the basic institutions of a society, and this limitation is a reflection of the special conditions under which he holds maximin to be the appropriate basis for rational choice: some choices have outcomes one could hardly accept, while gains above the minimum one can assure one's self matter very little, and so on. It follows, then, that in applying the Difference Principle—in identifying the limits of its applicability—we must fall back on the informal comparison of losses which is central to the form of contractualism I have described.

V

I have described this version of contractualism only in outline. Much more needs to be said to clarify its central notions and to work out its normative implications. I hope that I have said enough to indicate its appeal as a philosophical theory of morality and as an account of moral motivation. I have put forward contractualism as an alternative to utilitarianism, but the characteristic feature of the doctrine can be brought out by contrasting it with a somewhat different view.

It is sometimes said that morality is a device for our mutual protection.[25] According to contractualism, this view is partly true but in an important way incomplete. Our concern to protect our central interests will have an important effect on what we could reasonably agree to. It will thus have an important effect on the content of morality if contractualism is correct. To the degree that this morality is observed, these protection interests will gain from it. If we had no desire to be able to justify our actions to others on grounds they could reasonably accept, the hope of gaining the protection offered by morality would give us reason to try to instill this desire in others, perhaps through mass hypnosis or conditioning, even if this also meant acquiring it ourselves. But given that we have this desire for protection already, our concern with morality is less instrumental.

The contrast might be put as follows. On one view, concern with protection is fundamental, and general agreement becomes relevant as a means or a necessary condition for securing this protection. On the other, contractualist view, the desire for protection is an important factor determining the content of morality because it determines what can reasonably be agreed to. But the idea of general agreement does not arise as a means of securing protection. It is, in a more fundamental sense, what morality is about.

NOTES

1. Though here the ties between the nature of morality and its content are more important. It is not clear that an account of the nature of morality which left its content *entirely* open could be the basis for a plausible account of moral motivation.

2. See John Rawls (1974–75:8) and Daniels (1979:257–258). How closely the process of what I am calling philosophical explanation will coincide with the search for "wide reflective equilibrium" as this is understood by Rawls and by Daniels is a further question which I cannot take up here.

3. For expression of this dissatisfaction see Singer (1974) and Richard Brandt, *A Theory of the Good and the Right* (Oxford: Oxford University Press, 1979), pp. 16–21.

4. Sir William David Ross, *Foundations of Ethics* (Oxford: Oxford University Press, 1939), pp. 52–54, 315.

5. For purposes of this discussion I leave open the important questions of which individuals are to count and how "well-being" is to be understood. Philosophical utilitarianism will retain the appeal I am concerned with under many different answers to these questions.

6. "Average Utilitarianism" is most plausibly arrived at through quite a different form of argument, one more akin to contractualism. I discuss one such argument in section 4.

7. Here I am indebted to Gilbert Harman for comments which have helped me to clarify my statement of contractualism.

8. A point I owe to Derek Parfit.

9. On this view (as contrasted with some others in which the notion of a contract is employed) what is fundamental to morality is the desire for reasonable agreement, not the pursuit of mutual advantage. See section 5. It should be clear that this version of contractualism can account for the moral standing of future persons who will be better or worse off as a result of what we do now. It is less clear how it can deal with the problem presented by future people who would not have been born but for actions of ours which also made the conditions in which they live worse. Do such people have reason to reject principles allowing these actions to be performed? This difficult problem, which I cannot explore here, is raised by Derek Parfit.

10. Reasonably, that is, given the desire to find principles which other similarly motivated could not reasonably reject.

11. Kant (1785), section 2, footnote 14.

12. John Leslie Mackie, *Ethics: Inventing Right and Wrong* (London: Penguin, 1977), p. 42.

13. In discussing Harsanyi and Rawls I will generally follow them in speaking of the acceptability of principles rather than their unrejectability. The difference between these, pointed out above, is important only within the version of contractualism I am presenting; accordingly, I will speak of rejectability only when I am contrasting my own version with theirs.

14. The discussion which follows has much in common with the contrast between majority principles and unanimity principles drawn by Thomas Nagel in "Equality," chapter 8 of *Mortal Questions* (Cambridge: Cambridge University Press, 1979. I am indebted to Nagel's discussion of this idea.

15. For example, the intuitive argument against utilitarianism on page 14 of Rawls, *A Theory of Justice* (Cambridge: Harvard University Press, 1971) and his repeated remark that we cannot expect some people to accept lower standards of life for the sake of the higher expectations of others.

16. Though they must then check to see that the principles they have chosen will be stable, not produce intolerable strains of commitment, and so on. As I argue below, these further considerations can be interpreted in a way that brings Rawls' theory closer to the version of contractualism presented here.

17. Rawls, p. 137.

18. *Ibid.*, p. 152.

19. *Ibid.*, p. 153.

20. *Ibid.*, p. 154.

21. *Ibid.*, sec. 29, pp. 175ff.

22. *Ibid.*, p. 183.

23. E.G., Rawls, pp. 141, 148, although these passages may not clearly distinguish between this alternative and an assumption of benevolence.

24. Rawls, p. 141.

25. In different ways by Geoffrey J. Warnock in *The Object of Morality* (London: Methuen, 1971), and by John L. Mackie, *Ethics*. See also Richard Brandt's remarks on justification in chapter 10 of *A Theory of the Good and the Right*.

[13]
Revolutionary Action Today

SHELDON S. WOLIN

O NE OF THE CHAPTERS in Tocqueville's *Democracy in America* is entitled "Why Great Revolutions will become Rare." His thesis was that once a society becomes democratized in its political system and more egalitarian in its social institutions, it is unlikely that it will ever undergo the type of revolutionary upheavals experienced by France in 1789 and England in the 1640s. The great revolutions had resulted from gross political and social inequalities. Thanks to its system of equal political rights (i.e., for white males), and the ready availability of land, American democracy had eliminated the causes of revolution. He claimed that the revolutionary impulse would wither because for the first time in Western history the masses of ordinary human beings had a tangible stake in defending the status quo.

Tocqueville's conclusions have been restated in many ways. Democracy, it has been said, is the form of government that has had its revolution. Others claim that for the people to rebel against democracy is for them to rebel against themselves, or that a revolution against democracy in the name of democracy is a contradiction in terms. In each of these formulations the implication is that as long as a political system is democratic, it makes no sense to think of revolutionary activity as an appropriate or obligatory form of action for the democratic citizen. But the real problem is, is it right for the democratic citizen to undertake revolutionary action when the political system retains some of the formal features of democracy but is clearly embarked on a course that is progres-

Reprinted by permission from *Democracy* (Fall 1982, vol. 2, no. 4).

sively antidemocratic without being crudely repressive? What are the precise ways in which a system that is formally democratic conceals its antidemocratic tendencies? Are pseudodemocratic substitutes introduced that create the illusion of democracy? Was the idea of a democratic citizen partially skewed at the outset so that its development in America was truncated? And, finally, does it make sense even to discuss the possibility of revolution under the circumstances of an advanced, complex society? In what terms would it make sense to talk of revolution today—what would revolutionary action by democratic citizens be?

Democratic Citizen

Our starting point is with a significant silence. Although the United States has been repeatedly described as being in a condition of crisis, no one seems to have suggested that there is a crisis at the center of American democracy, in the idea of citizenship itself. While there are many voices, with varying degrees of good faith, ready to testify for democracy—especially when the purpose is to contrast the United States with the USSR—there is virtually no one who is given to reflecting about the democratic citizen, to asking what it is to be one, or why, if each of us is one and there are so many of us, the society seems to have so many antidemocratic tendencies.

In a speech last June to the British Parliament Ronald Reagan announced that the United States was about to throw its prestige and resources behind a program launched to strengthen "democracy throughout the world," but he made no reference to the idea of democratic citizenship or any suggestion that democracy might need strengthening at home. The silence on the subject is not peculiar to conservatives or reactionaries. The democratic citizen does not appear in any substantial form in the writings of Barry Commoner, the titular leader of the Citizens' Party, or Michael Harrington, the theoretician of Democratic Socialism of America. Most Marxists are interested in the "masses" or the workers, but they dismiss citizenship as a bourgeois cc eit, formal and empty, although Marx himself was much preoccupied 'th the idea in his early writings.

The present silence is a symptom of a crisis that has been in the making since the beginning of the republic. Its origins are in the one-sided conception of citizenship that was reflected in the Constitution. Beginning with the movement for a bill of rights, which was mounted in the midst of the controversy over ratification of the original Constitution (1787–89), and extending through the era of Jacksonian Democracy, the battle over slavery, and the adoption of Amendments 13, 14, 15, 17 (providing for the direct election of senators), and 19 (prohibiting the denial of suffrage on the basis of sex), a distinct pattern emerged in which each extension of rights was assumed to be an advance toward the realization of democracy. In actuality, the ideal of rights was usurping the place of civic activity. A liberal conception of citizenship was becoming predominant.

A democratic conception of citizenship, if it means anything at all, means that the citizen is supposed to exercise his rights to advance or protect the kind of polity that depends on his being involved in its common concerns. The liberal view was that citizenship is democratic in the United States because every citizen, regardless of cultural, social, economic, and biological differences, can equally claim the right to vote, speak, worship, acquire property and have it protected, and be assured of the elements of a fair trial. Unfortunately, the liberal civic culture never supplied any content to rights. A citizen was no less a citizen for espousing Klan doctrines than he was for joining the NAACP. To possess rights was to be free to do anything or say anything as long as one did not break the law or interfere with the rights of others.

Revolutionary Action Today

How could a democratic conception of citizenship be said to be fulfilled—as a liberal conception would be—by having rights exercised for antidemocratic ends, as the KKK choice would be? It is not that a liberal view of rights disposes one toward the Klan, only that liberalism is fulfilled by protecting those who are so disposed. The American Civil Liberties Union, with its commitment to defending the entire range of opinion, from the most liberal to the most illiberal, was, one might say, immanent in the historical failure of liberalism to create a vision of civic commitments and of common action that could furnish both content and guidance to the exercise of rights.

This failure was inevitable, given the nature of the original liberal project, which was to protect rights by limiting governmental power. That project was written into the Constitution. The Constitution was not designed to encourage citizen action but to prevent arbitrary power, especially the form of power represented by the will of the majority. Among several of the states, the majority principle was being actively tested in the period from the outbreak of the Revolution in 1776 to the ratification of the Constitution in 1789. The Constitution was intended to shatter the majoritarian experiment at the national level by incorporating several devices that were supposed to frustrate the natural form of democratic action: separation of powers, checks and balances, federalism, the Supreme Court, indirect election of the president and Senate, and brief tenure for representatives. At the same time, the Constitution made no reference to the right to vote or hold office or to the principle of equality. Save for a somewhat enigmatic clause that was later interpreted to prevent a state from discriminating against citizens of other states, citizenship hardly figured as a basic institution. When the first ten amendments were quickly added to the Constitution, the outline of the citizen began to emerge, but it was primarily as a bearer of rights than as a participant in a collective undertaking. Several rights in the original Bill of Rights were couched in language that was less suggestive of what a citizen might actively do than what government was prohibited from doing. ("Congress shall make no law . . . abridging the freedom of speech. . . . No person shall . . . be deprived of life, liberty, or property, without due process of law.")

The present silence about democratic citizenship is a sign of the disintegration of the liberal conception of rights and, necessarily, of the idea of citizenship dependent upon it. What happened is that in the twentieth century the liberal practice of politics rapidly undermined the liberal conception of rights. The theory of rights enshrined in the Bill of Rights conceived of special forms of freedom and protection that were to be beyond the ordinary reach of legislative or executive power. Once they had been given constitutional status, rights were not only beyond the scope of positive law, they were assumed to be "above" politics. Whenever an historical controversy arose about rights, the point was made repeatedly that constitutional guarantees were intended to protect rights against "transient majorities" and "temporary gusts of passion."

At almost the exact moment when the liberal theory of rights was about to be given the material form of the first ten amendments to the Constitution, James Madison, who was the prime mover of that effort, also produced what came to be the classical formulation of the liberal theory of politics. In Letter 10 of the *Federalist* papers he argued that one of the sternest tests for the proposed Constitution would be whether it could control "factions," the distinctive form of politics in a society founded on freedom. A faction was a group organized to promote its interests by political means. Inevitably factions would be in continual conflict with each other, not only over property rights but over political and religious beliefs as well. Thus the liberal conception of politics, with its conception of groups as pursuing interests that would conflict with other interests protected by legal rights, carried the presumption that politics was an activity that, by nature, posed a threat to rights. The task, as Madison and later liberals saw it, was to encourage institutional devices that would control the effects of politics, not to reconstitute politics. Citizens would be engrossed in private actions, for when men and women are given freedom they use it to promote their self-interests, and it would be unjust and oppressive to limit that pursuit in the name of encouraging common action for common ends.

There were at least two further respects in which the liberal conception of politics was at odds with liberal rights. First, the protection of rights presupposed that government would be their defender, intervening to prevent interest groups from violating the rights of other groups or individuals. For this presupposition to work, government itself would have to withstand effectively the pressures generated by interest-group politics, pressures that were guaranteed to be unrelenting by the system of elections, campaign contributions, and lobbying. The presupposition collapsed because once politics was reduced to interest groups, there was no general constituency to support government in its role of impartial defender of rights. Instead of playing the role of defender of rights, government assumed a function more consistent with the politics of interest groups, that of "balancing" rights against certain overriding matters of state. Thus when wider latitude was given to the CIA and FBI to conduct surveillance, or when First Amendment rights of the press were limited by the prohibition against disclosing the names of CIA agents, the government's justification was that there had to be balancing of national security needs with civil liberties, as though the setting were simply another instance of having to weigh the demands of conflicting groups.

Interest politics discourages as well the development of a civil culture favorable to the defense of rights and to the acceptance of integrative action as the activity definitive of citizenship. Interest politics dissolves the idea of the citizen as one for whom it is natural to join together with other citizens to act for purposes related to a general community and substitutes the idea of individuals who are grouped according to conflicting interests. The individual is not first and foremost a civic creature bound by preexisting ties to those who share the same history, the same general association, and the same fate. He or she is instead a business executive, a teamster, a feminist, office worker, farmer, or homosexual whose immediate identity naturally divides him or her from others. As a member of an interest group, the individual is given an essentially anticivic education. He is taught that the first duty is to support the self-interest of the group because politics is nothing but a struggle for advantage. In contrast, the citizen has to decide what to do, not in a setting where each has the same interest as the other, but in one where there are differences that have to be taken into account and, ideally, incorporated into the decision. The citizen, unlike the groupie, has to acquire a perspective of commonality, to think integrally and comprehensively rather than exclusively. The groupie never gets beyond "politics," the stage of unreflective self-interest.

The inability of liberals to develop either a tradition of the state as the consistent defender of rights—save, of course, property rights—or a civil culture that nourished political action rather than politics eventually led to the radical alteration in the status of rights. The underlying philosophy of the Bill of Rights, which drew heavily from the tradition of natural-rights thinking, was that the status of rights could be "settled" on a more or less permanent basis, that once a right was included in the Constitution it was "fixed" or, in the language of the eighteenth-century natural-law writers, "unalterable." But rights proved no less tractable to interest-group politics than did other lofty subjects, such as foreign polity or national defense. Throughout the nineteenth century and down to the New Deal, property rights, rather than civil or political rights, dominated American politics—even the issue of slavery was formulated as a matter of rights of ownership. But in the twentieth century, especially after World War II, it has been the civil rights of citizens that have been contested, not only in the courts and before administrative tribunals, but in the arena of interest-group politics.

Some of the most powerful groups are organized for the express purpose of using political and legal means to deprive other citizens of their rights or to restrict the exercise or scope of them. Rights to abortion, sexual freedom, freedom from censorship, public education free of religious influences, rights of privacy against sophisticated surveillance, affirmative action quotas—these and a multitude of other issues are an indication of how profoundly politicized rights have become, how unassured their status is. This is not, as the Founding Fathers or latter-day conservatives would have it, because of the tyranny of the majority. Many of the limitations imposed on rights through legislation or administrative rulings have been inspired by minorities obsessed with single issues. Society is now accustomed to the dangerous notion that rights, like crop subsidies or taxes, are part of the normal give-and-take of politics.

The transvaluation of rights from a quasi-absolute to a contingent status, from being constitutive of politics to being very nearly derivative or reflexive, is vividly illustrated by the recent fate of the system of "economic rights" that liberals had vigorously promoted and touted as the answer to socialism. Beginning with the New Deal, liberals argued that political rights were formal and ineffective if citizens did not have jobs, social security, unemployment compensation, the right to organize unions and bargain collectively, access to higher education, and, in general, a decent standard of living. The claim was frequently made that because material needs were primary, economic rights were more "fundamental" than political rights. This primacy should be given recognition by legislating an "economic Bill of Rights" that would supply a "real" foundation for the exercise of what would otherwise be formal or "legal" rights. Although this proposal was not explicitly adopted, it accurately foreshadowed the extraordinary growth of social benefits and services that evolved into the program of the welfare state. It proved to be a latter-day version of Esau's bargain, a selling of a political birthright for a mess of pottage.

Economic rights, or, as they more recently have been called, "entitlements," do empower people. There is a gain in dignity, autonomy, and well-being, and no democrat should believe otherwise. But this must not bind one to the antipolitical consequences resulting from the preoccupation with economic rights. Unlike the situation with political rights, where, for example, my possession of a right to form a voluntary association does not diminish your right to free speech, economic rights are contingent upon finite resources: your right to medical care will necessarily utilize resources that cannot be allocated to satisfy my right to job training. In the context of an expanding economy such as existed from roughly 1945–70 the political consequences of economic rights were temporarily suppressed, but with the onset of economic recession, stagflation, and unemployment, the diverse effects of basing the value of citizenship upon economic benefits became apparent. Given a capitalist economy and an increasingly harsh conception of it by the dominant groups, all of the solutions to the deepening crisis involved cutting back social benefits and thereby creating or exacerbating cleavages among the citizenry: racial, religious, class, ethnic, and regional prejudices moved closer to the surface as groups competed for survival in a declining economy.

Interest-group politics became intensified, while concern for shared values and a common fate seemed either incomprehensible or utopian and naive.

Yet this is not quite a complete description of our political condition because it omits one of the most striking and seemingly puzzling facts. Despite the deepening unemployment, the irrational level of defense expenditures, the utter hopelessness for millions of blacks and many Hispanics, and the brazenly business-oriented bias of the Reagan administration, there is an astonishing passivity among those who have been hurt most by the current economic policies. All of the elements for radical political protest appear to be present. And yet there has been no general mobilization of outrage, only a few parades.

There are, of course, many reasons for the political passivity of the unemployed and the permanently poor, but one of the most important is the depoliticization to which they have been subjected. For more than three decades the thinking behind as well as the substance of public policies dealing with the poor, the unemployed, and racial minorities, have treated them as having a pariah status quite unlike other interests. The tacit assumption of interest-group politics has always been that there was one common element among farmers, workers, employers, and teachers, etc.: they were all productive in one way or another. They might receive subsidies, benefits, or protections from the government, but after all, it was they who in the last analysis were contributing to what they were receiving. This is why farmers and businessmen have always been outraged whenever the federal government has attempted to use government aid as a justification for government regulation and intervention. Farmers and businessmen have never conceived of themselves as receiving handouts and therefore as being dependents. As a result, they have been able to retain a strong sense of dignity and have been able to act with others who share their interests.

Those who are poor, unemployed, and members of racial minorities can be treated differently, in ways that are divisive, that render them incapable of sustained political action. They are "targeted" by specialized programs that, in effect, fragment their lives. One agency handles medical assistance, another job training, a third food stamps, and so on *ad infinitum*. If a person's life is first flensed by bureaucrats whose questionnaires probe every detail of it, and that life is reorganized into categories corresponding to public programs that are the means of one's existence, the person becomes totally disabled as a political being, unable to grasp

the meaning of common concerns of even so small a totality as a neighborhood. This is because he or she has been deprived of the most ele-
mental totality of all, the self.

Depoliticization is more extreme among the poor and racial minorities
because they are the most helpless of all groups in the political economy,
the new social form that is replacing the older form of the political order.
The political economy has taken the liberal idea of the citizen one apol-
itical step farther. The conception of the citizen as a bearer of rights, who
in principle could exercise his capacities to speak, petition, write, and associate, gave way to a conception of a wholly new kind of being whose
existence consisted of indices which told him what his condition was objectively: an index for prices, another for wages, inflation, unemployment, consumer spending, and, most grandly, "a misery index."

However useful indices may be for those who have the power to make
decisions, they are simultaneously a symbol of powerlessness and a persuasive force toward further depoliticization for those who cannot. An
index, such as one representing inflation rates, does not tell the individual what he is *doing*, but rather what is *happening to him*. It registers forces
that are beyond his ability to influence or control.

Perhaps there is no more striking indication of the extent of depoliticization than the level of popular awareness concerning how the political
system really works. Most people understand that our system makes it
relatively easy for wealth and economic power to be translated into political power and influence, which are then retranslated into legislative
enactments, Treasury rulings, defense contracts, FCC policies, export li-
censes, and the like. They also know that money, especially corporate
money, buys candidates, finances campaigns, hires lobbyists, and keeps a
legion of experts, especially academic ones, on long retainers and short
leashes. What is so striking is not that people know these things, but that
the dominant groups in the political economy are now so confident of
their control that they encourage rather than suppress public knowledge
of their enormous power. It becomes the interest of corporate power,
not simply that ordinary citizens should perceive how money buys politicians and legislation, but that they should perceive how *much* money it
takes. That knowledge provides an invaluable lesson in powerlessness. Lurid
accounts of political scandals are doubly useful in this regard, especially
when large sums are involved; they teach how much money it takes to
purchase favors and how purchasable public officials are, and how utterly

cynical it has all become when government corrupts its own members. One Abscam is worth a thousand Mobil ads.

Corporate politics has perverted the forms of politics that meant to connect the institutions of government with the citizens. These changes have been recognized but not frontally challenged because—at the most obvious level—the political economy developed over the past century has been a spectacular success. The very functioning of a successful economy seems to transform political categories and expectations into economic ones, and thereby creates an illusion of "economic democracy." If we do not participate as citizens we do participate as consumers, exercising our freedom to choose our satisfactions whenever we wish—and as if by magic when new products suddenly materialize on the store shelves, we feel that the economy is responding to our every impulse and desire—which is more than we can say about our elected representatives and nonelected public administrators.

About seventy-five years ago, Elihu Root, a representative public figure of the age, remarked after surveying the state of American politics that "in the whole field of popular government I am convinced that one of the plainest duties of citizenship is hopefulness, and that pessimism is criminal weakness."[1] In a land where optimism is virtually a patriotic duty, pessimism is still taken as a symptom of resignation and despair. But pessimism is, I think, something else: the sign of suppressed revolutionary impulses. Pessimism is the mood inspired by a reasoned conviction that only a revolutionary change can ward off the consequences that are implicit in the tendencies in contemporary American society, but that such a revolution, while politically and morally justified by democratic standards for legitimate authority, is neither possible nor prudent—if by revolution we mean launching a campaign of violent insurrection or civil war. Revolutions of that nature are plainly pathological under contemporary conditions of interdependency.

Democrats need a new conception of revolution. Its text should be John Locke, not Karl Marx, because the problem is not to show that a social class should seize power—no social class in an advanced society can pretend to the universality of right which Marx presupposed in the workers of his day—but to reinvent the forms and practices that will express a democratic conception of collective life.

Locke is best remembered for the argument that when those who rule seem bent on acquiring "Absolute Power over the Lives, Liberties, and

Estates of the People," their power, which they hold on trust from the people, reverts, and the people are free to fashion new institutions. The right to revolution is not solely a right to overturn and destroy institutions but to fashion new ones because those who rule have perverted the old ones. The right to revolution is the right to create new forms.

Locke insisted that if that right was to be meaningful, people were not required to wait submissively until absolute power had been established:

> the State of Mankind is not so miserable that they are not capable of using this Remedy till it be too late to look for any. . . . Men can never be secure from Tyranny if there be no means to escape it, till they are perfectly under it . . . they have not only a right to get out of it, but to prevent it.[2]

When the right to revolution is conceived as justifying political creativity rather than violence, it is easy to understand why Locke was so insistent that people should and would not revolt over "every little mismanagement in publick affairs." Establishing new institutions was justified only after the rulers had engaged in "a long train of Abuses, Prevarications, and Artifices, all tending the same way." Elsewhere he alluded to a "general course and tendency of things" and to "a settled Design." Given the complex judgment required, Locke's discussion was remarkable for its democratic implications. At various times he referred to the right to revolt as an option that belonged to the "people," to "the majority," and even to individuals; but he never implied that it was so weighty a matter that only a high-minded elite could be entrusted with it. This last point is crucial for if the right to revolt is about devising new institutions, citizenship is more than a matter of being able to claim rights. It is about a capacity to generate power, for that is the only way that things get established in the world. And it is about a capacity to share in power, to cooperate in it, for that is how institutions and practices are sustained.

Under contemporary conditions, the Lockean question is: are there signs of rebellion, symptoms of disaffection but also examples of political creativity? For some years now social scientists have uncovered widespread civic apathy and pollsters have reported on the low esteem in which politicians and major political institutions are held. Now in a society where the official rhetoric and the rituals of political socialization are still heavily democratic, *incivisme* of the kind documented by voting studies is a serious matter. It is not alienation but disaffection and rejection. I want to suggest that "rejectionism" pervades our society and that its presence and intensity represents a form of rebellion, a gesture of defiance in the face of a system that is immovable and so interconnected as to be unreformable as a totality. We see rejectionism in the vast underground economy of illicit transactions; in the chronic insubordination that plagues the armed forces; and even, I would hazard, in the patriotic zeal of the Moral Majority: for if one looks at their rhetoric and actions, one finds a profound loathing for the current condition of the body politic. We see it among professional groups where the obsession with money and status seems inspired less by greed than by the inability to find any moral point to serving a society so wholly dominated by the corporate ethos. And it is present in its most exaggerated form among high school achievers and undergraduates who are convinced that if they can transform themselves into technical functions—law, medicine, public administration, and business management—they will be hermetically sealed off from the cynicism and corruption of society.

The origins of rejectionism lie in the 1960s. The turmoil of those years was not solely about the Vietnam war: it was about racism, imperialism, professionalism, affluence, moral codes, orthodox notions of sexuality and gender, and much more, from junk food to slick culture. It was revolutionary not because it was violent—the violence was exaggerated by the media—but because it was uncivil and yet civil: uncivil in withdrawing from and condemning the bourgeois forms of civility, but civil in inventing new ones, many of them bearing the marks of an obsession with participation and equality as well as an intoxication with the first experience of power, the experience of cooperation, common sacrifice, and common concern. "Sharing" threatened suddenly to lose its sentimental overtones and become a political word.

The truth of rejectionism is that it recognizes that it is naive to expect the initiative for reform of the state to issue from the political process that serves the interests of political capitalism. This structure can only be reduced if citizens withdraw and direct their energies and civic commitment to finding new life forms. Toward these ends, our whole mode of thinking must be turned upside down. Instead of imitating most other political theories and adopting the state as the primary structure and then adapting the activity of the citizen to the state, democratic thinking should renounce the state paradigm and, along with it, the liberal-legal corruption of the citizen. The old citizenship must be replaced by a fuller and wider notion of being whose politicalness will be expressed not in one or two modes of activity—voting or protesting—but in many.

A political being is not to be defined as the citizen has been, as an abstract, disconnected bearer of rights, privileges, and immunities, but as a person whose existence is located in a particular place and draws its sustenance from circumscribed relationships: family, friends, church, neighborhood, workplace, community, town, city. These relationships are the sources from which political beings draw power—symbolic, material, and psychological—and that enable them to act together. For true political power involves not only acting so as to effect decisive changes; it also means the capacity to receive power, to be acted upon, to change, and be changed. From a democratic perspective, power is not simply force that is generated; it is experience, sensibility, wisdom, even melancholy, distilled from the diverse relations and circles we move within. Democratic power, accordingly bears the marks of its diverse origins—family, school, church, workplace, etc.—and, as a result, everything turns on an ability to establish practices whose form will not distort the manifold origins of power.

The practical task is to nurture existing movements that can provide constructive forms for rejectionism and make it genuinely political. The most important of these are the grass roots movements that have become epidemic throughout the country. Their range and variety are astonishing. They include rent control, utility rates and service, environmental concerns, health care, education, nuclear power, legal aid, workers' ownership of plants, and much more. Their single most important feature is that they have grown up outside the state-corporate structure and have flourished despite repeated efforts to discredit them.

While it is of the utmost importance that democrats support and encourage political activity at the grass roots level, it is equally necessary that the political limitations of such activity be recognized. It is politically incomplete. This is because the localism that is the strength of grass roots organizations is also their limitation. There are major problems in our society that are general in nature and necessitate modes of vision and action that are comprehensive rather than parochial. And there are historical legacies of wrong and unfairness that will never be confronted and may even be exacerbated by exclusive concern with backyard politics.

During the last year hopeful signs of discontent have emerged at this more general level in the antinuclear movement, the opposition to an imperialistic foreign policy, and the defense of human rights. These developments are suggestive because they represent the first steps ever toward systematic popular intervention in the sacrosanct domain of state secrets and national security. This is new terrain for democratic politics and it is genuinely political, for the problems of war, rights, and imperialism concern us all, not only because our survival is at stake but also because our bodies, our labor, and our legitimating name are frequently used for purposes that implicate us in shameful actions.

NOTES

1. Elihu Root, *Addresses on Government and Citizenship* (Cambridge: Harvard University Press, 1916), p. 59.

2. John Locke, *Two Treatises of Government,* vol. 2, p. 220.

Afterword

The Politics of
American Neo-Pragmatism

CORNEL WEST

Pragmatism could be characterized as the doctrine that all problems are at bottom problems of conduct, that all judgments are, implicitly, judgments of value, and that, as there can be ultimately no valid distinction of theoretical and practical, so there can be no final separation of questions of truth of any kind from questions of the justifiable ends of action.

C. I. Lewis, *Collected Papers*

I revelled in the keen analysis of William James, Josiah Royce and young George Santayana. But it was James with his pragmatism . . . that turned me from the lovely but sterile land of philosophic speculation to the social sciences.

W. E. B. Du Bois, *Autobiography*

IN THE EYES of many, we live among the ruins of North Atlantic civilization. Major philosophical figures such as Hannah Arendt, Walter Benjamin, Martin Heidegger, Alasdair MacIntyre and Ludwig Wittgenstein echo this Spenglerian theme. Possible nuclear holocaust hovers over us. Rampant racism, persistent patriarchy, extensive class inequality, brutal state repression, subtle bureaucratic surveillance, and technological abuse of nature pervade capitalist, communist, and neocolonial countries. The once vital tradition of bourgeois humanism has become vapid and sterile. The emancipatory intent of revolutionary Marxism has been aborted and discredited. The shock effect of Catastrophic nihilism is now boring and uninteresting. As we approach the end of the twentieth century, the rich intellectual resources of the West are in disarray and a frightening future awaits us.

The most terrifying aspects of this contemporary situation fail to affect the discourses and practices of most American intellectuals—principally owing to unique geographical isolation, recent professional insularity, and relative economic prosperity. This is especially so in regard to American philosophers. Under the spell of Viennese-style logical positivism (whose major proponents migrated here), Oxford-inspired linguistic analysis, Continental phenomenology and existentialism, and homespun naturalism, post-World War II American philosophy became a legitimate academic discipline and respectable professional career. Similar to the singular roles of New Criticism in literary studies and structural-functionalism in the social sciences, these philosophical "schools of thought" not only produced intense intellectual activity, they also provided stable and secure self-images for new arrivals in the then-expanding stratum of university and college professors. This unprecedented expansion was regulated by professional norms and habits: easy transmittance of techniques, routine evaluation of performance, and widespread agreement on pertinent problems.

By the late fifties, the voices of something new could be heard. Thoroughly trained in the predominant paradigm of Anglo-American philosophy—diverse forms of atomism, reductionism, and empiricism loosely dubbed "logical positivism"—Willard Van Orman Quine, Nelson Goodman, and Wilfred Sellars reached conclusions which threatened the basic presuppositions of the paradigm. To put it crudely, logical positivism rested upon three basic assumptions. First, it assumed a form of *sentential atomism* which correlates isolated sentences with either possible empirical confirmation, logical necessity, or emotion. Second, it emerged with a kind of *phenomenalist reductionism* which translates sentences about physical objects into sentences about actual and possible sensations. Third, it presupposed a version of *analytical empiricism* which holds observational evidence to be the criterion for cognitively meaningful sentences and hence the final court of appeal in determining valid theories about the world. These independent yet interrelated doctrines—held at various times by Rudolf Carnap, Carl Hempel, and other logical positivists—were guided by distinctions between the analytical and the synthetic, the linguistic and the empirical, theory and observation.[1]

Quine's breakthrough, by far the most influential, accented an *epistemological holism* which shifted the basic units of empirical significance from isolated sentences to systems of sentences or theories; a *methodological monism* that abandoned the analytic-synthetic distinction; and a *naturalism* which rejected a first philosophy prior to science.[2] Goodman's project promoted a *logical conventionalism* which replaced accurate pictorial depiction with acceptable verbal description as the end and aim of constructing versions of the world; a *postempiricist antireductionism* that highlighted the theory-laden character of observation; and an *ontological pluralism* which relegated the notion of truth to that of fitness and encouraged diverse, even conflicting, true versions of the world instead of a fixed world and unique truth.[3] Sellars' major move was toward an *antifoundationalism* in epistemology which undermined attempts to invoke self-justifying, intrinsically credible, theory-neutral or noninferential elements in experience which provide foundations for other knowledge-claims and serve as the final terminating points for chains of epistemic justification. Furthermore, his *psychological nominalism* held that knowledge begins with the ability to justify—the capacity to use words—and since language is public and intersubjective, all "given" elements which purportedly ground knowledge are matters of social practice.[4] The common theme in the perspectives of these three American philosophers recovers and reiterates Charles Peirce's "first rule of reason": Do not block the way of inquiry.[5]

The major contributions of Quine, Goodman, and Sellars, though related in complex and sometimes conflicting ways and still quite controversial in some philosophical circles, signified the Americanization of analytical philosophy—like abstract expressionism Americanized modern art—and set the terms of the debate in contemporary humanistic studies. A distinctive feature of the various philosophical positions reached by Quine, Goodman, and Sellars was their elective affinities with the viewpoints of American pragmatists. Their conscious and often unconscious revival of aspects of American pragmatism opened new avenues in present-day philosophy.

Notoriously popularized by Thomas Kuhn in *The Structure of Scientific Revolutions* (1962) and controversially formulated by Richard Rorty in *Philosophy and the Mirror of Nature* (1979), epistemological holism led to a "distrust of the whole epistemological enterprise."[6] Quine quickly quipped that such scrapping of his underdetermined yet minimally foundational "observation sentences" results in "epistemological nihilism" which he unequivocally rejects.[7] For Kuhn and Rorty, methodological monism yielded a rapacious antirealism in ontology against which Sellars revolted and of which Quine recanted. Last, monocosmic naturalism blossomed into a polycosmic pluralism—dethroning the authority of science as the monopoly on truth and knowledge—which radically called into question Quine's ontological allegiance to physics and Sellars' neo-Tractarian defense of the correspondence theory of truth.[8] The patriarchal trio of postmodern American philosophy bickered among themselves, with Goodman and Quine (along with the brilliant, though then vacillating, Hilary Putnam) doing so quite publicly in their historic sessions on the third floor of Emerson Hall at Harvard. Yet, despite such fruitful disagreements, Pandora's box had been opened—and pragmatism returned with a vengeance.

The great contribution of Richard Rorty is that he constructs a powerful narrative history of modern North Atlantic philosophy in light of the Quine-Goodman-Sellars contributions and boldly draws the threatening implications for philosophy as a discipline. His *Philosophy and the Mirror of Nature* brings to light the deep sense of crisis within the profession of academic philosophy. Rorty's provocative and often profound meditations impel philosophers to examine the problematic status of their subject-matter—only to discover that modern North Atlantic philosophy has come to an end.

Rorty credits Wittgenstein, Heidegger, and Dewey for having "brought us into a period of 'revolutionary' philosophy" by undermining the prevailing Cartesian and Kantian paradigms and advancing new conceptions of philosophy.[9] And these monumental figures surely inspire Rorty. Yet, Rorty's philosophical debts—the actual sources of his particular anti-Cartesian and anti-Kantian arguments—are Quine's holism, Goodman's pluralism, and Sellars' anti-foundationalism. In short, despite his adamant attack on analytical philosophy—the last stage of modern Euro-American philosophy—Rorty feels most comfortable with the analytical form of philosophical argumentation.

From the disparate figures of Wittgenstein, Heidegger, and Dewey, Rorty gets a historicist directive: to eschew the quest for certainty and the search for foundations.

> These writers have kept alive the suggestion that, even when we have justified true belief about everything we want to know, we may have no more than conformity to the norms of the day. They have kept alive the historicist sense that this century's "superstition" was the last century's triumph of reason, as well as the relativist sense that the latest vocabulary, borrowed from the latest scientific achievement, may not express privileged representations of essences, but be just another of the potential infinity of vocabularies in which the world can be described.[10]

For Rorty, the Western philosophical tradition can be overcome principally by holding at arm's length the ahistorical philosophical notions of necessity, universality, rationality, objectivity, and transcendentality. Instead, we should speak historically about transient practices, contingent descriptions, and revisable theories.

The basic lesson Rorty learns from Quine, Goodman, and Sellars is an antireductionist one: to refuse to privilege one language, language-game, morality, or society over another solely by appealing to philosophical criteria. For the results will more than likely be apologetics, "attempts to eternalize a certain contemporary language-game, social practice, or self-image."[11] In cases of conflict and disagreement, we should either support our prevailing practices, reform them, or put forward realizable alternatives to them—without appealing to ahistorical philosophical criteria or standards. In short, Rorty rejects philosophical discourse as the privileged mode of resolving intellectual disagreements.

Rorty strikes a deathblow to modern North Atlantic philosophy by telling a story about the emergence, development, and decline of its primary props: the correspondence theory of truth, the notion of privileged representations, and the idea of a self-reflective transcendental subject. Rorty's fascinating tale—his-story—is regulated by three Quine-Goodman-Sellars shifts which he delineates in detail and promotes in principle: the move toward antirealism in ontology, the move toward anti-foundationalism in epistemology and the move toward dismissing the mind as a sphere of philosophical inquiry.[12]

The move toward antirealism in ontology leaves no room for a correspondence theory of truth (of any importance) in that it undermines the very distinctions upon which such a theory rests: the distinctions between ideas and objects, words and things, language and the world, propositions and states of affairs, theories and facts. The result is not a form of idealism because the claim is not that ideas create objects, words create things, language creates the world, and so forth. Nor is the result a form of Kantianism because the claim is not that ideas constitute objects, words constitute things, language constitutes the world, and so on. Rather the result is a form of pragmatism because the claim is that evolving descriptions and ever-changing versions of objects, things, and the world issue forth from various communities as responses to certain problematics, as attempts to overcome specific situations and as means to satisfy particular needs and interests. To put it crudely, ideas, words, and language are not mirrors which copy the 'real' or 'objective' world but rather tools with which we cope with 'our' world.

In a more philosophical vein—and as more pointedly argued in Rorty's influential essay "The World Well Lost"—the theory-laden character of observations relativizes talk about the world such that realist appeals to "the world" as a final court of appeal to determine what is true can only be viciously circular.[13] We cannot isolate "the world" from theories of the world, then compare these theories of the world with a theory-free world. We cannot compare theories with anything that is not a product of another theory. So any talk about "the world" is relative to the theories available.

The second move, toward anti-foundationalism in epistemology, takes the form of an attack on prelinguistic awareness and various notions of intuition.[14] This move precludes the notion of privileged representations because it views knowledge as a relation to propositions rather than as privileged relations to the objects certain propositions are about.

> If we think in the first way, we will see no need to end the potentially infinite regress of propositions-brought-forward-in-defense-of-other-propositions. It would be foolish to keep conversation on the subject going once everyone, or the majority, or the wise, are satisfied, but of course we *can*. If we think of knowledge in the second way, we will want to get behind reasons to causes, beyond argument to compulsion from the object known, to a situation in which argument would be not just silly but impossible, for anyone gripped by the object in the required way will be *unable* to doubt or to see an alternative. To reach that point is to reach the foundations of knowledge.[15]

For Rorty, the search for such foundations expresses a need to be gripped, grasped, and compelled. This holds for Plato's Eye of the Soul perceiving the World of Being, Descartes' Eye of the Mind turned inward grasping clear and distinct mental representations, or Locke's Eye of the Mind turned outward seeing "singular presentations of sense" as bases for our knowledge. All such models view ahistorical, terminal confrontation—rather than historical, fluid conversation—as the determinant of human belief. In short, the philosophical privileging of representations principally rests upon epistemological attempts to escape from history and put a closure upon human practices. Therefore Rorty concludes:

> When Sellars's and Quine's doctrines are purified, they appear as complementary expressions of a single claim: that no "account of the nature of knowledge" can rely on a theory of representations which stand in privileged relations to reality. The work of these two philosophers enables us . . . to make clear why an "account of the nature of knowledge" can be, at most, a description of human behavior.[16]

The third move, toward dismissing the mind as a sphere of inquiry or detranscendentalizing the transcendental subject, relies, in part, on Gilbert Ryle's logical behaviorism in *The Concept of Mind* (1949) and Quine's radical behaviorism in *Word and Object* (1960). Rorty's own epistemological behaviorism links Ryle's attack on the Cartesian disembodied ego and Quine's assault on the Kantian transcendental subject (and Husserlian nonempirical ego) to a wholesale rejection of ocular metaphors in epistemology.

> A behavioristic approach to episodes of "direct awareness" is not a matter of antimentalistic polemic, but a distrust of the Platonic quest for that special sort of certainty associated with visual perception. The image of the Mirror of Nature—a mirror more easily and certainly seen than that which it mirrors—suggests, and is suggested by, the image of philosophy as such a quest.[17]

Two crucial consequences flow from Rorty's historicist, antireductionist project. First, the distinction between the "soft" human sciences and the "hard" natural sciences collapses. The basic difference between the *Geisteswissenschaften* and the *Naturwissenschaften* is neither the self-defining character of the former nor the context-free facts of the latter. Rather the difference is between the relative stability of normal vocabularies in the natural sciences and the relative instability of normal vocabularies in the human sciences. And the irreducibility of one vocabulary to another does not imply an ontological distinction—only a functional difference.

> As Kuhn says in connection with a smaller, though obviously related issue, we cannot differentiate scientific communities by "subject matter," but rather by "examining patterns of education and communication."[18]

Needless to say, this rudimentary demythologizing of the natural sciences is of immense importance for literary critics, artists, and religious thinkers who have been in retreat and on the defensive since the Enlightenment. And the sparks generated by such a novel viewpoint in our technocentric culture are only beginning to fly.

Second, the conception of philosophy is no longer that of a tribunal of pure reason which defends or debunks claims to knowledge made by science, morality, art, or religion. Rather the voice of the philosopher is but one voice—that of the informed dilettante or polypragmatic, Socratic thinker—among others in a grand Conversation. Rorty's deconstruction

of philosophy as a subject, a *Fach,* a field of professional inquiry results
in equalizing (or depriviliging) the voice of the philosopher in this grand
Conversation.

> In this conception, "philosophy" is not a name for a discipline which
> confronts permanent issues, and unfortunately keeps misstating them,
> or attacking them with clumsy dialectical instruments. Rather, it is a
> cultural genre, a "voice in the conversation of mankind" (to use Michael
> Oakeshott's phrase), which centers on one topic rather than another at
> some given time not by dialectical necessity but as a result of various
> things happening elsewhere in the conversation (the New Science, the
> French Revolution, the modern novel) or of individual men of genius
> who think of something new (Hegel, Marx, Frege, Freud, Wittgen-
> stein, Heidegger), or perhaps of the resultant of several such forces. In-
> teresting philosophical change (we might say "philosophical progress,"
> but this would be question-begging) occurs not when a new way is found
> to deal with an old problem but when a new set of problems emerges
> and the old ones begin to fade away.[19]

Rorty's historicist, antireductionist perspective amounts to a self-styled
neo-pragmatism. His plausible yet objectionable uses of Wittgenstein,
Heidegger, and Dewey and his creative misreadings of Quine, Goodman,
and Sellars yield the most adversarial position in American academic philosophy since the fervent antiprofessionalism of William James. His controversial viewpoint is a move back not simply to American pragmatism,
but more fundamentally, to Ralph Waldo Emerson, in that we are left
with no philosophically authoritative traditions with which to re-create
and redescribe ourselves and the world.[20] Even Dewey's historically-de-
rived authority of science is rendered suspect—thanks to Thomas Kuhn
and especially Paul Feyerabend—hence merely one tradition among others.

> Pragmatism . . . does not erect Science as an idol to fill the place once
> held by God. It views science as one genre of literature—or, put the
> other way around, literature and the arts as inquiries, on the same foot-
> ing as scientific inquiries. Thus it sees ethics as neither more "relative"
> or "subjective" than scientific theory, nor as needing to be made "sci-
> entific." Physics is a way of trying to cope with various bits of the uni-
> verse; ethics is a matter of trying to cope with other bits. Mathematics
> helps physics do its job; literature and the arts help ethics do its. Some
> of these inquiries come up with propositions, some with narratives, some
> with paintings. The question of what propositions to assert, which pic-
> tures to look at, what narratives to listen to and comment on and retell,

are all questions about what will help us get what we want (or about what we *should* want).[21]

For Rorty, we are Emersonian sailors, self-rebegetting creatures, adrift on Neurath's boat—forever inventing and creating new self-images, vocabularies, techniques, and instruments in light of a useful backdrop of mortal beliefs and values which have no philosophical foundation or transhistorical justification. To put it bluntly, we are North Atlantic ethnocentrists in solidarity with a civilization (or set of contemporary tribal practices)—and possibly a decaying and declining one—which has no philosophical defense. In this sense, Rorty's neo-pragmatism is a form of ethnocentric posthumanism. He is unashamedly ethnocentric in that he holds that no other civilization is worth choosing over the modern West. Yet his viewpoint differs from Matthew Arnold's bourgeois humanism and John Dewey's plebeian humanism because he believes no philosophical case can be made for this civilization.

Rorty's neo-pragmatism ingeniously echoes the strident antihumanist critiques—such as those of Martin Heidegger, Jacques Derrida, and Michel Foucault—of a moribund bourgeois humanism. Yet his brand of neo-pragmatism domesticates these critiques in a smooth and witty Attic prose and, more importantly, dilutes them by refusing to push his own project toward cultural and political criticisms of the civilization he (and, in varying degrees, we) cherishes. In this way, Rorty circumscribes his ethnocentric posthumanism within a practical arena of bourgeois humanism.

Yet, from an ethical point of view—the central point of view for pragmatists—what is the difference that makes a difference here? Does Rorty's neo-pragmatism only kick the philosophical props from under bourgeois capitalist societies and require no change in our cultural and political practices? What are the ethical and political consequences of adopting his neo-pragmatism? On the macrosocietal level, there simply are none. In this sense, Rorty's neo-pragmatism is, in part, a self-conscious post-philosophical ideological project to promote the basic practices of bourgeois capitalist societies while discouraging philosophical defenses of them. Rorty's insouciance toward philosophy is coupled with his vigilance toward bourgeois American practices. In short, he throws the ball back into the leftist or rightist courts.

But, on the microinstitutional level, Rorty's neo-pragmatism makes a difference. This difference is that his viewpoint has immense antiprofessional implications for the academy—as enacted in his departure from, and refusal to be appointed in, an academic philosophy department. On his view, academic philosophers can neither justify their specialized activities nor legitimate their narrow results without the very philosophical defenses he undermines. In this way, Rorty's neo-pragmatism provides not an earth-shaking perspective for the modern West but rather is a symptom of the crisis in the highly specialized professional stratum of educational workers in the philosophy departments of universities and colleges. Rorty's antiepistemological radicalism and belletristic anti-academicism are welcome in a discipline deeply entrenched in a debased insularity and debilitating isolation. Yet, ironically, his project, though pregnant with rich possibilities, remains polemical and hence barren. It refuses to give birth to the offspring it conceives. Rorty leads philosophy to the complex world of politics and culture, but confines his engagement to transformation in the academy and apologetics for the modern West.

This political narrowness is exemplified in Rorty's seductive interpretation of the Western philosophical tradition in general and the Anglo-American analytical tradition in particular. This interpretation is itself symptomatic of the ahistorical character of Anglo-American philosophy. Rorty's historicist sense remains too broad, too thin—devoid of the realities of power; his ethnocentric posthumanism is too vague, too nonchalant—and unmindful of the decline of liberalism. Furthermore, Rorty's demythologizing of philosophy seems to retreat into the philosophical arena as soon as pertinent sociohistorical issues are raised.

For instance, is there a link between the emerging antirealism in ontology and the crisis of intellectual authority within our learned professional academies and educational institutions? Is there a relation between the anti-foundationalism in epistemology and the crisis of legitimacy among those subjected to our intellectual authority? Does the detranscendentalizing of the subject express the deep sense of impotence in contemporary capitalist societies, the sense of reaching a dead end with no foreseeable way out or no discernible liberating projects in the near future—hence the proliferation of prevailing apocalyptic forecasts, narcissistic living, and self-indulgent, ironic forms of thinking? If science is, as Rorty notes, a "value-laden enterprise,"[22] is there an ideological character intrinsic to the very methods of the natural sciences owing to an agreed-upon conception of and disposition toward nature which may promote the domination not only of our environment but also those people subsumed under the rubric "nature" such as women, non-Europeans and even "earthy" workers?

The central concern underlying these rhetorical yet crucial questions is that it is impossible to historicize philosophy without partly politicizing (in contrast to vulgarly ideologizing) it. Surely, the relation of philosophy to history and politics is complex. Yet embarking on a historicist project which demystifies philosophy entails dragging-in the complexities of politics and culture. To tell a tale about the historical character of philosophy while eschewing the political content, role, and function of philosophy in various historical periods is to promote an ahistorical approach in the name of history. To undermine the privileged notions of objectivity, universality, and transcendentality without acknowledging and accenting the oppressive deeds done under the aegis of these notions is to write a thin, i.e., intellectual and homogeneous, history—a history which fervently attacks epistemological privilege but remains relatively silent about political, economic, racial, and sexual privilege. Such a history which surreptitiously suppresses certain histories even raises the sinister possibility that the antiepistemological radicalism of neo-pragmatism—much like the antimetaphysical radicalism of poststructuralism—may be an emerging form of ideology in late capitalist societies which endorses the existing order while undergirding sophisticated antiepistemological and antimetaphysical tastes of postmodern avant-gardists.

Indeed, the relativist, even nihilist, implications of neo-pragmatism upset mainstream realists and old-style humanists. So the narrow though noteworthy battle within the academy between the professional avant-gardists and professional establishmentarians will continue to be intense. Yet after the philosophical smoke clears, the crucial task is to pursue thick, i.e., social and heterogeneous, historical accounts for the emergence, development, sustenance, and decline of vocabularies and practices in the natural and human sciences against the background of dynamic changes in specific (and often coexisting) modes of production, political conflicts, cultural configurations, and personal turmoil.

Rorty is highly suspicious of thick historical accounts. For example, when a provisional explanation—even a speculative one—seems appropriate for the centrality of ocular metaphors in Western thought, he asserts that:

> there was, we moderns may say with the ingratitude of hindsight, no particular reason why this ocular metaphor seized the imagination of the founders of Western thought.[23]

And when he contemplates questions about the acceptance and performance of modern science and moral consciousness in the West, he concludes that "in no case does anyone know what might count as a good answer."[24]

In light of such pessimism regarding historical accounts, one wonders whether Rorty takes his own neo-pragmatic viewpoint seriously. Is a "good answer" something more than a particular insightful interpretation based on an emerging, prevailing, or declining social consensus put to a specific purpose? Is not Rorty's narrative itself a "good answer" to Cartesians, Kantians, and analytic philosophers? In short, Rorty's neo-pragmatism has no place for ahistorical philosophical justifications, yet his thin historicism rests content with intellectual historical narratives and distrusts social historical narratives. This thin historicism—linked to the narrow ethical and political consequences of his narrative—is clearly illustrated in his frequent use of an all-encompassing and undifferentiated conception of society.

> Explaining rationality and epistemic authority by reference to what society lets us say, rather than the latter by the former, is the essence of what I shall call "epistemological behaviorism."[25]

It should be clear that Rorty's thin historicism needs Marx, Durkheim, Weber, de Beauvoir, and Du Bois; that is, his narrative needs a more subtle historical and sociological perspective.

Despite the limitations, Rorty's neo-pragmatism can serve as a useful springboard for a more engaged, even subversive, philosophical perspective. This is so primarily because it encourages the cultivation of critical attitudes toward all philosophical traditions. This crucial shift in the subject matter of philosophers from the grounding of beliefs to the scrutiny of groundless traditions—from epistemology to ethics, truth to practices, foundations to consequences—can lend itself to emancipatory ends in that it proposes the tenuous self-images and provisional vocabularies that undergird past and present social orders as central objects of criticism, as the primary subject matter for neo-pragmatic philosophers.

Rorty's perspective creates new discursive space—especially in the academy—for those on the underside of history. Its explicit ethnocentrism—of which there is much to preserve and reject—solicits critiques from those victimized by the North Atlantic conversation which often excludes them and by the North Atlantic societies which usually oppress them. These marginal voices and peoples are excluded and oppressed not because they have a monopoly on truth which frightens the dominant culture—though there is much to learn from marginal peoples—but rather because the historical development of the structural societal mechanisms, such as class exploitation, state repression, patriarchy, and racism, reproduce and reinforce such marginality.[26] Alienated intellectuals from marginal groups and subaltern classes often forget that their relative exclusion from the dominant conversation is a by-product of these mechanisms—not a personal conspiracy to silence their eager voices. Rorty's neo-pragmatism is significant for marginal intellectuals principally because oppressed peoples have more at stake than others in focusing on the tenuous self-images and provisional vocabularies which have had and do have hegemonic status in past and present societies.

Rorty's project should not be viewed as a nostalgic call for a pristine form of pragmatism nor a nativistic move toward Americanism in philosophy. Yet, as I noted earlier, his cosmopolitan conversation presupposes the fruits of bourgeois humanism: North Atlantic ethnocentrism. In this sense, his viewpoint resembles the earlier forms of American pragmatism. Like the first great pragmatists, Charles Peirce and William James, Rorty demystifies science—but he does not share their interest in updating religion. He shuns Peirce's attempt to save the notion of Reality by means of a communal eschatology and rejects James' obsession with the irreducibility of individuality and the mystery of plurality. Similar to John Dewey—the first world-historical figure in American philosophy—Rorty historicizes philosophy and Americanizes history. He frees philosophy from its illusions of transcendental quests and delusions of detached autonomy. Philosophy becomes an enabling device to enhance the capacity of men and women to create new and better self-images and vocabularies. Rorty and Dewey herald community and solidarity and reject nihilism, skepticism, and pessimism. Yet Rorty's neo-pragmatism contains neither the creative ambition nor the engaged activism of Dewey's historical theory of inquiry and reflective intelligence which is, in part, a theory of social reform and amelioration. Last, Rorty and Dewey both Americanize history in that for them the march of freedom in modern history is exemplified in the march of the best in America and the march of America in history is to be viewed critically in light of the best in American democracy. In this way, Dewey's libertarian democratic socialism and Rorty's revisionist liberalism view history through American lens.[27]

If American neo-pragmatism is to put forward an acceptable philosophic vision and project for contemporary North Atlantic civilization, it must built upon the Quine-Goodman-Sellars contributions, refine the conceptions of philosophy put forward by Dewey and Rorty and encounter more fully the classical and contemporary discourses in social theory, cultural criticism, and historiography. American neo-pragmatic philosophers should not settle simply for shedding old self-images and breaking out of professional modes; they also can contribute to the making of a new and better global civilization.

NOTES

1. The classic essays on the philosophical refinement and rejection of these various doctrines are Carl G. Hempel, "Empiricist Criteria of Cognitive Significance: Problems and Changes" and "The Theoretician's Dilemma: A Study in the Logic of Theory Construction" in his *Aspects of Scientific Explanation and Other Essays in the Philosophy of Science* (New York: Free Press, 1965), p. 101–122; 173–226.

2. For the powerful and often persuasive arguments for Quine's epistemological holism and methodological monism, see his classic essay, "Two Dogmas of Empiricism" in *From a Logical Point of View* (New York: Harper & Row, 1963), pp. 20–46 and his more personal reflections in "The Pragmatists' Place in Empiricism," in Robert J. Mulvaney and Philip M. Zeltner, eds., *Pragmatism: Its Sources and Prospects* (Columbia: University of South Carolina Press, 1981), pp. 23–39. For Quine's naturalism, especially his conception of philosophy as being continuous with science, see "Epistemology Naturalized" and "Natural Kinds" in *Ontological Relativity and Other Essays* (New York: Columbia University Press, 1969), pp. 69–90; 114–138.

3. Nelson Goodman arrived at his logical conventionalism after his long and tortuous struggle with Rudolf Carnap's *The Logical Construction of the World* as portrayed in the revision of his Harvard dissertation, *The Structure of Appearance* (Cambridge: Harvard University Press, 1951). Goodman's postempiricist anti-reductionism is best seen in his powerful essay, "The Test of Simplicity" and his classic piece, "The Way The World Is" in *Problems and Projects* (New York: Bobbs-Merrill, 1972), 279–294, pp. 24–32 respectively. His full-blown ontological pluralism is put forward in his *Ways of Worldmaking* (Indianapolis: Hackett, 1978).

4. Sellars' classic statement is "Empiricism and the Philosophy of Mind" in Herbert Feigl and Michael Scriven, eds. *Minnesota Studies in the Philosophy of Science*, vol. 1 (Minneapolis: University of Minnesota Press, 1956), pp. 253–329.

5. *Collected Papers of Charles Sanders Peirce*, Charles Hartshorne, Paul Weiss, and Arthur Burks, eds. (Cambridge: Harvard University Press, 1933–58), 1:135.

6. Richard Rorty, *Philosophy and the Mirror of Nature* (Princeton: Princeton University Press, 1979), p. 181.

7. For Quine's defense of observation sentences and the intimation that Kuhn is an epistemological nihilist and cultural relativist, see Quine, *Ontological Relativity and Other Essays*, pp. 86–90.

8. For Sellars' neo-Tractarian theory of "logical picturing," see his *Science and Metaphysics* (New York: Humanities Press, 1968), pp. 116–150, 169–174. For Quine's full-scale defense of what he calls his "ontological line of naive and unregenerate realism" and "robust realism"—which recants his earlier pragmatic claims

in "On What There Is" in Quine, *From a Logical Point Of View,* pp. 1–19—see *The Roots of Reference* (Lasalle, Canada: Open Court, 1973) and *Theories and Things* (Cambridge: Harvard University Press, 1981), especially his responses to Donald Davidson, Nelson Goodman, Saul Kripke, Grover Maxwell, and David Armstrong, pp. 38–42; 96–99; 173–178; 182–184.

9. Richard Rorty, *Philosophy and the Mirror of Nature,* p. 6.

10. *Ibid.,* p. 367.

11. *Ibid.,* p. 10.

12. I have explored these shifts in detail in Cornel West, "Nietzsche's Prefiguration of Postmodern American Philosophy," *Boundary 2,* special Nietzsche issue, Daniel O'Hara, ed., (Spring-Fall 1981), 9(10):241–270.

13. Richard Rorty, "The World Well Lost," in *Consequences of Pragmatism* (Minneapolis: University of Minnesota Press, 1982), pp. 3–18. This essay first appeared in *The Journal of Philosophy,* (1972), 69:649–665.

14. For Rorty's more direct and technical attacks on the various forms of intuition, see his important essays, "Intuition" in the *Encyclopedia of Philosophy,* vol. 4, pp. 204–212; "Wittgenstein, Privileged Access, and Incommunicability," *American Philosophical Quarterly* (1970), 7:192–205; and "Criteria and Necessity," *Nous* (1973), 7:313–329. It also should be noted that Rorty learned historicist and antireductionist lessons from and in response to his early teachers at the University of Chicago, Richard McKeon and Robert Brumbaugh, and his thesis adviser at Yale, Paul Weiss. His first two major essays, published in 1961, bear witness to such lessons: "The Limits of Reductionism" in Irwin C. Lied, ed., *Experience, Existence, and The Good: Essays in Honor of Paul Weiss* (Carbondale: University of Illinois Press, 1961), pp. 100–116 and "Pragmatism, Categories, and Language" in *Philosophical Review* (1961), 70:197–223. The impact of Rorty's maternal grandfather, Walter Rauschenbusch, the great social gospel advocate, upon his neo-pragmatism remains unexplored.

15. Richard Rorty, *Philosophy and the Mirror, of Nature, op. cit.,* p. 159.

16. *Ibid.,* p. 182.

17. *Ibid.,* p. 181.

18. *Ibid.,* p. 331. Rorty's quote from Kuhn is in Thomas S. Kuhn's *The Essential Tension* (Chicago: University of Chicago Press, 1977), p. xvi.

19. *Ibid.,* p. 264.

20. Rorty's neo-pragmatism also is of an Emersonian sort in that poetic activity tends to regulate his conception of human redescription and constitute the most noble of human practices. For his constant praise of self-redescription, see Rorty, *Philosophy and the Mirror of Nature,* pp. 358–359, 362, 367, and 378. This Emersonian theme should come to the fore in Rorty's book on Heidegger that will appear in the Cambridge University Press *Modern European Philosophy* series. In his unpublished essay, "Heidegger Against the Pragmatists," Emerson already has an absent presence.

21. Rorty, *Consequences of Pragmatism,* p. xliii.

22. Rorty, *Philosophy and the Mirror of Nature,* p. 341.

23. *Ibid.,* p. 38.

24. *Ibid.,* p. 341.

25. *Ibid.*, p. 174.

26. The most intellectually underdeveloped state of academic philosophical articulation among marginal peoples may be that of Afro-Americans and Africans—owing to severe conversational exclusion and societal oppression. But presently black philosophical voices are emerging with power and perspicacity. Note the collection of essays on "Philosophy and the Black Experience" in *The Philosophical Forum*, vol. 9, nos. 2–3 (Winter 1977–78) and those in Leonard Harris, ed. *Philosophy Born of Struggle: Anthology of Afro-American Philosophy from 1917* (Dubuque, Iowa: Kendall/Hunt, 1983). For exemplary African texts, see Kwasi Wiredu, *Philosophy and an African Culture,* (Cambridge: Cambridge University Press, 1980); Paulin J. Hountondji, *African Philosophy: Myth and Reality* (Bloomington: Indiana University Press, 1983); and Theophilus Okere, *African Philosophy: A Historico-Hermeneutical Investigation of the Conditions of Its Possibility* (New York: University Press of America, 1983).

27. American pragmatism has moved beyond such lens primarily in the philosophical journalism of Max Eastman in the late twenties and thirties, the sophisticated pragmatic Marxism of Sidney Hook in the thirties and moments in the eclectic yet learned texts of Richard Bernstein. Eastman was the first noteworthy left pragmatist but ultimately became captive to a vulgar Americanism. Hook has fought the major ideological battles of this century, holding his social democratic ground, taking a few courageous stands yet making major mistakes. His Americanism retains a tempered and hardly discernible critical cutting edge. Bernstein writes well about the major philosophical minds of our time, yet he is reluctant to specify in any detail his progressive politics. Yet he, along with the early Eastman and Hook, provide inspiration to young left neopragmatist philosophers. Of course, this holds for high moments in Dewey.